BICYCLE TOURING
IN
TUSCANY

A Guide to the Best rides in
Tuscany, Umbria & the Marches

by
David Cleveland

CHAINRING PRESS
Boulder, Colorado

BICYCLE TOURING IN TUSCANY

A Guide to the Best Rides in Tuscany, Umbria & the Marches.

Copyright © 2004 David L. Cleveland

Published in the United States by the Chainring Press,
PO Box 2371, Boulder, CO 80306-2371

ISBN 0-9755002-0-1

Contact Information:

Chainring Press
PO Box 2371
Boulder, CO 80306-2371
http://chainringpress.com
(303) 956-1597

TABLE OF CONTENTS

PART TWO

PART THREE

INTRODUCTION

The jet taxied down the runway. The voice explaining where to find the nearest exit switched from English to Italian. The bikes were boxed and checked, the panniers stuffed into the overhead compartments. This was it! We were finally on our way — our first bike tour of Italy.

Despite all the dreaming and planning, all the guide books and maps, I really had no idea what to expect when we arrived in Rome. I knew where we wanted to go, I just wasn't sure how to get there. How would I get out of the airport? Should I take that big, straight road directly to our first destination, or set off into the web of secondary roads that weave through the countryside? And what about all those little towns and villages sprinkled along the way. None of them were mentioned in the guide books, but wouldn't some of them be just as charming as the ones that were? We were going to Italy to ride through the marvelous scenery we'd seen in magazines and coffee-table picture books, to explore the winding cobblestone alleys of medieval towns, to stop for a cappuccino and pastry under the stripped awnings of cafes, and to picnic on green hillsides with views over olive trees and vineyards. But mostly we were going to ride. There are guide books to Italy for driving tours and for walking tours, for garden tours and cooking tours. What I needed was a guide book for bicycle tours!

This book was born of that need. It is designed to take the guess-work out of a bike tour of Italy, or at least a bike tour of Tuscany, Umbria and the Marches. It is a guide to bike routes, the most enjoyable routes I could discover and piece together into a multi-day tour. It is not a guide to restaurants or hotels. With one exception I do not suggest where you should stay or where you should eat or even what you should do off the bike. There are already too many guide books that cover those topics. *Bicycle Touring in Tuscany* is about the ride.

Travel by Bike

Not knowing what to expect at the airport on that first trip to Italy, we had decided to spend our first day Rome. We would take a bus downtown and spend the night, and then catch a train out of the city the next day. We planned to start our bike tour in Orvieto a few hours north of the city.

It seemed like a reasonable plan. The next morning we bought our train tickets. The ticket agent assured us that putting the bikes on the train would be "no problem." The bikes would go in the baggage car and we could pick them up at the Orvieto train station when we arrived. We were then directed to the baggage department to check the bikes. Here the jovial attendant confirmed that the bikes would go to Orvieto, but for reasons beyond the reach of my Berlitz Italian they would not arrive until the next day.

The next day?! That would throw off the whole schedule I had so carefully worked out. Months of planning and map reading gone in a bureaucratic shrug. I briefly thought of cashing in our tickets and trying to ride out of the city, but one look at Roman traffic extinguished that idea. In the end we caught the train to Orvieto. Our bikes were duly waiting for us the next morning (although they looked like they'd been there all night), and we at last began our bike tour. Rule number one of bike touring: Don't lock your self into a schedule. What if you just can't get there?

Two days later we were struggling up steep cobblestone streets into the town of Spoleto. This beautiful city has a long history and the architecture to prove it. Twisting alleys and stairways lead to a magnificent cathedral and a fearsome medieval fortress. But before seeing the sights what we really craved was a cold drink and a hot shower. We finally spotted a down-at-the-heels hotel above a quiet café. It was just what we were looking for.

But the proprietor was shaking his head as he looked over the hotel register, and we resigned ourselves to looking elsewhere. Then he noticed our bikes in the doorway. "Ah, ciclistas!" he said. He suddenly came alive with enthusiasm. He pointed excitedly at the faded black and white photographs of bike racers behind the desk. Apparently he was one of the "tifosi," the maniac Italian bike racing fans. We were instantly elevated to celebrity status. A vacancy magically appeared in the hotel registry, and he insisted on storing our bikes behind the front desk where he could personally keep an eye on them.

The next morning over steaming cups of cappuccino the proprietor wanted to know where we were heading next. When we mentioned Assisi he threw up his hands in protest and insisted that we had to ride to Norcia. We had never heard of Norcia, but he said, "You came to Italy to ride, no? Then you must ride to Norcia!"

He pulled out maps and tourist brochures and gave us a long enthusiastic description of riding up the Nera River valley to Norcia. After plying us with more cappuccino he insisted on leading us to the intersection where we could pick up the route.  Soon we were following him on his Bottechia mountain bike on a wild ride down alleys and one-way streets. He frantically waved aside on-coming traffic and finally brought us to an intersection outside the old city walls. Gesticulating at the sign for Norcia he bid us good luck and wheeled around to rush back to his hotel. We stood waving on the roadside wondering what to do next.

We studied the map more carefully. It looked like a great ride — up a long river valley into the hinterlands of Umbria. We didn't know anything about Norcia. It was barely mentioned in any of our guide books. But what the heck—when in Rome, ride where the Romans ride.

It turned out to be an unforgettable ride. From Spoleto the road climbed up through lush meadows of wild flowers past tumble-down farm houses. From high above the Nera River we sailed down serpentine switchbacks into the narrow valley below. In the quaint village of Vallo di Nera we enjoyed a picnic lunch on a stone bench beneath a sprawling shade tree. This is what we came to Italy for — beautiful rides on quiet roads through magnificent scenery. Rule number two of bike touring: Don't lock yourself into a schedule. What if you learn of a better ride?

One week later we woke up to rain showers and a blustery wind in Gubbio. Neither of us were anxious to pedal into the mountains in these conditions. We decided to declare a holiday from our holiday, a day for laundry, long breakfasts, postcards, and some TLC for the bikes. Those annoying clicks and clacks and squeaks were beginning to bug me. In the process of going over the bikes I found that my derailleur cable was frayed and in danger of snapping. The hotel proprietor had his son lead me to a bike shop, which turned out to be no more than a dark cellar off an alley. The shop owner was short and jolly and loved to shove and slap on the back. Luckily he spoke some English. He deftly replaced the cable, adjusted the brakes, and tuned the wheels as he regaled me with tales of his racing days. He chided me over my Japanese bike components—hadn't I heard of Campagnolo? Rule number three of bike touring: Don't lock yourself into a schedule. What if it rains?

Rules 1-3 of Bike Touring: Don't lock yourself into a schedule.

You will notice that this guide book seems to provide you with just such a schedule. It lays out daily itineraries for 8 different bike tours. It suggests how far you should ride each day and in which town you should stay each night. But you should remember these are only suggested itineraries. The routes themselves I can vouch for. They all offer good cycling with a minimum of traffic and maximum of scenic value. The lengths of each ride are up to you. Some of you may want to reel off 100 mile days; others may wish poke along at a more leisurely pace. In either case remember to factor in some float time. You may not be able to do in 7 days what I suggest. You may do it in 5 days, or you may get rained out. See Rules 1-3 above.

I have bike-toured through almost every country in Europe from Norway to Sicily and Slovakia to Portugal. Without a doubt central Italy is my favorite destination on a bike. Tuscany, Umbria, and the Marches combine spectacular scenery, magnificent architecture, history, culture, good food, warm people and great riding. The roads are smooth, the towns are close together, and the drivers are friendly. On the weekends you will encounter scores of riders out on the road. A pack of 40 or more splendidly clad men of all ages will suddenly swarm up on you. For five minutes they will pepper you with questions about where you're from and where you're going. And then they will roll off down the road chattering away among themselves. Occasionally you will encounter other pannier-laden cyclists, and hours can pass while you exchange stories of your adventures and favorite rides.

To me this is what bicycle touring is all about. It's about the journey, not the destination. And that's what this book is about—the journey, not the hotels or restaurants or museums you will see when you get there. For that you will need another guide book. *Bicycle Touring in Tuscany* is about the ride.

Bike Tour Options

There are lots of ways to tour Italy by bike. You can go by yourself, with a group of friends, or as part of a commercial tour. You can carry your own gear or rent a car and take turns driving. You can bring your own bike, you can rent one, or you can buy one over there.

The Commercial Tour

The easiest way to see Tuscany by bike is with one of the commercial bike touring companies. There are literally dozens of companies that operate tours in this region. These companies can book your flight, provide the bikes, reserve the hotel rooms, tell you where eat and where to ride. They provide guides, carry your bags, and will even carry you if necessary. All you do is show up and have fun. But these are for-profit companies, and you will pay a fairly high premium for the services they provide. For the first-time bike tourist or the inexperienced cyclist, a commercial tour might be a good choice. Personally I prefer the independence and cost-efficiency of a self-supported tour. I can choose where I want to go, where I want to eat, and where I want to sleep. I can go at my own pace, with friends, or alone. And I can decide to change my itinerary due to the weather, local advice, or just because I want to. Best of all, this freedom costs nothing.

The Self-supported Tour

Touring on your own means carrying your own gear, and those panniers can be heavy. A self-supported tour is all about weight. Too much can ruin one. The bike is harder to pedal, it handles differently, and if your are over-loaded, you can have one flat after another. I know, I've done that. An ex-racer friend of mine advocates touring with no more than a credit card and a pocket comb. But while I won't go quite that far, I definitely strive for the ultra-light end of things. More on that later.

The Rental Car Tour

If the idea of loading down your sexy road bike with heavy panniers dismays you, another option is to rent a car to serve as a sag wagon. In a group you can each take turns driving, or you can drive to a central location and take day trips from there. I have done it both ways, completely self-supported and by rental car, and both have their merits. A self-supported tour will give you greater personal satisfaction and sense of accomplishment. It can also be done on a tight budget. On a rental car tour you can cover a lot more ground, zoom in and out of larger cities where the riding is not the best, and be less at the mercy of the weather. The down side is obviously the cost, although it is nowhere near as much as a commercial tour, and you will have to take turns driving. This is no small matter as no one wants to be stuck behind the wheel driving one of the epic rides. I know, I've done that too.

The Train/Bike Tour

A variation on the rental car/bike tour theme is the train/bike tour. I met a pair of cyclists once, who more or less used their bikes as baggage carts. They had a ton of gear and quickly abandoned their planned self-supported bike tour from Amsterdam to Athens. Instead they took trains everywhere, and once at a destination they would unload their bikes at a hotel and ride around to see the sights.

I have found, however, that train schedules are generally too unwieldy for a short term tour. Not all trains take bikes, and the ones that do, sometimes don't. Relying on trains is mostly useful for making long transits between destinations. It can also be very expensive for both you and the bike. You might find that renting a car is a cheaper alternative.

Bring, Buy, or Rent

On any bike tour to Europe you can bring your own bike, buy one over there, or rent one. Renting a bike is usually the poorest choice because (1) few shops rent bikes, (2) almost no shops rent bikes suitable for self-supported touring, and (3) it is highly recommended that you get used to your bike before you strike off into the hills. Having said that, I have listed in the Appendices several bike shops that do rent bikes in the Tuscany region. You may find they can supply what you need.

You can also buy a bike at any bike shop after you arrive, but again you would have little opportunity to try it out before taking off on your tour. If you really wanted to go in style, you could the order the custom-made bike of your dreams, built and equipped to your specifications, and arrange to pick it up at the factory. But both bikes and components tend to be much more expensive over there, and bike touring gear, like racks, panniers, etc., can be hard to find. I've never seen anything other than heavy commuter gear sold at an Italian bike shop. But if you were really going to strap a rack and panniers on that custom-made frame, you could bring all the gear with you.

By far the best and most sensible option is to bring your own bike. You will know it fits, that it is properly equipped, and how it handles. You will know the saddle is comfortable, that the gearing is correct, and that you have the right tires. More importantly you can do several shake down rides fully loaded and decide if you really need all that stuff. If you buy or rent over there, you won't have this opportunity. The only complication to bringing your own bike is getting it over there and back. This really isn't a big deal. You have several options which are discussed later in this section.

What Kind of Bike

As you probably know there are basically two types of bikes: road and mountain. There are also tandems and recumbents, but if you ride one of those, you already know more about them than I do. Under the road bike category there are racing bikes, touring bikes, and hybrid bikes. Racing frames tend to be lighter, quicker, and less forgiving. Touring bikes generally have a longer wheel base for a more comfortable ride, sturdier (heavier) construction, and all the attachment points for racks and fenders.

Hybrid bikes are more or less an adaptation of mountain bike components on a road bike frame. They are comfortable to ride, have a broad range of gears, and can be quite light-weight. Mountain bikes divide into categories of suspension. If you look hard you can still find mountain bikes without shocks, but they are usually very low end (that means heavy and with cheap components). Almost every mountain bike is now sold with front shocks. And the most recent trend is towards bikes with full suspension - shocks front and rear.

The Best Bike for Touring

You can tour on virtually any bike so long as it is comfortable to ride for hours at a time. Otherwise the choice of bike is defined by how much weight you want to carry. If you intend to carry a heavy load with a full set of panniers, then a purpose-built touring bike might be best. Touring bikes have a relaxed geometry that ensures both efficient handling and a smooth ride. They are robustly built to carry heavy loads, and they usually have mountain bike-type brakes to accommodate wider tires. On the down side they can be relatively expensive. Production touring bikes from Cannondale, Bianchi, and others start at about $700 and go up to about $2,000. Custom-made touring bikes from specialty builders start at about $2,000 and go up from there.

The Hybrid
The next best type of bike for touring could be the hybrid. These are usually marketed to bike commuters as an around town bike, but the term can also include cyclocross racing bikes. Generally they have lightweight road bike frames, mountain bike-type gears and brakes, and straight mountain bike style handlebars which allow for a more comfortable upright riding position. Unlike mountain bikes they take 700C wheels which are much lighter and quicker than 26 inch mountain bike wheels. They also usually come with the eyelets for attaching fenders and racks.

The Racer
A normal racing-type road bike can also be fine for touring, especially if you are on a credit-card-and-pocket-comb or rental car-supported tour. The more you load down these thoroughbreds the more you will sacrifice performance. Strapping forty pounds on a bike will make it handle sluggishly no matter what kind of frame you have. When bike touring, it's all about weight, and less is more, especially if you have a high perform-

ance bike. Higher end, more specialized racing bike frames also do not have the eyelets for racks, but you can get adapters from a good bike shop or one of the mail order catalogs (see Appendices). If you are going to load down your road bike pay attention to the gearing. Most racers come with go-fast gears which are great on the flats but a real grind in the hills. Before you jet off to Tuscany with your road bike, you should seriously consider fitting some climbing gears. More on that in a moment.

Mountain Bikes

Although they can be a little heavier, mountain bikes can also be a good choice for touring. They are generally sturdy and have the proper gearing for climbs. Some have the eyelets for racks and fenders. They are limited to one hand position on the handlebars, but that can be alleviated by adding bar ends. The front shocks aren't necessary for riding on paved roads, and they make carrying front panniers more complicated, but you can replace the shocks with a solid fork inexpensively. At the very least you will want to replace the knobby mountain bike tires with narrower "street" tires. Those low pressure knobby tires are meant for traction in the dirt and will just create a lot of rolling resistance on the pavement. Higher pressure smooth-treaded tires will be much more enjoyable to pedal on paved roads. There is no easier way to add horsepower to your bike than to get lighter wheels and tires.

Full suspension mountain bikes are perhaps least suitable for touring. They are designed for a completely different environment, which, if you follow the directions of this book, you will never encounter. They are meant for big bumps, and in Italy you will find very few on the paved roads. The flexible frame is great for hammering down hill but actually robs you of efficiency when climbing. It absorbs the force you put into the pedals rather than transferring it to the wheels. Nevertheless some people, particularly those with sore backs, find them more comfortable to ride, and so for them they may be the best choice.

The bottom line for whatever bike you choose is that it must be comfortable to ride. If your shoulders and neck knot up after an hour or two of riding, it's time to visit the bike shop. Simply raising the handlebars can sometimes eliminate this problem. If your butt hurts after a long ride, or certain appendages go numb, look into getting a new saddle or adjusting the one you have. On a long tour you're going to be in that saddle for hours and hours and you want it to be comfortable. If your knees ache at the top of a long climb, you need to adjust the height of your seat. If the front of your knees hurt, it means you have to raise your seat. If the back of your knees hurt, it means you must lower it. In either case an adjustment of just 1/8 of an inch can cure the problem. Of course there may be other reasons your knees hurt, and if adjusting the seat doesn't help, visit the bike shop again or see a medical professional. Whatever the problem, you will want to fix it before you set off on a bike tour. Bike touring is about the ride, and if it's not fun to ride, it's not fun to tour.

Gears

This guide promises to take you to all the famous, and some not-so-famous, hilltowns of Tuscany, Umbria and the Marches. The operative word here is "hilltown." These towns are mostly found at the top, not at the bottom. You will be doing a lot of climbing. Unless you are extremely fit, you will enjoy this climbing much more with lower gears. Most touring, hybrid, and mountain bikes have the range of gears to make climbing easier. They have triple chain rings in the front and big pie plate sprockets in the rear to give you really low gears. If you're taking a road bike make sure you have it fitted with climbing gears. This means a rear sprocket with at least 28 teeth, 32 would be better. You should also consider installing a triple chain crank. In either case you may also have to get a new front or rear derailleur to accommodate the new gears. Having ridden all of the rides described in this book, I can guarantee that you will not regret installing easier gears.

Tires

Regardless of the type of bike you choose or its gearing, the wrong type of tires can ruin your tour. If you use skinny racing tires (e.g. 700 x 20C) on a fully-loaded bike, you will have one flat after another. If you bring your gnarly mountain bike with its soft knobby tires to ride the smooth pavement of Italy you will be doing three times the work to pedal anywhere. There is a reason that road bikes do not come with fat, knobby tires. They have much more rolling resistance, and that means they are slower and harder to pedal.

Tires also affect riding comfort. Skinny, high pressure racing tires are quick and light and give you a better "feel" for the road, which is another way of saying that they transmit every crack and bump in the road up through the wheels and the frame to your spine. Wider tires will absorb more of the bumps and give you a smoother, more comfortable ride— but they are not light and quick. Remember that bike touring is about the ride. If it is more fun to ride, it's more fun to tour. Therefore get the tires suited to your type of bike tour.

If you are on a rental car tour, use the skinny racers; they are fast and fun. If you are on a self-supported hotel tour with panniers but not a lot of weight, get wider tires to take the load but still spin well (e.g. 700 x 28C). If you are on a fully loaded camping tour, go for the big fats (700 x 38C). They are not light or quick, but with 40+ lbs strapped to your bike nothing is. If you are hauling a trailer, you can use the mid-fats (700 x 28C) because most of the weight is resting on the trailer axle. If you will be riding a mountain bike, *get rid of the knobby tires!* Several companies offer narrower, smooth-treaded mountain bike tires (e.g. 26 x 1.25 in.). They are specifically designed for riding on pavement. They are higher pressure and can be almost as light as road bike tires. Except for bike fit, nothing will do more to improve the quality of your ride than the proper tires.

Regardless of what kind of tires you choose, if you plan a self-supported tour you should bring at least one foldable spare tire. If you get a bad puncture or tear a sidewall, it can be a long walk to the nearest bike shop. If you have an older bike with 27 inch wheels, you will want to bring two tires, as you are unlikely to find one of those in Europe.

Racks, Panniers, and Trailers

I have a theory that people will pack exactly as much stuff as they can fit into their bags. The usual answer to the question of whether to bring something is if you have room for it. The trick then is to only buy small panniers. The less gear you bring, the less weight you will have to haul up those Tuscan hills. But the real answer to what to bring and how to carry it all depends on what kind of tour you will be doing: (1) a car supported tour, (2) a self-supported hotel tour, or (3) a self-supported camping tour.

On a car-supported tour you can bring pretty much anything you want and load it in the car each morning. On the bike at most you might need a handlebar bag to carry maps, food, a windbreaker, and a camera. You can also get away with just a fanny pack or even the rear pockets of your cycling jersey. You should also carry tools, a pump, and a spare inner tube. This is a great way to tour because it maximizes the pleasure of riding.

On a self-supported hotel tour you will need a rear rack and panniers to carry clothes and toiletries, guide books, spare parts, and anything else you think you might need. Remember, get small panniers; otherwise you will find yourself dragging all kinds of junk around with you. A handlebar bag for maps, food, and camera is also handy. You can also use it to carry all your important documents, passports, plane tickets, money, etc., and slip it off the bike to take with you into stores or restaurants. On a hotel tour you should not need front panniers. These will affect steering and just mean more weight.

It's on the camping tour that you will need all the room to carry gear. With a sleeping bag, sleeping pad, tent, stove, pots and pans, and all the other attendant camping gear plus clothes, etc., you can expect to be hauling 40 pounds or more around with you. There are two ways to do it: front and back panniers plus handlebar bag, or use a trailer.

Panniers

Panniers are the traditional way to go. You drape them all over the bike and load them down. Look for panniers with a draw-string top and a flap that cinches down over it. These allow expansion and contraction of loads and are more water resistant. Avoid zippers as they will jam when they get dirty. Despite manufacturers' claims of waterproofness, line your panniers with plastic garbage bags, and bring spares, as they will rip. You can also use heavy-duty zip-lock freezer bags, which also help to organize things. Pack the heaviest items in the bottom of the panniers where they will have the least effect on bike handling. Put the things you will want during the ride on the top where they will be accessible. Be sure the panniers you select have metal hooks or similar type of attachment to secure them to the rack. Straps alone will fray and work loose.

Racks

Both front and rear panniers require racks that bolt to the frame. A rear rack with at least four attachment points to spread the load is best. You can also buy rear racks which bolt only to the seat post. These might work well for very light loads. If you are going to use a mountain bike with shocks, at least one manufacturer, Old Man Mountain Products, Inc., (see Appendices) makes front and rear racks that work with mountain bike suspension systems. Be sure to bring along several spare nuts and bolts for the rack as they will work loose and disappear. This only seems to happen during rain storms.

Trailers

Trailers are the other option for hauling a heavy load of gear. They attach to the rear fork and come with either two wheels or one. The advantage to trailers is that you can preserve some bike handling performance without the burden of panniers. They work well with full-suspension mountain bikes, and you can pile them high with gear. A trailer also costs about the same as a full set of panniers and racks, and they can be used with virtually any bike. The disadvantage is that  sometimes you feel like you are attached to a ball and chain, and they are awkward to transport on planes, trains and in hotel lobbies. If you decide to use a trailer, remember to bring spare tubes and spokes for it as well as your bike.

Whether you choose panniers or a trailer be sure to take a few shake-down rides before you fly off to Europe. Riding a heavily loaded bike or tugging a trailer takes some getting-used-to. The first time you ride your fully loaded bike you will be shocked at how sluggishly it handles. The main thing to get used to with a trailer is the longer turning radius and the effect on braking. You don't want to discover this on your first descent down a steep set of hairpins.

What to Bring

What you should bring is again defined by what sort of tour you are planning—a rental car tour, a hotel tour, or a camping tour.

On a rental-car tour, you can bring anything you want. In addition to the obvious things, don't forget to bring a bike rack for the rental car. It is very unlikely that the car rental agency can provide you with one. Get one that hangs off the back of the car and is adaptable to both wagons and sedans. It must also fold flat for packing. They are available at any good bike shop or from a mail order house (see Appendices).

On a self-supported hotel tour where weight and volume are an issue, you have to be more disciplined. At minimum you will need tools and spares for the bike and clothing for you. For tools you will need those necessary to assemble the bike at the airport, to make minor adjustments to brakes and gears, and to change a flat. For spares you will need two or three extra spokes and nipples in the two sizes that fit your wheels (the rear wheel uses two different length spokes), a spare folding tire, and two spare tubes. How long you intend to be out touring of course also affects what tools and spares you might want, but for a tour of the length contemplated by this guide, the following list should be sufficient.

Tools

1. A small box wrench for removing pedals.
2. Allen wrench or screw driver for adjusting brakes and derailleur.
3. Allen wrench for loosening and tightening handlebars and seat post.
4. A small wrench or pliers for tightening the rack bolts.
5. Tire irons for removing the tire from the wheel.
6. An inner tube patch kit.
7. Tire pump

In addition to these you may want to bring a spoke wrench, but only if you know how to true your own wheel. If you have an older bike you may want a freewheel puller for replacing broken rear spokes, but again only if you know how. I have several times broken a spoke and continued riding by adjusting the brakes to clear the wobble. Almost every town in Italy will have a motor scooter or bike shop where someone can replace a spoke for you. But they may not have the right size spoke which is why you must bring your own. And that leads to the following list of spare parts.

Spares

1. Spokes in two sizes with nipples.
2. One folding tire.
3. Two inner tubes.
4. Several sets of nuts and bolts that fit your rack.
5. A small spray can of de-greaser to clean your chain.
6. Chain lube.

This list should be sufficient for a two or three week tour. Remember you are in Italy; there are bike shops everywhere, and there is no need to overdo it.

Okay, so the bike is covered, now for you. What are the bare necessities for a self-supported tour? My racer friend would say a credit card and pocket comb, but at least one bicycle touring guide recommends including two evening ensembles with appropriate accessories for women and a coat and tie for men. I don't know about a neck tie, but I definitely would bring more than a pocket comb. There are few more luxurious feelings on a bike tour than peeling off clinging, sweaty cycling clothing and pulling on something loose, comfortable, and dry. But more clothes means more weight and more laundry. In Italy laundramats are both rare and expensive. It is best to limit yourself to clothes you can wash in a sink and hang to dry.

Basically you will need two sets of clothes: one to ride in and one for everything else. For riding I favor lycra because it dries quickly and doesn't flap in the wind. And it looks good; this is Italy after all, where fashion rules! Others may shy away from such natty attire and choose to wear cotton (which stays damp and flaps...). Bottom line: Ride in whatever feels comfortable, will rinse out in a sink, and be dry in the morning.

The clothes you wear off the bike have to meet this wash-and-wear criteria as well, plus they have to pack easily. That means no jeans, which are too heavy and bulky. You need material that compacts well and colors that won't show the smears of chain grease. For pants I recommend Dacron trousers with legs that zip off into shorts. A couple of T-shirts, a light fleece pullover, and you are set.

For shoes you will also need a pair for on and off the bike. For the bike use mountain bike-style cleats with rubber soles that allow you to walk around with a measure of safety. If you have or prefer toe clips, cycling cleats are still a good idea, but you can get by with sneakers if you don't mind having your feet go numb. For off the bike I recommend sandals, because they're light and pack easily.

For inclement weather (cold or rain or both) I just pack a light water-resistant shell. It is mostly for cutting the wind. I find that if it rains I get soaked either by the precipitation or by perspiration. In sunny Italy you can get away with this; I would not recommend this for cycling in northern Europe.

So here is my bare bones list of clothing and other sundries for the self-supported touring cyclist:

Clothing

A. On the bike
1. Two pairs of lycra bike shorts.
2. Two lycra cycling jerseys.
3. One nylon shell.
4. One pair cycling cleats.
5. Two pairs of socks.
6. Helmet and cycling gloves.

B. Off the bike
1. One pair of light-weight trousers.
2. Two cotton T-shirts.
3. One light-weight fleece pull-over.
4. Underwear.
5. One pair of light-weight shoes or sandals.

Toiletries

1. Toothbrush, toothpaste, etc.
2. Plastic bottle of shower gel soap (can use as shampoo, shaving cream, and to wash clothes too!).
3. Pocket comb (okay, maybe a hair brush).
4. Ear plugs (for the flight, those thin hotel room walls, or the generator in the next campsite).
5. Sun block.

First Aid kit

1. Aspirin, Ibuprofen, or the like.
2. Antibiotic ointment
3. Band Aids in several sizes
4. Waterproof tape
5. Sterile pads
6. Mole skin or Spenco 2nd Skin
7. Tweezers
8. Chemical cold packs

There are, of course, many more items you can add. This list is designed to take care of road-rash, blisters, and the other common injuries you might encounter on the road. For more serious ailments, remember that you are in Italy, not the Third World; they have pharmacies and medical clinics just like home. There is no need to carry a large scale medical kit with you. However, if you take prescription medication, you should bring a sufficient supply with you.

Miscellaneous

1. Guide books. This one, of course, plus your choice among the many tourist guides covering museums, cathedrals, restaurants, hotels, etc. (see Appendices).
2. Maps, the smallest scale you can find (see below).
3. One roll of clear packing tape, the wider the better, for mending all the tears you will get in paper maps and for packing up your bike at the end of the tour.

4. Plastic zip-lock freezer bags for pretty much everything, but particularly maps, passports, and plane tickets.

5. A cable bike lock.

Hydration is extremely important when cycling long distances. This is particularly true in the humid summer heat of Italy. If your bike only has one water bottle holder, fit a second one. I also carry a third bottle in the rear pockets of my jersey. Like those climbing gears, you will not regret having an extra bottle of water in the hills of Tuscany.

Maps

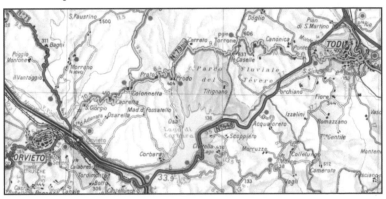

This one item can make or break your tour of Tuscany. In order to enjoy the best riding and avoid traffic, and incidentally to follow the routes described in this book, you will need the smallest scale maps you can find. This means maps on a scale of 1:200,000. Anything larger, such as the 1:400,000 Michelin maps of Italy, do not have enough detail to show the smaller roads and towns. They can be useful for planning or to get an overall view of the region, but are not much help when you are out on the road.

The only 1:200,000 maps I know of that are available in the U.S. are the Touring Club Italiano (TCI) maps. You can sometimes find them in specialty map or travel stores, or they can be ordered from several sites on the Internet (see Appendices). The relevant portions of TCI maps have been reprinted by permission in the tour descriptions of this book, but you will need the original full-size maps to orient yourselves. These maps are also readily available in Italy along with several other brands, but be sure to buy 1:200,000 scale maps.

TCI maps in common with other brands use a color code to denote the size of roads. Red roads usually mean heavy, high-speed traffic and no shoulder — but not always. Yellow roads usually mean good riding, but sometimes they can seem a lot like red roads and sometimes they can turn to dirt. White roads can be either paved or dirt, and sometimes little more than jeep trails, but generally they have very little traffic. Roads highlighted with green are designated as particularly scenic, but occasionally you will wonder what they could have been thinking. Arrows on the road designate steepness of grade. One arrow means a grade of 4-7%; two means 7-12%; and three means 12% and above. An absence of arrows, however, does not mean an absence of hills, and many steep grades are unmarked. A good rule-of-thumb is that if the road writhes back and forth like a serpent, it is going to be steep. Luckily with this guide book you get the benefit of all my wrong turns. I can't promise that you will avoid all the steep climbs, but at least I will warn you when they are coming.

The Bike Box

There are several ways to get your bike to Europe. The most common method is to take it on the airplane as checked luggage. Most international flights do not charge extra for bikes unless they exceed certain dimensions. You should check with the airline before buying your ticket to find out their policy on bikes.

You don't strictly need a bike box to check your bike as luggage. They will accept it if you simply turn the handle bars sideways and remove the pedals. I only do this on the return trip, because it is often too difficult to locate a bike box at the airport. Some airlines do sell them, but it can very time-consuming to track them down. And there is a school of thought that the bikes are handled with more

care, if they are not boxed up. For one thing nothing can be stacked on top of them, so they usually wind up on top of the pile. Cardboard bike boxes on the other hand almost never survive the journey. They will arrive at your destination gouged and ripped in many places. The only damage suffered by my bike when checked without a box was a broken spoke. This is why I resort to this option for the return trip only. If the bike is damaged on the way home, it won't ruin my long-planned bike tour. On the way over I always box up the bike. I've got plenty of time to do it. I can pad the frame and wheels to my heart's content. And I can stuff most of my gear into the box too.

There are basically two kinds of boxes: new and used. The new ones are built like a giant hard-shell suitcase. They are quite expensive, and you have to find a place to store them while you are on the bike tour. Airports no longer have "Left-Luggage" departments where you can check a bag until your return due to the threat of bombs. Some train stations still offer this service, such as the main Termini station in downtown Rome, but you have to figure out how to get your giant suitcase there and back to the airport. It is also possible that a nearby hotel would store it for you, but you would want to confirm that in advance.

Used bike boxes are available for free from your local bike shop. These are the cardboard boxes that new bikes are shipped in. You can usually find them stacked up by the dumpster in back of the shop. The trick with a used box is to find the largest one you can. A box for a 15 inch mountain bike may not fit your 25 inch touring bike. The bigger the box, the more stuff you can cram into it. New bikes are shipped with foam padding and fork braces that you can re-use. If you don't find any in the boxes out by the dumpster, ask the shop employees. They sometimes remove all this stuff if the cardboard bike boxes are going to be recycled. You should definitely use the fork braces on your bike. They are plastic wedges that fit between the forks to prevent them from being bent. Use the foam and anything else you can find to pad the frame and wheels.

To fit your bike into a bike box you need to remove the wheels, the handlebars, the seat, and the pedals. You should also remove the rear derailleur to prevent the tang it hangs on from being bent or broken. As you disassemble your bike be sure to clean all the parts. Apply a new coat of grease to the pedal threads, seat posts, and handle bar stem. Take special care with the brakes while disassembling and packing your bike. It is easy to tweak these and have to spend many jet-lagged minutes trying to re-adjust them at the airport after your arrival. Lastly remember to put the tools you will need to reassemble the bike into the bike box too.

When to Go Where

The cycling season in central Italy is basically April through October. The best months in terms of weather and crowds are May and October. The average high temperature in Firenze (Florence) in May and October is 75 degrees, the average low is 52. By July and August the average high climbs to 92 degrees. In the higher elevations of the Apuan and Apennine mountains it can of course be much cooler. There are ski areas throughout these mountains and the wild flowers still look fresh in August.

 With the warmer mid-summer temperatures come proportionately larger crowds. The main tourist destinations, such as Firenze and Siena, will be packed. If you want to stay in the hotel of your choice during June, July, and August, you will have to reserve months ahead of time. By way of example, I have had trouble reserving a room in January for a July stay in Firenze. Farther off the beaten track there is almost never a need to book ahead, and in general I would encourage you to avoid advance reservations in order to preserve your independence. See Rules 1-3 of bike touring. In the tour descriptions I will suggest where you might want to consider making advance reservations.

 With these parameters in mind, if for instance you were to choose Tour 5 which takes you from Firenze to San Gimignano, Siena, Montalcino, and back to Firenze, you would be better off doing this tour in May or October, because it will not only be cooler but the crowds will be less, and accommodations will be easier to find. If you were to choose Tour 8 which winds its way over the high passes of the Apennines, you would be better off in July or August when it will be warmer high in the mountains. This route is far enough off the beaten path that finding accommodations should not be as great a concern.

Summers are generally dry in the Tuscany region, but you can always encounter rain. Rarely will you have more than a day of rain unless you are particularly unlucky. If it does rain, take a day off the bike, read a book, write postcards, explore, drink wine with lunch. Whichever tour you decide to take, always factor in a day or two of float time to allow for bad weather, mechanical breakdowns, lost luggage, etc.

Accommodations

 Accommodations in Italy range from luxury hotels to hiding in the woods. Hotels are classified from 1 to 5-stars with 5-stars being at the deluxe end of the spectrum. The rates charged are fixed by agreement with the Provincial Tourist Board. With one exception I will not recommend any specific hotel to you. For this you should consult one of the main-stream travel guides like *Let's Go Italy*, or the Michelin Red Guide for Italy. You can also research hotels and book on line at www.italiantourism.com, the website of the Italian Government Tourist Board.

The next category of accommodations are the ubiquitous "Agritourismos." These are roughly equivalent to "Bed and Breakfasts," but can be quite grand with the prices to match. The concept was originally for farmers to let out vacant rooms and get a share of tourist dollars, but now the "farms" have lawns and pools and electronic gates at the foot of the driveway. Generally speaking they are geared more for one week stays rather than overnight stops. They can also be far, far out of the way. I have followed cheerful agriturismo signs for miles and miles up and down dirt roads only to find they were full or too expensive. If you want to stay at an agriturismo it is best to research them ahead of time and make an advance reservation. A good place to start is at www.agriturist.it. This is an Italian website with an English language version that lists 1700 agriturismo "farms" all over Italy.

Hostels are found in some of the larger towns in Tuscany and Umbria. Some are wonderful, like the one in Cortona, which occupies an old monastery; some are more like college dormitories and can be far from the town center like the one in Firenze. Anyone can stay there. You do not need a membership card, although it is cheaper if you have one. To find out more about hostelling and where they are located go to www.hostel.com which claims to list "every hostel, everywhere," more than 6,000 worldwide.

Another option is "affittacamere," rooms for rent in private homes. Often this is your only option if you arrive in a place like Siena in the high season without a reservation. The tourist office will have a list of available rooms and will sometimes call ahead to reserve it for you. If you see a hand-painted sign in someone's driveway for "zimmer" or "camere" ("rooms" in German and Italian), it means they have a room for rent, and you can just knock on the door.

Next there is camping at commercial campgrounds. This is rarely a back-to-nature experience. For a little less than you'd pay for a hotel room you are given a gravel parking space on which to pitch your tent. On the plus side they sometimes have amenities like a pool, a café or store, and laundry facilities. This is also a great way to meet Europeans, particularly the Dutch and Germans who flock to these campgrounds each summer for their month-long holiday. Unfortunately campgrounds are pretty scarce away from the coast and the large cities. Two websites list commercial campgrounds in Italy: www.icaro.it and www.camping.it. Both have English-language versions.

Finally you can camp in the woods, although you didn't hear that from me. Camping in the rough is illegal without the landowner's permission. There are plenty of beautiful places to camp, and the price is right, but you have to get used to sleeping with one ear cocked for the approach of the farmer and his dog. After a few days of this you may also find that people move away from you when you enter a store. When this happens it may be time to check out the showers at the commercial campground.

Safety: The Rules of the Road

Driving in Italy has been described by some as a "blood sport." And while it is true that Italian drivers treat speed limits and stop signs as polite suggestions I have found that for cyclists the roads are generally safe. I think this is due to two factors. First, drivers are used to sharing the road with cyclists. Coming upon a group of cyclists daring to ride two or even three abreast does not provoke episodes of road-rage. Drivers may politely tap their horns some distance behind you to signal that they would like to pass. This is all done with pleasant waves and nodding. I don't know where you live, but I find this a refreshing change from the usual behavior of drivers.

The second thing that makes the roads safer on a bike is that it is easier to get out of the way. Driving a car on narrow, winding roads can be highly stressful. The Italians will tailgate you relentlessly and pass on blind curves, and they seem to think nothing of cutting into the on-coming lane as they round corners. On a bike this doesn't affect you as much. They can wiz around a blind corner half in your lane and miss you cleanly. In a car it is another matter, but the shot of adrenaline as you jerk the wheel into the ditch does help keep you alert. On a rental car tour the designated driver is often more exhausted at the end of the day than those who rode.

The rules of the road for a cyclist in Italy are basically the same as anywhere else: Always watch out for cars; make eye-contact at intersections; hug the shoulder when a car passes. The one additional rule I'd pass along is not to anticipate that cars will actually stop for stop signs and stop lights, especially if there is no other traffic in sight. Cars generally detract from the cycling experience, which is why I guide you whenever possible onto the quiet back roads.

Signs

In Italy directions are given in reference to the principal cities. For instance in the darkest hinterlands of Umbria the signs at an intersection may direct you to "Roma" in one direction and "Macerata" in the other. There may also be signs for the next town or series of towns. Sometimes these "towns" do not appear on your map, even the detailed TCI maps, and sometimes they turn out to be no more than a single house beside the road. In order to navigate across central Italy you need to know the names of the various towns you will be passing through. Even then you will constantly need to refer to your map.

Signs in Italy are also color-coded. Green signs lead you to the Autostrada. You don't want to go there on your bike. Blue signs generally direct you along secondary roads to a named town. Brown signs indicate something of cultural interest like a monastery or castle. Yellow signs usually refer to some commercial establishment. A sign with a red circle around something means that the designated activity is prohibited, much like US signs with a red circle and a slash through it.

A few Italian traffic signs you should know about:

IL CENTRO

No Bikes Allowed!　　　To Downtown　　　Tourist Information Office

Security

Bike security in Italy is about like it is anywhere. Lock up your bike any time it is out of your sight. Don't bring a heavy steel U-shaped lock. You need something more versatile. A heavy steel cable that coils up like a spring works well and packs away easily. A combination lock is probably better than a key lock, because keys can be lost. If possible set the combination to your street address or phone number or some other easily remembered number.

If you stop at a café, get a table where you can see your bike, even if it is locked up. Use a handlebar bag that slips off easily to carry your valuables. You can attach a strap and convert it into a shoulder bag. There is not much you can do to secure your panniers, but in my travels all over Europe I have never had them tampered with. Still, I would not leave anything particularly valuable in them.

When you check into a hotel *always* ask if they have a garage ("garage" in Italian) where you can lock up your bike overnight. If they don't, tell them you want to bring the bike into your room; this usually results in an offer to leave it behind the front desk. *Never* leave your bike locked up on the street overnight. Even in the quietest country village the hotel proprietor will often be the first to suggest you put your bike in his garage for safe-keeping.

As for your personal security the greatest risk is from pickpockets, but you should only encounter these in the cities. They sometimes appear as beggars, and while they distract you with their appeal, they deftly go through your pockets. If you see a beggar approach, you can do as the Romans do and yell "Via, via!" (basically "Get lost!").

Money

You are not supposed to leave home without them, but I don't see any need to carry travelers' checks. You often pay a fee for them up front, and then get a lower exchange rate when you cash them in. Credit and debit cards are now universally accepted throughout Italy. In all the larger towns there are ATM machines you can use to get cash. In places like Firenze and Siena there are ATM machines that accept American dollars and convert them to Euros. You are no longer beholden to seemingly arbitrary banking hours, those weird locking double doors, and long lines at the currency exchange counter — unless you are using travelers checks.

Credit cards often get a better exchange rate on purchases than cash because the banks give each other wholesale rates. At ATM machines, however, any savings can be negated by transaction fees. A credit or debit card can simplify almost all transactions. If you don't have one, consider getting one before you leave for Italy.

On bike tours I always carry photocopies of the front and back of my credit card (and my passport too) in case it is stolen or lost. The phone number to call if your card is lost is on the back of the card, where it won't do you any good if it's lost. You should of course carry these photocopies separately from the credit card for the same reason.

Preparation

As with most things the key to success is in the preparation. For a bike tour that means getting in shape. More than anything else (except maybe the weather), your degree of fitness will be the key to an enjoyable tour. The fitter you are, the more fun you will have. The panniers will seem light, the pedaling will seem effortless, and you will revel in the scenery. You may even forget that all those towns in Tuscany are preceded by "hill."

While you are out getting into shape be sure to take at least one shake–down ride with your bike fully loaded for touring. Nothing else will convince you more completely of the wisdom of taking less stuff. The fitter you are the less important this will seem, but you still have to figure out how to fit all your gear into panniers.

Between rides take some time to learn a little Italian. Buy a Berlitz tape or a phrase book and study it. Although the Chianti region has been called "Chianti-shire" because of all the British tourists there, you will find few people who speak English away from the major tourist towns. I have included a bike-oriented vocabulary list in the Appendices to help out in the bike shop, but you will also need to memorize a handful of survival phrases. You need to be able to ask for directions, for a cup of cappuccino, and where to find the toilet. Few things will seem more miraculous than mouthing something unintelligible and have the person you're speaking to nod in comprehension.

Lastly you need to study the guide books—not just this one, but the ones that tell you all about what you're going to see. I just tell you how to get there on a bike. You will need other guide books to tell you why you should go there. You can then decide which of the tours described in this book suits your interests. Some tours take you on the hit parade of hill-towns. They include all the big names like Firenze, Siena, and San Gimignano. Others take you to lesser lights like Gubbio and Bibbiena. And some will take you to places you are unlikely to even find in guide books, like Barga, Anghiari, and Roccatederighi. Take it from me, these places are well worth the ride.

There are more than 300 tourism guides to Italy, so there is plenty to choose from. I have listed a very few in the Appendix that I have used and found helpful. Some are better on accommodations, some are better on art history, some just seem more readable. I suggest you go to a book store with a good travel section and spend some time paging through them until you find one you like. For bike routes you need this book; for everything else you will need one of those books.

Nutrition: Beware of the Bonk

On a bike your body is the engine that drives you over the hills. When your engine runs out of gas, you "bonk." This is that disagreeable sensation of being unable to make another pedal stroke and not caring either. You basically collapse on the side of the road. This is not a good thing and to be avoided at all costs.

After careful research I have developed a multi-phase early warning system for an impending bonk. At the beginning of a ride in a place like Tuscany everything will look incredibly quaint and photogenic. You will find yourself constantly stopping to snap photographs. As the day wears on things look less quaint and you stop less often to take pictures. Soon things look down right ordinary and you find yourself just staring down at the road oblivious to your surroundings. This is the first sign that the tank is getting low, and it is time to eat something.

The next warning sign is when you begin to notice mysterious squeaks and clicking noises coming from your bike. No amount of fiddling with the gear shifters seems to make any difference. It really gets bad when you find yourself stopping to try to track down the annoying sound. These mysterious noises seem to go away if you eat something. So as soon as you notice that irritating clicking noise, the quickest way to fix it is to eat.

The final sign of imminent bonk is when virtually everything bugs you. The only car to pass you in the past half hour came by too close. The cows along the side of the road *stink*. That shopkeeper this morning pretended not to understand English and shorted you on your change. And that *clicking noise is driving you nuts!* By this point things are no longer fun, and it's time to stop, take a break, and eat something. In 10 minutes the noise will be gone, the cows will be wonderfully photogenic, and the people in shops will seem *so* nice.

The key to getting the most enjoyment out of your bike tour is to eat. Don't worry about gaining weight; you will be burning it off with every pedal stroke. This doesn't mean stopping for a three course meal for lunch. You might start hearing that clicking noise by mid-morning and be raving by lunch time. It means taking food along with you to eat while you ride. It can be candy bars, fruit, sandwiches, whatever you like. In Italy you will find that there are a lot of exotic foods that you may never have tried. It is fun to nose around the shops and try new things. It will also keep the pedaling fun.

Water

If food is the gas, then water is the oil for your engine. If you run out, the engine will seize up. The summer months in Italy are warm and humid. You can expect to sweat a lot while climbing all those Tuscan hills. It is vital that you carry water with you on the bike and refill the bottles frequently.

Tap water is perfectly safe to drink in Italy. This means you can fill your water bottles at any water faucet. You can walk into any café and hand over your water bottles with hardly a word to get them refilled. If you want to go high-end you can fill your water bottles with pricey mineral water. Just be sure to order "acqua naturale." This is the kind without the bubbles.

The water in fountains is also safe to drink unless it is marked "non potabile" (not safe for drinking). In many towns and villages there will be a fountain in the town square where you can fill water bottles. You will also sometimes see people lined up on the side of the road holding empty jugs. They are waiting their turn to fill up their bottles at a natural spring. These can be elaborate affairs with fountains and troughs or just a spigot sticking out of a rock. You should always keep your eye out for them and fill your water bottles as the opportunity arises.

Carbo-loading Italian Style

Italy is of course famous for its cuisine. That is one of the prime attractions to cycling there. You really have to be unlucky to have a bad meal anywhere except in tourist traps. But Italian eating habits can nevertheless present a challenge for the touring cyclist.

First, Italians don't really eat breakfast. This meal seems to consist of a cappuccino and a puff-pastry covered in powdered sugar. This isn't going to get you very far down the road before you start to notice that clicking noise. Hotels that cater to foreign tourists will sometimes provide a more substantial breakfast of juice, cereal, and sometimes even soft-boiled eggs. This is great when you can get it, but you will pay a premium for it. The best option for a cyclist is to hit a market the night before to stock up on real food. You can go the cappuccino and puff-pastry route first thing in the morning then pull out the good stuff when you find the scenery is starting to look dull.

Second, lunch is the really big meal of the day in Italy. Why? Because they skipped breakfast. For the cyclist you can find yourself presented with a four course menu and a nice Chianti that will leave you snoozing by the roadside. That can make for a great day, but it does not get you very far down the road. To avoid this predicament you need to avoid sit-down restaurants for lunch. That means make your own lunch in the morning, buy something in a shop for a picnic (my favorite), or try to find a cafe that sells reasonable-looking "pannini" (sandwiches). For some sinister reason pizzerias are generally not open for lunch except in tourist areas.

Lastly, there is dinner. This is why you came to Italy, so go wild! Carbo-load to your heart's content…because there may be no breakfast.

How to Use this Book

Route Descriptions

There are eight tours described in this book. Each tour is broken down into days and destinations. For instance, Tour 1/ Day 4 takes you from San Gimignano to Firenze. Firenze is what English-speakers call Florence. I use the Italian spelling throughout this book, because among other reasons you will see no signs for "Florence" in Italy.

The distance of each daily stage is set out in miles and kilometers along with the degree of difficulty. The daily routes are described in narrative form giving specific road directions where necessary, intermediate mileage, and riding conditions. If there is a hill, I will tell you how long it is and how steep. If there is a quaint village or a ruined castle along the way, I will point it out. Each daily route includes an altitude profile and a TCI map excerpt with the route marked on it. There is also a table listing each town you will be passing through with their respective distances and amenities.

Unfortunately not every ride is perfect despite my best efforts. Generally, any large town with its attendant traffic and suburban sprawl doesn't offer perfect riding. But if you want to see Lucca, Pisa, Firenze and Siena, you have to put up with it. There are no really good rides in or out of these towns, but I think I have found the most reasonable routes.

You are of course free to deviate from the routes described here. They have all been worked out to achieve the maximum quality ride, but you may hear of or discover a better ride. A few words of caution: First, beware of doing the daily routes in reverse order. Many of the climbs are much steeper going the other direction. Second, do not succumb to the temptation to take the more direct highways marked in red on TCI and Michelin maps. With a few exceptions these routes are terrible for cycling. They usually have no shoulder and are plagued by heavy, high speed traffic.

Degree of Difficulty Ratings

Each daily tour stage is assigned a degree of difficulty rating. The scale I use is based on movie ratings. I don't know why or how I came up with this particular ratings system except that while researching this book I found myself referring to the climbs in these terms. A "G" climb was fun for the whole family, no swearing or violence involved. A "PG-13" climb could involve some profanity and physical violence mostly to yourself on the steeper sections. An "R" climb was serious stuff likely to provoke gratuitous profanity, with wanton violence, and some strictly adult situations. "X" climbs? Only for the connoisseur of the truly steep. Adults only, and don't bring your mother. There are only two of these in the book.

Unfortunately these ratings are completely subjective, and you should not put absolute faith in them. My PG-13 may be your G, or my R may be your X. I am reasonably certain someone will curse me for grossly under-rating a particular climb. If you think about it, it is impossible for difficulty ratings to be anything other than the subjective opinions of the author. I rated them based on how hard I thought they were. How hard I thought they were was based on my degree of fitness and not yours. The ratings are useful only in a relative sense. What I rated G will be easier than what I rated PG-13, and what I rated PG-13 will be easier than what I rated R. In that sense they should be consistent and useful.

	Difficulty Ratings Guide
G	Suitable for general audiences. Easy riding. The few hills will be short and sweet.
PG	Parental guidance suggested. Some material may not be suitable for novice riders. Mild profanity possible. Longer hills, but no walls.
PG-13	Parents strongly cautioned. Some material may be inappropriate for out-of-shape riders. Some profanity and physical violence likely. Long sustained climbs but generally moderate grades.
R	Restricted. Some adult situations. Gratuitous profanity and prolonged physical violence likely, particularly if you did not train for this tour. Longer distances with a lot of sustained climbing.
X	No one under Olympian status admitted unless they really like to suffer. Explicit profanity, excessive physical violence, strictly adult content. Wicked long and wicked steep.

Altitude Profiles

 Each daily stage has an altitude profile graphically depicting the relative altitude gains for the day. Like the Degree of Difficulty ratings these too should not be taken too literally. These graphs show the absolute altitude gains, but not how the road climbs up to that altitude. In other words, the road does not climb up those really steep sections; it winds back and forth up switchbacks that go at an easier grade. The altitude profiles are most useful for showing when you are going up and when you are going down, not how steep it is.

Distances

Each daily stage states the distance along the route described. When figuring out how long it will take you to ride this distance you can use the very conservative figure of 10 miles per hour (16 kph). Your actual mileage will vary depending on the degree of difficulty, the load you are carrying, your level of fitness, etc. In a group your mileage will be no faster than that of the slowest member.

Castiglione di Garfagnana

AIRPORTS

There are three international airports easily accessible to the Tuscany region: Rome, Pisa, and Firenze. Your choice of which to use will depend upon convenience, cost, time, and the tour you choose. All of the tours described in this book originate at one of these airports. If you wanted to do a tour starting in Firenze, you'd be better off flying into Firenze. But time, cost, and convenience might dictate flying into Pisa or Rome. For instance if flying into Firenze meant a day lay-over in Amsterdam or London, you might opt to fly to Pisa and take the train to Firenze.

You can also fly into the international airport in Milan, but this requires an all-day train or car ride to and from the Tuscany region. Unless there is some other compelling reason to fly into Milan, I would not recommend it.

Rome's Leonardo Da Vinci International Airport at Fiumicino has the benefit of direct flights from the United States. If you fly into Pisa or Firenze, you have to change planes at another hub in Europe. None of the three airports are particularly fun to bike into or out of. Rome's may be the easiest to negotiate since it is well out of the city. The airports in Pisa and Firenze are near the city centers, and upon leaving the terminal you are thrust into urban traffic.

Trans-Atlantic flights into Rome generally arrive between 7:00 and 9:00 a.m. This gives you plenty of time to assemble the bikes and set off on your first leg. Connecting flights into Pisa and Firenze will likely arrive later in the day and may not allow enough time to reach your first destination. On the other hand, this allows you to work off the jet lag by spending the first day exploring either of these fascinating cities.

Trans-Atlantic flights depart Rome's airport between 10:00 a.m. and 1:00 p.m. In most cases this means you will have to spend the night at a hotel near the airport in order to get the bikes and gear packed and checked. My recommendation is to stay in the sea-side town of Fregene, 16 km (10 mi.) from the airport. More on that below.

How to get out of the airport was always the hardest part of any tour I planned. I have solved that dilemma for you here by mapping out the escape routes from each of the three choices. I won't claim they are scenic or even any fun, but they do get you in and out of the airports with a minimum of difficulty.

Roma/ Leonardo Da Vinci International Airport

Rome's Leonardo Da Vinci International Airport is located 26 km (16 miles) west of the city near the coastal town of Fiumicino. It is connected to Rome by train and divided highway. Fortunately there is a back way out of the airport that provides a convenient escape route for cyclists. This route is not unknown to motorists, so don't expect a tranquil country lane. Nevertheless it beats riding on the highway.

From the international arrivals and departures terminal you push off into traffic on a big one-way boulevard. You will soon come to a traffic circle where you bear right following a blue sign for **Ostia** and **Fiumicino**. At a second traffic circle you again bear right following the blue Ostia/ Fiumicino sign. You are now on a long straight-a-way past non-descript one-storey office buildings. You will be able to see gas stations ahead. At the end of the straight-a-way you cross directly over a third traffic circle. Now look for a black on white sign saying "**Fiumicino Nord**." It is on the right immediately before a Shell gas station.

This road bears off to the right along the fenced edge of the airport. Just past a series of large fuel tanks you will merge onto another road which continues along the edge of the runways. After a short distance you will come to a 4-way intersection. There will be a blue sign for **Focene** and a white sign for **Fregene** pointing to the right. Turning here you leave most of the traffic behind and are on your way.

You are now pedaling down a long, straight road with the airport runways on one side and a dense pine forest on the other. Seven kilometers (4.3 mi.) from the 4-way intersection you will reach a junction where you turn right to go around the end of the runways in the direction of Fregene. There is a small café on the left, and a sign for Focene straight ahead.

The road jogs around the end of the runways next to a canal. After about 2 km (1.2 mi.) the road crosses over the canal and strikes off due north. This is board-flat agricultural land and is easy riding.

After a few kilometers you will pass a flashing yellow traffic light at a right turn for Roma; continue straight. At the second flashing yellow light you can turn left to go into Fregene. To continue on to the first destination of your tour, you keep straight on this road until you reach the town of Maccarese. From here refer to the tour description for further directions.

On your return to the airport simply retrace your route around the outside of the runways to the 4-way intersection. Here you turn left following the sign for **Aeroporto.** After a short distance there will be a left turn for Ostia and Roma. Continue past it to the second left turn which has a yellow sign for Ostia and a green Autostrada sign for Roma. At the top of the ramp you will find yourself back on the long straight-a-way past the gas stations that leads into the airport. You simply follow the signs through the three traffic circles to the airport terminal buildings.

If you need to spend the night at the beginning or end of your tour at or near the Rome/ Fiumicino airport, you have three options. First, you can stay at the airport Hilton Hotel which is connected to the terminal buildings. This is very expensive, but you cannot beat the convenience.

Roma/ Leonardo Da Vinci International Airport

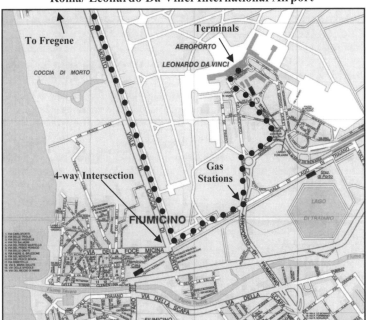

Touring Club Italiano, Auth. 04 November, 2002

Your second option is to take the train into downtown Rome. The train station is also connected to the terminal buildings and has regular service to downtown. Getting your bikes on and off the train will be the challenge. Unfortunately there is no longer a baggage storage facility at the airport.

Your third option is to stay in Fregene. This is a quiet seaside resort 16 km (10 mi.) from the airport. It has three hotels and a pleasant main street lined with shops. Fregene is a popular weekend destination for Romans. If you intend to stay there on a summer weekend it is best to book well ahead. Contact information for these hotels is listed in the Appendices.

The towns of Ostia and Fiumicino are also near the airport. Each has a few very expensive hotels. Both towns are seedy and commercial, and the traffic can be horrific. I would not recommend either one as an overnight stop on a bicycle tour.

Pisa Galileo International Airport

Pisa's international airport has the benefit of being on the edge of the old section of the city. It is a short ride into the downtown area, or you can peel off into the countryside. Pisa is a bustling place, and as with any of the large towns or cities in Italy there is no easy way in or out on a bike. You will have to deal with heavy traffic until you emerge from the suburbs that surround the historical sections.

This guide contains three tours that depart from Pisa. One goes north through the city-center and on to Lucca. The other two head south out of the city and into the hills to the spa town of Casciano Terme. Each route out of the city is marked on the map below.

The Pisa airport terminal is a long, one story building. A one-way street runs in front of it and leads you to a traffic circle where you follow the white signs with the black bull's eye symbol. This is the universal Italian symbol for the city-center or "il centro."

After passing under a highway overpass you are now on **Via dell' Aeroporto**. This wide, tree-lined boulevard leads you north towards the old section of the city. After a kilometer or so you come to a square, **Piazza Giusti.** If Lucca is your destination, you should continue straight across the square and up over a railroad overpass into the old section of town. Refer to the specific tour description for detailed directions from here.

If you are going south to Casciano Terme you must make a sharp right turn when you reach Piazza Giusti onto **Via Giuseppe Montanelli**. After several blocks you will come to a fork where you bear left onto **Cavalcavia S. Ermete Ovest**. After crossing an overpass above a set of railroad tracks you will come to an intersection with route **N 206**, the **Via Emilia.** Turn right here and you are now on your way towards Casciana Terme. Refer to the specific tour for directions from this point.

Pisa is a fascinating city and well worth exploring beyond the shadow of its famous tower. As one of the principal tourist attractions in Italy and a university town, there is no shortage of hotels to choose from. Conventional tourist guides cover Pisa thoroughly.

Pisa Galileo International Airport

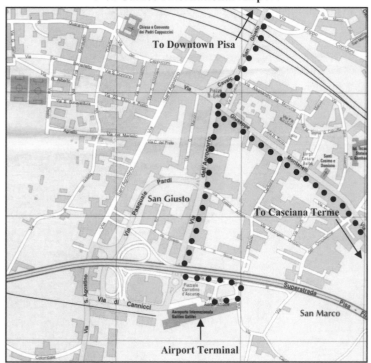

Touring Club Italiano, Auth. 04 November, 2002

Firenze Amerigo Vespucci International Airport

The international airport in Firenze is enveloped in the urban sprawl of the city. And while it is easy to navigate your way down the wide boulevards, you will have to contend with horrendous city traffic. To reach the old section of the city from the airport you want to get on **Via Francesco Baracca**. This is a wide one-way boulevard that rolls downtown. From the airport entrance dash across **Viale XI Agosto** and under a highway overpass. Any one of several streets leading away perpendicularly from the airport will put you on Via F. Baracca. Once on this wide boulevard you just go with the flow of traffic. Via F. Baracca fizzles out at **Piazza Puccini** and becomes **Via del Ponte alle Mosse**. Continue to pedal with the one-way traffic until you reach **Porta al Prato,** an impressive medieval gate surrounded by equally impressive traffic. You are now on the edge of the old section of the city.

In order to reach the main tourist area around the **Uffizi** museum and the **Ponte Vecchio** you need to turn right at the Porta al Prato. This takes you to the banks of the Arno River. Once at the river you turn left onto **Lungaro Amerigo Vespucci**, a one-way along the river's edge. You can follow this all the way to the Ponte Vecchio.

Firenze Amerigo Vespucci International Airport

Touring Club Italiano, Auth. 04 November, 2002

PART TWO
TOURS 1-8

TOUR 1: Firenze—Siena—Firenze, 250 km/ 155 mi.
TOUR 2: The Garfagnana, 353 km/ 219 mi.
TOUR 3: Pisa—Firenze—Pisa, 397 km/ 246 mi.
TOUR 4: Roma/ Fiumicino—Orvieto—Fiumicino, 377 km/ 234 mi.
TOUR 5: Firenze—Montalcino—Firenze, 446 km/ 277 mi.
TOUR 6: Pisa—Elba—Pisa, 498 km/ 309 mi.
TOUR 7: Firenze—Urbino—Firenze, 700 km/ 434 mi.
TOUR 8: Roma/ Fiumicino—Norcia—Fiumicino, 845 km/ 524 mi.

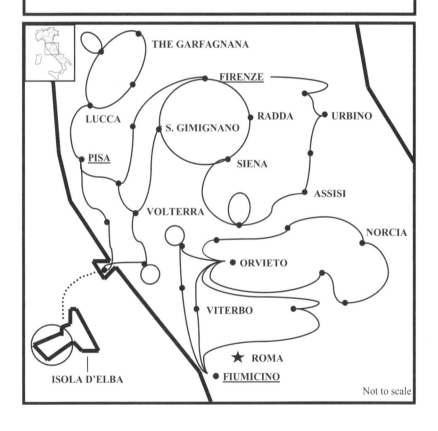

Bolsena

TOUR 1

FIRENZE—SIENA—FIRENZE
4 Days, 250 km/ 155 mi.

If you had just one week to spend in Italy and wanted to see the crown jewels of Tuscany, this could be the tour for you. Four days of relatively easy riding take you from Firenze through the Chianti region to Siena and then on to San Gimignano and back to Firenze. Don't be misled; the riding is easy only relative to other rides in Tuscany. These are still the Tuscan hills, and you will be going up and down many of them. Nevertheless the distances are not long, and you should be in the saddle for no more than three or four hours each day leaving you plenty of time to enjoy the sights at your destination.

Day 1: Firenze—Radda in Chianti, 54 km/ 33.5 mi., PG.

Day 2: Radda in Chianti—Siena, 62 km/ 38.5 mi., G.

Day 3: Siena—San Gimignano, 62 km/ 38.5 mi., PG-13.

Day 4: San Gimignano—Firenze, 72 km/ 44.5 mi., PG-13.

TOUR 1/ DAY 1

FIRENZE-RADDA IN CHIANTI
54 km/ 33.5 mi. Degree of Difficulty: PG

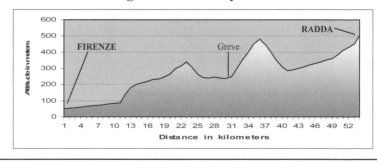

From the beautiful monuments and bustling crowds of **Firenze** this ride takes you out of the city and into the lovely rolling hills of the Chianti region. This isn't an especially long route, but there are a couple of memorable climbs. It follows the famous **Via Chiantigiana**, the Chianti road. It winds past famous vineyards and villas and ends at one of the quintessential hilltowns of Tuscany: **Radda in Chianti.** The stone houses of Radda are crowded inside circular walls on top of a hill with awesome views over the surrounding countryside. Its narrow traffic-free lanes are the perfect counterpoint to the hot confusion of Firenze.

This route description begins at the **Ponte Vecchio** in downtown Firenze. Strike off up the river along the **Lungarno Torrigiani.** This is a one-way against you, but there is a wide sidewalk along the river. Continue up river past **Ponte alla Grazie** to **Ponte San Niccolo.** Here at the confusing **Piazza F. Ferrucci** you go straight across onto **Via G. Orsini**, a one-way in your direction. After four blocks you bear right onto **Via di Ripoli,** another one-way going your way. You stay Via di Ripoli until you reach a large traffic circle at **Piazza di Badia a Ripoli.** Here you turn right onto **Via Chiantigiana, N 222.** You follow the signs for N 222 as it winds its way through the suburbs of Firenze. After several kilometers you will pass under the Autostrada. A short distance beyond the highway you will pass a huge modern Sheraton Hotel. Beyond the hotel there are two traffic circles where you continue to follow signs for N 222. After the second traffic circle a broad tree-lined boulevard rolls you into the modern town of **Grassina.**

Grassina marks the outer limits of the city congestion and the first climb of the day. Staying on N 222 you swing through town and begin a long gentle climb in the Chianti hills. A couple of broad switchbacks draw you up to the top of a ridge where there are views over rolling vineyards on each side. The road continues along the top of this ridge all the way to **Strada in Chianti** at about 19 km from downtown Firenze. It is lovely, quiet riding with relatively few cars through the classic postcard scenery of Tuscany. Strada has a large central square and many shops and cafes. Just past the edge of town the road descends gently for about a kilometer before gradually starting to climb. There is a steep section up to the village of **Chiocchio**, but it doesn't last long. Beyond Chiocchio the road meaders up and down a series of short climbs. At about 5 km from Strada you hit the very top of the hill marked by spectacular views and begin a steep descent into the forested valley below.

About 3 km down a steep winding descent you hit an intersection where you bear left following the sign for **Greve in Chianti**. From here the road follows the shady Greve River valley upstream to its name-sake. On the outskirts of Greve you pass by a few modern apartment buildings, but if you bear right when you reach the traffic light, you can find your way into the pretty central square. This marks the half-way point of the ride and makes a good place for a break — especially since the big climb of the day is up next.

From Greve you follow the signs for **Siena** on N 222. A few kilometers outside of town the road begins the prom-ised climb. It starts out gently but gets steeper and steeper until at last you reach the pleasant town square of **Panzano in Chianti.** This pretty town sits high on a hill with magnificent views over vineyards and forested hills in every direction.

On the far side of Panzano the road drops away abruptly. It descends steeply through tight switchbacks into a forested valley. After about 3 km watch for a left turn with a sign for **Radda in Chianti.** Don't miss it, or you will have to turn around and ride back up to it. From this turn the road continues to descend down to the valley floor. At the bottom nestled among shady trees is the hamlet of **Lu-carelli.** It consists of a single restaurant/ bar which serves among other things delicious gelato to weary cyclists.

From Lucarelli the road meanders up a shady river valley through vineyards and pasture land. You can see the towers of Radda high above on the ridge just as the road begins to climb again. The climb out of the valley is pretty steep but short. You soon top out on a saddle where you have to weave around a curious brick overpass. The final kilometer up to the gates of the town may be the steepest yet, but at least the end is in sight.

Radda has the freshly-scrubbed feel of a tourist town, and you will not have the place to yourself, especially during the summer months. Walled hilltowns do not get any quainter than this, and it is easy to see what all the fuss is about. Inside its fortified gates are narrow streets lined with shops and cafes. It has all the intimacy and charm lacking from the spectacle of Firenze. But as with any of the popular tourist destinations in Tuscany, it is wise to book a room in advance.

Degree of Difficulty: Overall this is a pretty hilly route. In addition to all the usual ups and downs there are three climbs of note: Above Grassina, above Greve, and up to Radda. But between these climbs there is wonderful, quiet riding in shady valleys. It is not especially long, and there are many quaint towns to stop in along the way for rest and refreshment. Rating: PG.

Highlights: The beautiful rolling countryside of the Chianti region and the peaceful stillness of Greve and Radda combine to be the perfect antidote to the congestion of Firenze.

km	Place Name	Cafes	Shops, Mkts	Lodging	Camping	Bank	Bike Shop	Quaintness Rating
12	Grassina	●	●	●		●		
15	Poggio Ugolino	●	●			●		*
17	Poggio alla Sala	●						
19	Strada in Chianti	●	●	●		●		*
30	Greve in Chianti	●	●	●		●	●	***
36	Panzano in Chianti	●	●	●		●		**
41	Lucarelli	●						*
54	Radda in Chianti	●	●	●		●	●	*****

Tour 1/ Day 1 Firenze—Radda in Chianti

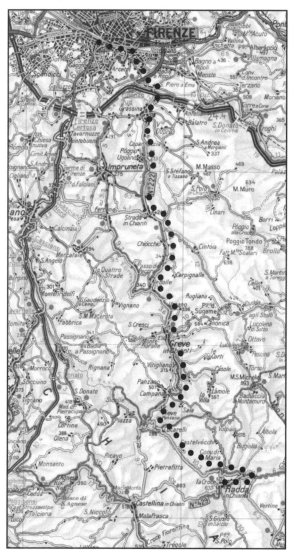

Touring Club Italiano, Auth. 04 November 2002

TOUR 1/ DAY 2

RADDA IN CHIANTI—SIENA
62 km/ 38.5 mi. Degree of Difficulty: G

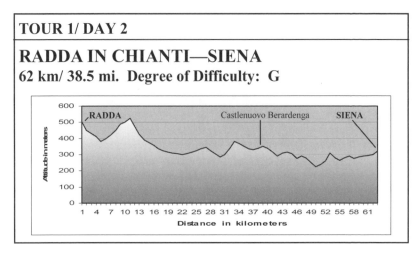

This is a great ride — easy, scenic, with little or no traffic. You will have plenty of time to savor the shady forests, the well-tended vineyards and olive groves, and the great, rambling villas overlooking it all. You will pass through villages of lovely stone houses and inviting outdoor cafes. You will pass one great picnic spot after another. And you will finish the ride before the gates of one of the great cities of the Middle Ages. Siena is a tastefully understated version of Firenze. It has comparable monuments but in a quainter, quieter, and more manageable setting.

From Radda you ride back down to the saddle below town following signs for **Firenze** and **Montevarchi.** You pedal past the brick overpass and the turn for Firenze. Beyond this turn the road begins to climb. You will soon reach a right turn with signs for **Siena.** Go past this turn and continue in the direction of Montevarchi. The road winds up into the forested hills above Radda. There are wonderful views back over the town and the surrounding hills. This should be enough to distract you from what becomes fairly steep climbing.

About 11 km from Radda you will reach another right turn with signs for **Gaiole in Chianti** and Siena. Turning here you zoom down past vineyards and elegant villas into the forested valley. The road whips back and forth in tight switchbacks as it makes its way down the steep hillside. After about 4.5 km of descending you roll into the pleasant town of Gaiole. As you enter town bear off to the left so you go down the main street of the old section of town. There are shops and cafes here if you feel like a break. Below the old section the main street merges back with the main road and you continue descending down a shady valley past vineyards and olive groves and thick stands of trees. Stately villas at the top of cypress-lined driveways overlook neat rows of grape vines. This is a beautiful section of road with very little traffic.

A few kilometers below Gaiole you will pass a right turn that would take you back to Radda. You bear left and continue down the lovely wooded valley in the direction of Siena. About 5 km below Gaiole you will come to a well-marked left turn for **Castel Brolio** and **Castelnuovo Berardenga.** Turning here the road begins to climb very gently up through beautiful forest; the branches arch over the road forming a dark green leafy tunnel. As the road climbs the forest gives way to pasture and finally vineyards. About 5 km from the turn you will see the spectacular towers of Castel Brolio ahead. The road meets an intersection below the castle walls where you turn left following the sign for Castelnuovo Berardenga.

From Castel Brolio the road circles around below the walls and then drops down into a valley beyond it. For about 3 km you descend down an easy, smooth grade through beautiful countryside. You then begin to climb again up through olive groves towards the lovely medieval village of **Villa a Sesta.** The road passes below this town and continues through more open country to Castelnuovo Berardenga.

Castelnuovo Berardenga is a wonderful medieval town with narrow streets and tiny shops. It is well worth a stop to explore, and it makes a good lunch stop. To continue on follow the road around the west side of town following the signs for Siena and **Pacina.** The road rolls up and down through hills dotted with ancient olive trees. At Pacina you turn right following the sign for **Pianella.** At each successive intersection just keep following the Pianella signs. About 11 km from Castenuovo Berardenga you will reach **N 408,** the main road between Siena and Radda. Turn left here which takes you into Pianella. There is nothing exciting here but you will find a few shops in case you need an energy boost. From Pianella all signs point to Siena and you just follow the main road through town.

The final 12 km from Pianella to Siena are up and down. There are some short, steep climbs at the top of which you can see the spires and towers of Siena. And as you get closer you enter the modern suburbs with its attendant traffic. You will soon reach a large traffic circle just below the heights of the old city. Here you follow the bulls-eye sign to the city center. This brings you to another traffic circle where you follow the bull-eye sign to the left. You pass through the marvelous city walls at the fortified gate of **Porta Ovile,** and wind your way up the steep streets into the city center. As one of the principal tourist destinations in Italy you will need to book months in advance if you wish to stay in the old section of the city.

Degree of Difficulty: This route has a lot of rolling hills, but only one long sustained climb. That one is from the base of the hill below Radda up to the turn for Gaiole. Nevertheless it is not particularly steep and comes early in the day when it is cool and you are fresh. The rest of the ride is easy cruising. Rating: G.

Highlights: This is beautiful riding — quiet shady river valleys, wonderful gentle climbs up through olive groves, magnificent castles crowning hilltops. This is the kind of riding you come to Tuscany for. Gaiole is quaint, Castelnuovo Berardenga is dramatic, and Siena is unforgettable. If you could only do one ride in Tuscany, this might be it.

km	Place Name	Cafes	Shops, Mkts	Lodging	Camping	Bank	Bike Shop	Quaintness Rating
16	Gaiole in Chianti	•	•	•		•		**
27	Castel Brolio	•						****
39	Castelnuovo Berardenga	•	•	•		•		****
50	Pianella	•	•					
53	San Giovanni	•						
55	Ponte Bozzone	•	•					
62	Siena	•	•	•	•	•	•	*****

Tour 1/ Day 2 Radda in Chianti—Siena

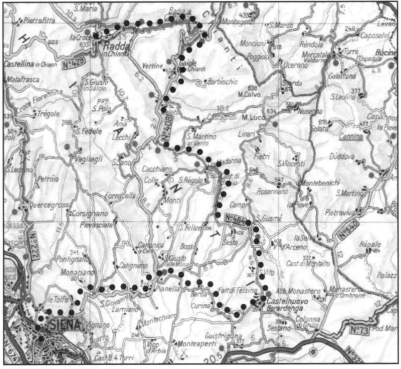

Touring Club Italiano, Auth. 04 November 2002

TOUR 1/ DAY 3

SIENA—SAN GIMIGNANO
62 km/ 38.5 mi. Degree of Difficulty: PG-13

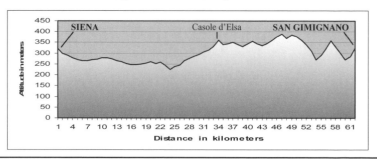

This route takes you through the beautiful rolling hills of Tuscany past the walled medieval towns of Monteriggioni, Strove, and Casole d'Elsa and finally to the famous towers of San Gimignano. The first half of the ride is fairly easy; the second half will have you working pretty hard; but the whole way you will be treated to the classic scenery that has made this region famous.

To leave **Siena** navigate your way to the **Porta Camollia** at the west end of the old city. Once beyond the protection of the city walls you are plunged into traffic. Follow signs for **N 2**, the **Via Cassia** to **Firenze.** You will soon come to a busy traffic circle with signs for N 2 to **Monteriggioni** and **Poggibonsi**. There is a slight climb away from this traffic circle for about 1.5 km. At next intersection continue straight following the sign for Monteriggioni. By now you will have escaped most of the heavy traffic. About 1 km from this intersection you begin a long descent down into open countryside.

The descent goes for about 3 km and finally flattens out in a broad valley. For the next several kilometers you will pedal easily past stands of corn and sunflowers. There are a few little ups and downs but mostly the road trends down. At about 14 km from Siena you will pass a sewage treatment plant on the left (you will know you are approaching this facility well before you see it…). Just beyond the plant you will see the walls and towers of Monteriggioni sitting picturesquely up on its hill overlooking the road.

Monteriggioni is a wonderful example of medieval architecture. The turn for the access road is marked by a collection of hotel signs. You will see the road snaking up the hill to the walls. There is a short steep section just past a car park which takes you to the main gate into the central square of the town. It is well worth the detour.

From Monteriggioni you continue north on N2 towards Poggibonsi. About 1 km from the Monteriggioni turn there is an intersectiuon with signs for **Colle Val d'Elsa** and **Volterra** to the left. Turning here the road stikes off across a broad flat valley with open fields of wheat and sunflowers on both sides. After about 1.5 km you will come to a left turn with a sign for **Strove**. This takes you off the main road and into rolling rural countryside. The road is board-flat and lined by columnar evergreens. After a few kilometers you pass through the wonderfully quaint village of **Abbadia Isola**. Its crumbling stone buildings have a wonderful time-worn air of having witnessed 800 years of Tuscan history.

The road climbs gently away from Abbadia Isola and across rolling fields of sunflowers. The nearby hillsides are combed with careful rows of grape vines. Ahead in a grove of cypress trees you can see the crenulated towers of the **Castel Petraio**, once a fortified manor and now a swanky hotel. And just past the castle you will come to the delightful walled village of **Strove**. This is another well-preserved gem of medieval charm, and you should not miss the chance to pedal through its narrow streets. It won't take long—it's a tiny place— unless you are lured into its inviting café.

The road rolls on through beautiful landscape and finally drops down a steep hill to a "T" intersection with signs for **Scorgiano** to the left and Colle Val d'Elsa to the right. You turn right and go a short distance to another intersection where you turn left following the sign for **Grosseto.** About 100 meters down the road in this direction you will see a right turn with signs for **Mensanello** and **Lano.** Turning here you climb gently away from the main road into rolling wheat fields. The road continues to climb up through these villages at an easy grade. Ahead you can see the walls of **Casole d'Elsa** dominating the ridge line. It is 10 km of climbing from the main road up to Casole, but only the last kilometer is really steep. The final 100 meters up to the town gate are the worst. But once inside the walls you are treated to a wonderful, quiet, un-touristy medieval village that among other things makes a great stop for lunch.

Continuing on from Casole d'Elsa you leave town following the signs for **Castel San Gimignano.** This takes you down a steep hill to the north of town. For the next 12 km you pedal up and down rolling hills through rugged country of forest and pastures. A few kilometers from Casole just past the hamlet of **Il Murlo** you will reach an intersection marked by a huge abandoned factory. Bear left here following the sign for Castel San Gimignano. After a short descent the road begins a long climb through scrub forest. After 2 km of gentle climbing the road contours along below the ridge line. You will pass a left turn for the village of **Posano.** Shortly afterwards you begin another long climb up to the main road, **N 68.**

At this intersection there will be signs for Volterra to the left and Castel San Gimignano to the right. Turning right you roll along the top of a ridge with magnificent views in every direction. Rows and rows of grape vines climb every nearby hill. After about 4 km you reach Castel San Gimignano, a fairly large town with many shops and a quaint old section. The main road skirts around the town and just beyond it you will see a left turn with a sign for San Gimigano.

From this turn you begin a wonderful 3 km plunge down through beautiful vineyards and wheat fields. Unfortunately at the bottom you begin a 3 km climb up the other side. On the way up you pass a prison with watch towers and barbed wire-topped walls. It couldn't look more out of place in the lovely landscape. At the top of this climb you pass through the village of San Donato and immediately plunge down another wonderful 3 km decent. Ahead you can see the famous towers of San Gimignano on top of the next hill, and it is this hill that you will soon be climbing. Three more kilometers of climbing through beautiful olive groves and vineyards, past immaculate villas, and rolling fields of wheat eventually bring you to the busy main road that takes you up to the walls of the city.

San Gimignano is a busy place. It is teeming with fellow sight-seers and has a festive air. There are many hotels in the immediate vicinity, but during the summer months you will definitely want to reserve a room well in advance.

Degree of Difficulty: The first half of this ride—as far as Casole d'Elsa—is the warm up for the second half. The 32 km from Casole to San Gimignano is an up and down grind with several long steep climbs. By the top of the last hill you will be very glad to see the city gates. Rating: PG-13.

Highlights: This route takes you through the scenery that has made Tuscany a favorite destination since the time of the Visigoths. You will be pedaling through beautiful fields of sunflowers and grape vines and up and down hills dotted with olive trees. You will pass by several quaint walled towns which so far have escaped plunder by tour bus hordes.

km	Place Name	Cafes	Shops, Mkts	Lodging	Camping	Bank	Bike Shop	Quaintness Rating
15	Monteriggioni	●	●	●		●		*****
28	Abbadia Isola	●	●					***
20	Strove	●	●	●				****
26	Mensanello	●	●					*
34	Casole d'Elsa	●	●	●		●		****
36	Il Murlo	●						
50	Castel San Gimignano	●	●	●		●		*
62	San Gimignano	●	●	●	●	●	●	*****

Tour 1/ Day 3 Siena—San Gimignano

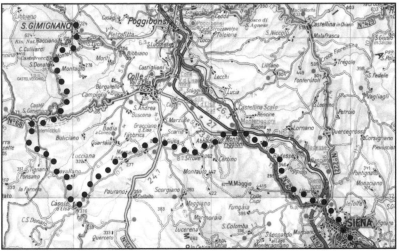

Touring Club Italiano, Auth. 04 November 2002

TOUR 1/ DAY 4

SAN GIMIGNANO—FIRENZE
72 km/ 44.5 mi. Degree of Difficulty: PG-13

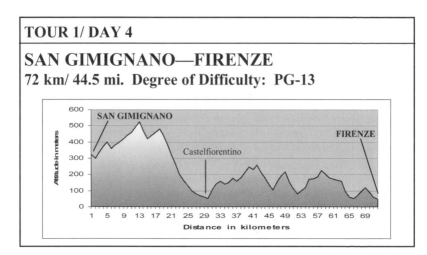

This ride goes up or down all day; there are very few flat stretches. It also goes through some of the most beautiful countryside you will find anywhere in Tuscany. From the bucolic panoramas of San Gimignano it delivers you back to the cosmopolitan atmosphere of Firenze.

Beginning at the gates of **San Gimignano** follow the signs for **Certaldo** west out of town. After about one kilometer you will reach an intersection marked by a lovely abbey surrounded by vineyards. Here you turn left following the sign for **Volterra**. The road begins to climb up a ridge with vineyards cascading down to the left. The view back at the towers of San Gimignano is as picturesque as you will find. The road continues to climb for about 4 km but at a gentle grade. After reaching the crest it begins to roll along the top of the ridge with several short descents and climbs. About 9 km from San Gimignano you will pass a left turn with a sign for Volterra. Continue past this turn for another 2 km to a right turn with a sign for **Castelfiorentino.**

After making this turn you pass through the village of **Il Castagno**. On the far side there is a fork where you bear right following the sign for **Gambassi Terme**. The road immediately begins to climb. After about one kilometer of steep you top out and begin a wonderful descent down through a dense shady forest. After about 2 km the descent bottoms out and you face a short steep climb up through the trees to an intersection where there is a sign for Gambassi Terme to the right. Turning here you continue climbing up through the shady forest. As you reach the top of the climb there is a left turn for Castelfiorentino which skirts around

Gambassi Terme. The next 6 km are a long sweeping descent down through vineyards and rolling fields of wheat into the broad valley of the Elsa River. The view across the valley as you descend is breathtaking.

At the bottom of the descent you merge with the main road from the modern town of **Montaione**. Cross directly over the main road and follow a narrow lane into a neighborhood of shops and apartment blocks on the outskirts of Castelfiorentino. This allows you to avoid the high speed traffic entering town. Wind your way through this modern part of town following signs for **Empoli.** This will take you across a bridge above the Elsa River to the old section of town. Turn left on the far side and continue to follow the signs for Empoli.

You are now on the main road which follows the river through town. As you reach the edge of the old section begin looking for a right turn with signs for **Firenze** and **Montespertoli**. Turning here you climb a very steep grade up to a saddle above the old section of town, and at the "T" intersection at the top you should turn left following the signs for Firenze.

From this intersection the road continues to climb, but more gently. You are on top of a ridge with wonderful views both left and right over rolling fields bordered by columnar evergreens. The road rolls up and down short climbs and descents along the ridge top. At 13 km from Castelfiorentino (43 km from San Gimignano) you reach Montespertoli. This mostly modern town sits on top of a hill with spectacular views in every direction. It has a pleasant central piazza with lawns and park benches which makes a good stop for lunch.

From Montespertoli the road descends down a steep hill. At the bottom you pass through the town of **Baccaiano.** This lovely descent is followed immediately by a steep 2 km climb up the opposite hillside. At the top you pass the village on **Montagnana** and begin another roller-coaster ride down into the next valley. Here the road is lined by cypress trees and has a wonderfully European feel. You cross the Pesa River at the town of **Cerbaia.** At every intersection you simply follow signs for Firenze.

Following another a short, steep climb up above Cerbaia you get a break as the road meanders through a pretty valley of trees and pasture land. About 4 km from Cerbaia the grade steepens and you begin a long haul up to the town of **Chiesanuova.** As you top out in this nondescript town take heart because all of the climbing is now behind you.

You are now rewarded by a marvelous 7 km descent. Broad sweeping switchbacks take you down through olive groves and vineyards into the Arno River valley. You sail past ancient abbeys and get a spectacular view over the hazy sprawl of Firenze.

This memorable descent ends below the walls of the citadel-like **Certosa di Galluzo.** Just past the entrance to this complex of medieval buildings you reach an intersection with the busy **Via Sienese.** This is your route into downtown Firenze.

Turning left here you run down a gentle hill into the town of **Galluzo**, a forgettable suburb of apartment blocks. You pass straight through town on Via Sienese. This is not especially enjoyable riding, but it is direct. After 6 km you descend down the broad busy boulevard to the walls of the old city at **Porta Romana.** Here you can duck through the gate onto **Via Romana** to escape the worst of the traffic. This one-way street takes you to the **Pitti Palace.** Here you hit a one-way street going against you. You have to jog down a few side streets to find your way back to your starting point at the **Ponte Vecchio.**

Degree of Difficulty: This ride is all up and all down. Fortunately it is mostly down, but it is still fairly challenging. Discretion advised; some material may be inappropriate for out-of-shape riders. Rating: PG-13.

Highlights: This ride is about landscape — beautiful tree-lined vistas that ache for an easel and paint or at least a disposable camera. This is 5-star scenery and great cycling.

km	Place Name	Cafes	Shops, Mkts	Lodging	Camping	Bank	Bike Shop	Quaintness Rating
11	Il Castagno	●	●	●				**
30	Castelfiorentino	●	●	●		●	●	*
43	Montespertoli	●	●	●		●		*
47	Baccaiano	●		●				
53	Cerbaia	●	●					*
59	Chiesanuova	●	●					
66	Galluzzo	●	●	●		●	●	
72	Firenze	●	●	●	●	●	●	*****

Tour 1/ Day 4 San Gimignano—Firenze

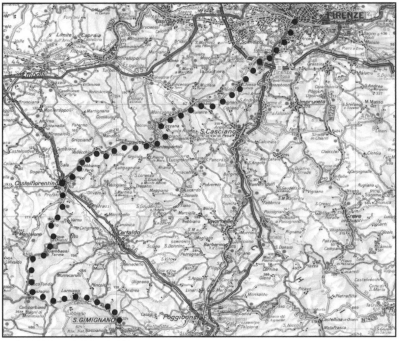

Touring Club Italiano, Auth. 04 November 2002

Montalcino   Photo by Geri Walsh

TOUR 2

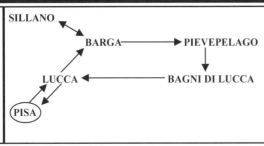

THE GARFAGNANA
6 Days, 353 km/ 219 mi.

This is a climbing tour. After an easy day from Pisa to Lucca, each succeeding day involves at least one big climb. Two of these climbs are rated X: wicked steep and wicked long. These are the kind of climbs that have words of encouragement spray-painted on the pavement, where every passing rider cries out a greeting, and where the triple chain ring rules. You will want to be in shape for this one.

The remote Garfagnana region lies between the coastal Apuan Alps and the central Apennine mountain chain. It is barely mentioned in most guide books and thus retains an unpretentious and genuine atmosphere. This is not the area to search for famous frescoes and gargantuan cathedrals. A tour of the Garfagnana is more about scenery than culture, more about smooth roads, no traffic, grueling climbs, and exhilarating descents. If you've "done" the classic Tuscan landscapes of columnar evergreens, olive trees and wheat fields and want to try something a little different and a bit more challenging, then this is the tour for you.

Day 1: Pisa—Lucca, 33 km/ 20.5 mi., G

Day 2: Lucca—Barga, 52 km/ 32 mi., PG-13

Day 3: Barga—Sillano—Barga, 82 km/ 51 mi., X

Day 4: Barga—Pievepelago, 62 km/ 38.5 mi., X

Day 5: Pievepelago—Bagni di Lucca, 52 km/ 32 mi., PG-13

Day 6: Bagni di Lucca—Pisa, 72 km/ 45 mi., PG-13

TOUR 2/ DAY 1

PISA—LUCCA

33 km/ 20.5 mi. Degree of Difficulty: G

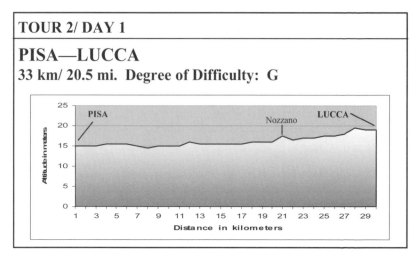

Pisa and **Lucca** are among the most famous destinations in Tuscany. Pisa's **Piazza dei Miracoli** (Field of Miracles), home of the famous Leaning Tower, has been drawing tourists since the 12th century—about 900 years. Lucca on the other hand seems to accept its fame reluctantly. Its massive 16th century walls were built to repel invaders, not attract them. The shops and markets along the narrow streets inside the walls cater to local clientele more than tourists. Both cities deserve their popularity and are well worth taking the time to explore.

The route from Pisa to Lucca is easy. You can fly into Pisa, assemble your bike, explore the city, and pedal the 20 flat miles to Lucca even under the influence of jet lag. The hardest part of your day will be negotiating the traffic in and out of the cities.

This tour begins at the Pisa International Airport. As outlined in the Airports chapter you should follow the bull's eye city center signs from the terminal building to **Via dell'Aeroporto**. This broad tree-lined boulevard takes you to **Piazza Giusti**, which has a raised grassy island in the middle. You continue straight past the traffic island and up over a railroad overpass. The street name now becomes **Via Antonio Fratti**. Street names are usually mounted on the corners of buildings at intersections. Continue straight on Via Antonio Fratti to **Piazza Guerrazzi,** a large square with an imposing fortress, the **Bastione Sangallo**, on one corner. Navigate your way around the traffic circle and continue in the same direction on **Via Giovanni Bovio**. After a block or so a one-way street, **Via Ceci,** bears off to the left. Via Ceci is a narrow street that takes you through a picturesque medieval section of Pisa. It eventually intersects with a pedestrian zone at **Corso Italia.** Here you turn right and cross over the Arno River on the **Ponte di Mezzo.** On the other side you must cross a busy boulevard before reaching another pedestrian zone. This leads you all the way to the Leaning Tower and the Piazza dei Miracoli.

After admiring the Field of Miracles and the equally large field of trinket shops ride along the pedestrian boulevard next to the expanse of lawn towards the original medieval walls of the city. Pass through a fortified gate and take an immediate right. Ride parallel to the outside of the walls through a parking area and cross over busy **Via Contessa Matilde**. On the other side you will find **Via Leonardo Da Vinci.** This narrow street curves around to the left and intersects with **Via Tino da Camaino,** where you turn right. After about 200 meters you will come to an intersection with **Via Ugo Rindi**. On the far side of the intersection there is left turn onto **Via San Jacopo**. You turn here and follow signs for **Vecchiano** and **Pontasserchio**.

Eight kilometers on this flat, straight road will bring you to Vecchiano on the Serchio River. After crossing the river you should turn right following signs for Lucca. About 4 km from Vecchiano you will cross over the A-11 Autostrada. On the other side bear right following signs for Lucca. You will shortly come to another bridge across the river, but you should bear left under a highway overpass and follow the signs for **Nozzano Castello.**

At the castle town of Nozzano again bear right and follow signs for Lucca . At the suburb of **Ponte San Pietro** you have the option of turning right and heading directly into Lucca on the very busy **Via Sarzannese**, or you can cross over Via Sarzannese to **Via della Chiesa** and then bear right after a few blocks onto **Via di Sant'alessio**. This will lead you around to the north side of Lucca to the village **Monte San Quirico** where entry into the city is easier. Either route will get you into the old section of the city, but the latter will have less traffic. Just follow the bull's eye city center signs and soon you will reach Lucca's massive 16th century walls. Advance reservations are advisable if you want to stay inside the old city. Otherwise follow the signs to the Tourist Information Office at the **Porta San Donato** gate for help in finding a room.

Degree of Difficulty: The riding will be easy; it's the traffic that will wear you out. Rating: G.

Highlights: The Leaning Tower of Pisa; the walled village of Nozzano; the city walls of Lucca; the first day on the bike.

km	Place Name	Cafes	Shops, Mkts	Lodging	Camping	Bank	Bike Shop	Quaintness Rating
8	Vecchiano	●	●					
13	Filettole	●	●					
21	Nozzano	●	●					***
24	Ponte San Pietro	●	●	●				
31	Monte San Quirico	●	●	●		●		
33	Lucca	●	●	●	3 km	●	●	*****

Tour 2/ Day 1 Pisa—Lucca

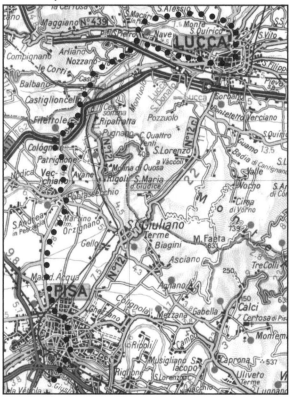

Touring Club Italiano, Auth. 04 November 2002

TOUR 2/ DAY 2

LUCCA—BARGA
52 km/ 32 mi. Degree of Difficulty: PG-13

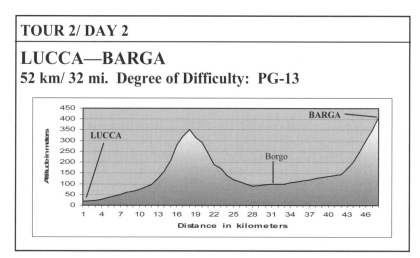

This stage begins at the north gate of the old section of Lucca, the **Porta Santa Maria.** Follow the signs for **Camaiore.** They will lead you on a circuitous route through the northern outskirts of the city, but it is generally well-marked and easy to follow. You will eventually reach the bridge across the Serchio River to the village of **Monte San Quirico.** Once across the bridge turn right still following the signs for Camaiore. By this point you will have left most of the traffic behind and be on quiet country roads.

About 11 km from Lucca you will enter the town of **San Martino in Freddana.** As you roll through town look for a blue sign marking a right turn for the village of **Torcigliano.** From this turn the road begins to climb up through a pretty side valley. About 15 km from Lucca you will begin a steep climb up a series of switchbacks which go on for about 1.5 km. From the top of the climb you drop like a stone into the valley of the Pedogna River, a tributary of the Serchio. At the intersection with the main road down in the valley there is a bar/ restaurant where you can re-fill water bottles or get a bite to eat. Turn right here and continue down the wooded valley towards the Serchio River.

This road eventually intersects with a four-lane highway from Lucca at the town of **Diecimo.** To avoid at least a portion of the high speed traffic turn left into the town. Its narrow cobble-stoned streets take you past cafes and shops and shorten your highway ride by a few kilometers. The 4 km stretch on the highway into **Borgo a Mozzano** isn't so bad as there is a wide shoulder, but the cars that pass are going fast.

Borgo a Mozzano is a bustling town with a famous medieval bridge that you will see on postcards throughout Tuscany. The so-called Devil's Bridge is wonderfully picturesque but not suited for riding. It is very narrow and steep and you will have a difficult time wrestling your bike over it. A better option is to cross the river by the bridge downstream near the center of town.

Once you have crossed to the east bank of the Serchio turn left and continue upstream. The road narrows to two lanes here and you lose the shoulder. But the traffic dissipates in about 3 km at the intersection for **Bagni di Lucca.** To reach Barga you should bear left continuing up the east bank of Serchio River following signs for **Aulla** and **Castelnuovo.** Just past the town of **Fornoli** you will see a huge lumber mill on the left. Just beyond this there is an intersection where you must bear left again in the direction of Aulla and Castelnuovo. The road to the right bears off into the hills away from the river.

Continue up the valley on the east bank of the river. The road narrows further and there is less traffic. You pass through several pleasant small towns. As you enter the town of **Fornaci** look for a right turn with a sign for **Barga**. Turning here the next 4.8 km climb steeply, but the magnificent view across the valley at the peaks of the Apuan Alps should be enough to distract you. At the top of the grade you will reach an uncut gem of medieval town. The upper section of Barga retains its medieval walls and gates. Its steep narrow streets lead down to the "new" part of town where most of the shops are located. You are well off the beaten tourist track here, but there are several hotels in town and some excellent restaurants.

Degree of Difficulty: While this is a relatively short day, there are two significant climbs. The first is at San Martino in Fredana 15 km from Lucca, and the second comes at the end of the day when you must ascend to the heights of Barga. Rating: PG-13.

Highlights: Once you are away from the suburban sprawl of Lucca the road to Camaiore takes you through beautiful vineyards where Colline Lucchesi wine is produced. There are long straight stretches of road bordered by trees whose branches grow together to form a leafy green tunnel. On weekends you will encounter packs of racing enthusiasts out for training rides along this route. After conquering the first steep climb up from San Martino you will be treated to a screaming descent of 17 km to the town of Diecimo. The Devil's Bridge at Borgo a Mozzano will not fail to captivate you, but the prize of the day will be arriving in the picturesque hilltown of Barga. It has a wonderful non-touristy flavor which can be all too rare elsewhere in Tuscany.

km	Place Name	Cafes	Shops, Mkts	Lodging	Camping	Bank	Bike Shop	Quaintness Rating
2	Monte San Quirico	●	●	●		●		
11	San Martino in Fredanna	●	●					
20	Piegaio	●						
28	Diecimo	●	●					
34	Borgo a Mozzano	●	●	●		●		***
37	Fornoli	●	●					
41	Calavorno	●	●			●		*
43	Ghivizzano	●	●					**
45	Lucignana	●	●	●				**
47	Fornaci	●	●	●		●	●	
52	Barga	●	●	●		●	●	****

Tour2/ Day 2   Lucca—Barga

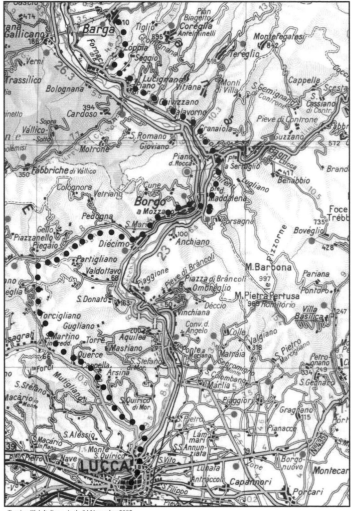

Touring Club Italiano, Auth. 04 November 2002

TOUR 2/ DAY 3

BARGA—SILLANO—BARGA
82 km/ 51 mi. Degree of Difficulty: X

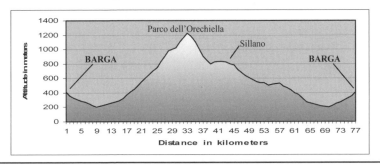

This stage is an out and back loop from **Barga**. This means you can leave the panniers behind in the hotel room, and when you see some of the grades you will be climbing, you will be glad you did. This route takes you up the Garfagnana Valley to **Castelnuovo**, the commercial center of the area. You then begin a long climb up to the **Parco dell' Orecchiella** nature reserve high on the flanks of the Appennine Massif. From there you plunge back down to the Garfagnana Valley through some of the most lovely scenery you will find anywhere in Tuscany. Although you will encounter some X-rated climbing, the spectacular scenery, ancient stone villages, and lush chestnut forests that you pedal through will more than make up for the effort. Do not miss this opportunity; this is one of the very best rides you will find in Italy.

You should make an early start today, for while the 82 km (51 mi.) may not seem long, it will be slow going up the steeper hills, and there are many interesting stops along the way. You begin with a beautiful descent out of Barga. You will be departing in the opposite direction from which you entered town. Follow signs for Castelnuovo and **Aulla.** The road courses down through forest and farmland past the hamlet of **Ponte di Catagnana** and then **Castelvecchio Pascoli,** which has an excellent bike shop, and finally to **Ponte di Campia** where you join the main road to Castelnuovo. Here the traffic increases in volume and speed, but there is a wide shoulder. The valley narrows down to a gorge and there are ancient stone farmhouses perched above you on the steep hillsides.

The road climbs gradually for 8 km up the valley along side the Serchio River. Around a bend in the river you suddenly find yourself at a busy intersection at the edge of Castelnuovo, a gritty, unremarkable town. The road forks here with signs for Aulla to the left and **Corfino, San Romano,** and **Modena** to the right. You should bear right crossing the bridge over the river. The traffic intensifies here as you make your way through the commercial section of town. About one kilometer beyond the intersection the road hits a series of tight switchbacks which vault you up onto a plateau above the river. Just beyond the top of this climb you reach another intersection marked by a café. In front of the café there is a blue sign pointing towards Modena to the right and San Romano and Aulla to the left. You want to bear left off the main road.

The road descends gently for about a kilometer to a lovely medieval convent in the village of Pontardeto. Just beyond the convent there is an intersection with blue signs to the right for Corfino and **Orecchiella.** Bearing right you begin climbing steeply up through forested switchbacks to the hamlet of **Pian di Cerreto.** Here the views open up across the patchwork fields of the Garfagnana Valley to the Apuan Alps beyond. You continue climbing past the ancient villages of **Pianacci, Magnano,** and **Canigiano,** and at 26 km from Barga you reach the town of Corfino.

Corfino is above the main road which continues towards Orecchiella. You have to pedal up a steep incline to reach it, but it is worth the effort. Corfino has a quaint, unpretentious air. There is a fountain at the edge of town where you can fill water bottles or simply dunk your head to cool off. Its ancient medieval buildings are not newly tricked-up for the tourist trade. The gray soot-stained stone buildings have the time-worn air of continuous occupation over many generations. There are several shops and cafes where you can buy a snack or a cold drink. There are spectacular views across the valley from the inviting benches in the town square — if you can find a seat among the gnarled old men in black suits and battered fedoras. After 26 km of more or less continuous climbing you may feel it is time for a rest. Unfortunately the real climbing only begins at Corfino — another reason for taking a break.

From Corfino you return to the main road and follow the brown signs for **Parco dell'Orecchiella.** The road takes you past the incongruous "Hotel California," and you run the risk of having this song stuck in your head for the next several hours. Just beyond the hotel you hit the first wall which earns this ride its "X" rating. The 15% grade claws its way up through thin mountain forest for 3.5 km. In several places you will see "FORZA" (strength!) spray-painted on the road along with the names of local cycling heroes. The grade finally moderates briefly at the hamlet of **Pruno,** a collection of stone houses with thatched roofs.

About one kilometer later, just beyond a turn for the village of **Sulcina,** you are back to the granny gears and crawling up another wall. Two kilometers of X-rated climbing brings you at last to the park headquarters of the Orecchiella Nature Reserve. There is a visitor center and a lake bordered by lawns and inviting park benches, but you must pay a fee to enter. Across the parking area there is a café in a stone hut. It has tables inside and out and makes a great place for a cold drink and a snack. From here it is all downhill (almost) back to Barga.

Continuing on from the Parco dell'Orecchella the road curves around below the parking area and drops into a dark pine forest. After a kilometer or so you come to a gushing fountain called the "Fontanone" where you can refill water bottles with pure mountain spring water. About 100 meters beyond the fountain you will reach a fork with a sign for "La Greppia," a restaurant that you can just see to the left. You should bear right here and continue on the paved road which plunges into the lush chestnut forest below.

The next 8 km take you down a steep winding grade through a forest of huge chestnut trees. You will pass ancient stone farm houses and may encounter sheep blocking the road. This is one of the most wonderful descents you will find anywhere, and it will more than compensate for the X-rated grind you had to endure to reach it. The screaming decent ends momentarily at a dam holding back a small reservoir. At the far side the road enters what appears to be a long dark tunnel. Fortunately it is only about 50 meters long and you will have no difficulty passing through it. A short distance beyond this tunnel you reach another short tunnel and then an intersection with signs for the town of **Sillano** to the left.

From this intersection a few tight switchbacks bring you to the bottom of the valley below the village of **Villa Soraggio.** After a short climb up through its narrow streets you descend once again down what becomes a narrow gorge. Two kilometers from Villa Soraggio you come to **Rocca Soraggio.** This is a collection of fortified medieval buildings perched high on a rock commanding access up the valley. The road goes through a tunnel under this rock. On the far side there is a café which has absolutely spectacular views from its terrace.

From Rocca Soraggio the road clings to the steep valley wall as it continues to descend. The valley finally opens up at the town of Sillano. This is a prosperous hilltown with many shops and cafes. The road winds through town and finally intersects with the main road at a small square with a café. There are no road signs at this intersection, but you want to turn left and continue downhill. Another 8 km of winding descent through beautiful olive groves and wheat fields bring you to the intersection with the main road from Castelnuovo. **Piazza al Serchio** is just across a bridge to the right. You want to turn left following the signs for **Lucca.**

A short distance down the road you will come to the village of **San Donnino.** This village is mostly remarkable for streets so narrow that it does not allow for two-way traffic. You will recognize the place by the line of trucks all gunning for their chance to squeeze through and continue on their way. Even on your bike you will have to carefully time your passage through this bottleneck.

Just beyond San Donnino the road begins to descend quite steeply. A short way down the hill you will come to a left turn with a sign for **San Romano**. Taking this turn gets you off the main road and away from its traffic. This quiet side-road rolls along the eastern slopes of the Garfagnana Valley. You pass below the steep streets of quaint San Romano. The road then begins a long descent back to Pontardeto where you began your climb up to Corfino. From Pontardeto you retrace your steps through Castelnuovo back to Barga. At Ponte Campia you turn left off the main road to begin the final climb back up to Barga.

Degree of Difficulty: The Garfagnana Valley seems to be all up or all down. You start the day with a pleasant 6 km descent from Barga down to the main road at Ponte di Campia. From there you will be climbing (but not always steeply) for the next 27 km. The section above Corfino is truly daunting especially after the 20 km warm-up climb to get there. But in a wonderful example of Newtonian physics, from the top of that climb it is all down hill back to Ponte di Campia — 43 km with hardly a pedal stroke. Nevertheless the 6 km or so of 15% grade above Corfino is serious adult entertainment. This is X-rated riding at its best.

Highlights: The scenery that unfolds before you as you climb to the Parco dell' Orechiella is nothing short of spectacular. All of the Garfagnana Valley and the Apuan Alps are displayed in all their glory. The several quaint villages you pass through are blissfully free of pandering to tourists. These are genuine hilltowns without a single postcard of the statue of David. The plunging descent from the Parco dell'Orecchiella through dark pine forests and brilliant green chestnut groves makes this one of the most exhilarating rides in all of Tuscany.

km	Place Name	Cafes	Shops, Mkts	Lodging	Camping	Bank	Bike Shop	Quaintness Rating
2	Ponte di Catagnana	●						**
4	Castelvecchio Pascoli	●	●	●			●	
6	Ponte di Campia	●						
14	Castelnuovo	●	●	●	●	●	●	
19	Pian di Cerreto	●	●					
21	Pianacci	●	●					
22	Magnano	●	●					*
24	Canignano	●	●	●				***
26	Corfino	●	●	●		●		***
30	Sulcina	●						
33	Parco dell' Orecchiella	●			●			****
40	Villa Soraggio	●	●					*
42	Rocca Soraggio	●						***
45	Sillano	●	●	●		●		**
52	Piazza al Serchio	●	●	●	6 km	●		
53	San Donnino	●	●					
58	San Romano	●	●	●		●		**
59	Sillicagnana	●						

Tour 2/ Day 3 Barga—Sillano—Barga

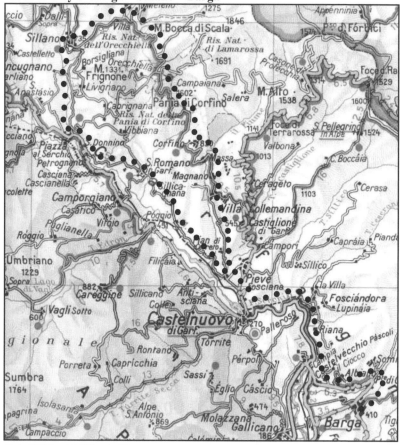

Touring Club Italiano, Auth. 04 November 2002

TOUR 2/ DAY 4

BARGA—PIEVEPELAGO
62 km/ 38.5 mi. Degree of Difficulty: X

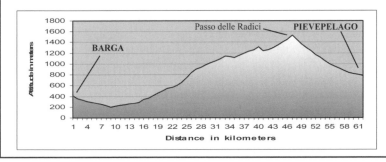

This ride takes you high up into the Appinine Massif and down the other side to the pleasant town of **Pievepelago.** Depending on your fitness and motivation, it can be combined with the following day's route up to the ski resort of **Abetone** and then down to **Bagni di Lucca.**

The route begins with the same gentle descent from **Barga** down to **Ponte di Campia.** At the main road you turn right and continue up the valley to **Castelnuovo.** At the main intersection as you enter town you cross the bridge on the same route you took to Sillano, but at the turn for San Romano you continue straight following signs for **Modena.** Although the map shows this to be a major road the traffic diminishes as you leave Castelnuovo behind.

About 3 km above Castelnuovo (17 km from Barga) just beyond the town of **Pieve Fosciana** you come to a "Y" intersection with signs for **Passo Radici** in both directions. You want to go left in the direction of **Castiglione di Garfagnana.** Going the other way takes you up a nearly 20% grade and an additional 130 meters in altitude to **San Pellegrino in Alp** before descending to Passo delle Radici. This route is said to be spectacular and was featured in the 1989 Tour of Italy, but mere mortals will prefer the easier alternative. Besides you would otherwise miss Castiglione which is one of the gems of the Garfagnana Valley if not all of Tuscany.

Taking the left turn for Castiglione the road immediately begins to climb more steeply. A series of long switchbacks take you up through rolling pasture to the town walls. Tucked behind its intact medieval walls and burly bastions, Castiglione will beg you to explore its "streets" which are too narrow for cars. It features a tumble-down castle above the village and wonderful views across the valley.

Continuing on, the main road skirts around the base of the walls and continues to climb. About one kilometer from Castiglione you will reach a sharp hairpin. A small road goes off to the left with signs for Pianacci, Magnano, and Corfino. You continue climbing on the main road in the direction of Modena. The next 2 km take you up several steep switchbacks through hardwood forest. At 28 km from Barga you will reach the village of **Cerageto.** It features a restaurant/ bar, a market, and even a hotel. Above Cerageto the grade moderates and you enter a shady forest with the branches of trees arching over the road to form a leafy green tunnel. In another 4 km you pass by **Casina Rossi** with two roadside restaurants. And then 2 km farther on you top out on the **Foce di Terrarossi**, a kind of false summit; you still have 13 km to go to the Passo delle Radici. The road actually descends from here for about 2 km giving you a bit of a break before once again beginning its inexorable march upward.

About 40 km from Barga you pass by a restaurant/bar/pensione at **Col d'Arciano**, a tiny village of only three or four houses. Here the road levels out for about a kilometer until **Casone di Profecchia**, a wide spot in the road hardly worth a sign. Its only building is an inviting-looking hotel/ restaurant set among tall dark pines. The road descends slightly here for about one kilometer and then you begin the final 5 km slog up to the Passo delle Radici.

Unfortunately the Pass is not particularly scenic. There is an unassuming hotel just off the road. The real reward is the coming 15 km descent down to Pievepelago. It starts off steep and stays that way almost all the way to the bottom of the valley. Five kilometers from the summit (52 km from Barga) you will pass a hotel/restaurant sign and a campground. Two kilometers later you roar through the pleasant alpine-looking town of **Sant'Anna Pelago**. You have now left Tuscany and entered the province of Emilia. Below you spread dark evergreen forests and rolling alpine meadows. The houses on this east side of the mountains are built with exposed beams and stucco — more Swiss chalet-like than the gray stone and tile roofs of the Garfagnana Valley.

The long descent comes to an end at a busy intersection at the edge of Pievepelago. This is not the most picturesque town you will see on your travels, but it has several hotels, markets, and restaurants, and makes a good over-night stop before the stiff climb up to Abetone. If you get stuck for a place to stay, there are hotels at intervals all the way up to the ski resort at Abetone.

Degree of Difficulty: At 62 km (38.5 mi.) this stage is not especially long, but of that distance more than 40 km (25 mi.) are up hill. There are few really steep sections, but the climbing is relentless. The brief descents on the way up to Passo delle Radici give you a break but also mean you have to regain that altitude. This stage is not as hard as the climb to the Parco dell'Orecchiella, but the 25 miles of continuous uphill pedaling push it into the category of strictly adult entertainment . Rating: X.

Highlights: Castiglione di Garfagnana gets five stars on the quaintness scale. That puts it on the "do not miss" list. Although the climbing goes on and on, periodically you are treated to spectacular views across the Garfagnana Valley. Where there are no views you are immersed in the deep shade of hardwood and pine forests. Surprisingly there is very little traffic on this route and you should have the road mostly to yourself. Finally all your labors are rewarded by a 15 km straight-down descent to Pievepelago.

km	Place Name	Cafes	Shops, Mkts	Lodging	Camping	Bank	Bike Shop	Quaintness Rating
2	Ponte di Catagnana	•						**
4	Castelvecchio Pascoli	•	•	•			•	
6	Ponte di Campia	•						
14	Castelnuovo	•	•	•	•	•	•	
17	Pieve Fosciana	•	•					
21	Castiglione di Garfanana	•	•	•				*****
28	Cerageto	•	•	•				
32	Casina Rossi	•						
39	Col d'Arciano	•		•				
40	Casone di Profecchia	•		•				*

km	Place Name	Cafes	Shops, Mkts	Lodging	Camping	Bank	Bike Shop	Quaintness Rating
47	Passo delle Radici	●		●				
55	Sant'Anna Pelago	●	●	●	3 km			*
62	Pievepelago	●	●	●	5 km	●	●	

Tour 2/ Day 4 Barga—Pievepelago

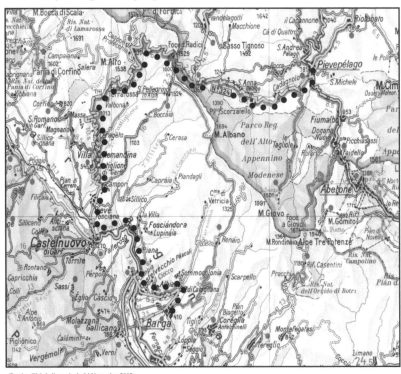

Touring Club Italiano, Auth. 04 November 2002

TOUR 2/ DAY 5

PIEVEPELAGO—BANGI DI LUCCA
52 km/ 32 mi. Degree of Difficulty: PG-13

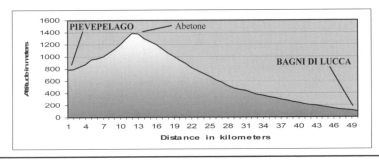

In some respects this stage is an ideal ride: You get all the climbing out of the way in the morning when it is cool, and you spend the rest of the day cruising down a river valley taking in the scenery. The day starts out steep right out of Pievepelago. Five kilometers of steep climbing brings you to medieval-looking **Fiumalbo**. The road levels out briefly above this quaint town before once again ramping up. At eight kilometers from Pievepelago you reach **Dogana**, a modern accessory to the **Abetone** ski resort above. The road climbs steeply here past grim concrete condominiums. Maybe they are more picturesque in the wintertime. **Faidello** is next, 2 km below the summit. The switchbacks come steep and tight, but soon you crest out at a broad square surrounded by shops, hotels and empty chair lifts. Abetone gets no style points at least in the summer, but the views across the rolling wooded mountains are inspiring. And now your work is done; the rest of your day is all downhill, 40 km (25 mi.) worth!

The road drops quickly away from Passo delle Abetone and dives into a beautiful pine forest. Four kilometers from the summit (16 km from Pievepelago) you will pass through **Le Regine**, another satellite of the ski resort with its own hotels, shops and restaurants. Below Le Regine the grade steepens and you a hit a series of tight switchbacks which drop through a park-like forest. Nine kilometers from Abetone (21 km from Pievepelago) you will pass by **Pianosinatico**, a collection of modern shops and restaurants. Finally at **Ponte Sestaione** the grade lessens and you can take your hands off the brakes. For the next 25 km or so you will be cruising easily down the Lima River valley.

Nineteen kilometers down from the summit of Passo delle Abetone and 31 km from Pievepelago you will pass through the town of **La Lima**. It has a few restaurants and roadside cafes but is a gritty, industrial spot, and if you are looking for a break a better option is 3 km down the road at **Popiglio**. This quaint stone village offers a few roadside cafes and a market, and has dramatic views down the valley where it narrows into a gorge.

Three kilometers below Popiglio you will see the village of **Lucchio** stacked up on a high ridge across the river to the left. Rows of stone houses march up the unbelievably steep hillside to a ruined fortress overlooking the valley. It has to be one of the most dramatic sites for a hilltown in all of Tuscany. And while it begs to be explored, it would be a long way up there on a bike.

Your 40 km of coasting comes to an end at **Bagni di Lucca.** This not particularly picturesque spa town reached its zenith about 1920. It has managed to preserve a kind of old world grace. There are scores of hotels and a pleasant downtown area with shops and cafes. It makes a good overnight stop before the push over the mountains on the last leg to Pisa.

Degree of Difficulty: There are only 12 km of climbing on this stage, but they are continuous and steep. However, you do get it all over with in the cool of the morning, so it shouldn't ruin your day. Rated: PG-13.

Highlights: Forty kilometers (25 mi.) of downhill! Beautiful mountain views, dark pine forests, 40 km of downhill!

Watch for traffic.

km	Place Name	Cafes	Shops, Mkts	Lodging	Camping	Bank	Bike Shop	Quaintness Rating
5	Fiumalbo	●	●	●		●		***
8	Dogana	●	●	●	●			
10	Faidello	●		●				
12	Abetone	●	●	●		●		
16	Le Regine	●	●	●	●			
20	Pianosinatico	●	●	●	●			
24	Ponte Sestaione	●	●					
31	La Lima	●	●					
34	Popilio	●	●					**
38	Lucchio	●						****
48	Fabbriche	●						
52	Bagni di Lucca	●	●	●		●		*

Tour 2/ Day 5 Pievepelago—Bagni di Lucca

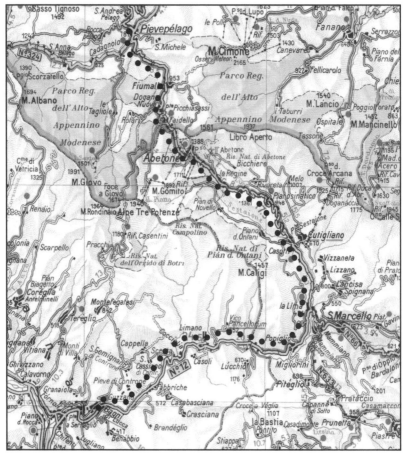

Touring Club Italiano, Auth. 04 November 2002

TOUR 2/ DAY 6

BAGNI DI LUCCA—PISA
70 km/ 43 mi. Degree of Difficulty: PG-13

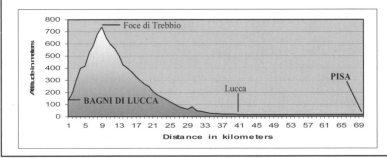

The route back to Pisa begins with a long 10 km (6 mi.) climb up to the **Foce di Trébbio** pass. This is a favorite route for local riders, and you are likely to encounter a pack out on a training ride particularly on weekends. Once over the top of the pass you face a long descent down into the broad valley of the Arno River. Soon you are back in the urban congestion of Pisa where the riding really gets challenging.

From Bagni di Lucca the road up to the pass begins across the river on the main road back towards Abetone. To find it, cross the river and head east towards Abetone. As you are leaving town look for blue direction signs on the right for **Benabbio** and **Villa Basillica**. A narrow lane veers away from the main road past some houses, makes a sharp hairpin turn, and then begins to climb. It climbs very steeply at first up a series of switchbacks through a shady forest. After 4 km of tough going the grade lessens briefly as you reach the wonderful little village of Benabbio. In addition to providing a welcome break from the climbing, Benabbio offers the authentic charm of an undiscovered Tuscan hilltown. It is well worth a stop to explore its narrow streets and alleys.

From Benabbio the road gets back to the business of climbing. Six kilometers of sustained uphill brings you at last to the top of the Foce di Trébbio pass. There is a pleasant café here set off the road, but otherwise your conquest of this pass will be unremarkable. The road meanders along

Benabbio

through the trees, then suddenly drops down several steep switchbacks past the village of **Boveglio**. Below this village the grade is less steep as the road carves along the edge of a steep wooded valley. A sharp hairpin brings you into the gritty town of **Colognora**, a step-child of the industrial revolution complete with sooty mills and crumbling company housing. Two kilometers later you pass through **Pracando**, which if anything is worse.

The road continues to descend down the wooded valley. You will pass through **Biecina,** a wide spot in the road but featuring a café and some shops. At the next town, **Botticino**, there is a fork with the left turn going towards **Pescia** and the right towards **Villa Basillica.** You want to bear right up a short hill. After a kilometer or two you will come to a right turn for Villa Basillica. The town is at the top of a very steep set of switchbacks, and while pleasant it is not really worth the climb.

Next down the road is the town of **Collodi**, famous as the birthplace of the author of Pinocchio. You can stop here and explore the Parco di Pinocchio complete with life-size statutes of the various characters from the book, but the place is pretty much a tourist trap There are several cafes and shops full of must-have collectables. Just below Collodi you hit **N 435**, the main road between Lucca and Pescia.

The best route back into Pisa is by way Lucca retracing the route of your first day. Turning right, N 435 will take you right up to the walls of Lucca. It is a busy road and not at all scenic, but it is direct. At Lucca you can loop around the old city on the broad boulevard that circles the walls and join up with your out-bound route back to Pisa. Since that route is covered in Tour 2/ Day 1, it won't be recounted here. You will have ridden that route once already, so the return trip into Pisa should be fairly easy.

Degree of Difficulty: The climb from Bagni di Lucca to Foce di Trébbio is long, but you can take a break at charming Benabbio. Once at the top of the pass the rest of your day is downhill or flat. PG-13.

Highlights: The screaming descent off of the Foce di Trébbio through the wooded valley on a mostly deserted road will be the highlight of your day. It will taste all the sweeter after the long slog to get up there. Lucca will remain as enchanting as ever should you decide to stop there, and you end your day and your tour at Pisa and its incomparable Piazza dei Miracoli. If you didn't climb the Leaning Tower on the first day, now's your chance.

km	Place Name	Cafes	Shops, Mkts	Lodging	Camping	Bank	Bike Shop	Quaintness Rating
5	Benabbio	•	•					***
10	Foce di Trebbio	•						*
11	Boveglio	•	•					*
15	Colognora	•	•					
17	Pracando	•						
20	Biecina	•	•					
21	Botticino	•	•			•		
24	Villa Basillica	•	•	•		•		**
27	Collodi	•	•	•		•		*
37	Lucca	•	•	•	3 km	•	•	*****
39	Monte San Quirico	•	•	•		•		
46	Ponte San Pietro	•	•	•				
49	Nozzano	•	•					***
57	Filettole	•	•					
62	Vecchiano	•	•					
70	Pisa	•	•	•	11 km	•	•	*****

Tour 2/ Day 6 Bagni di Lucca—Pisa

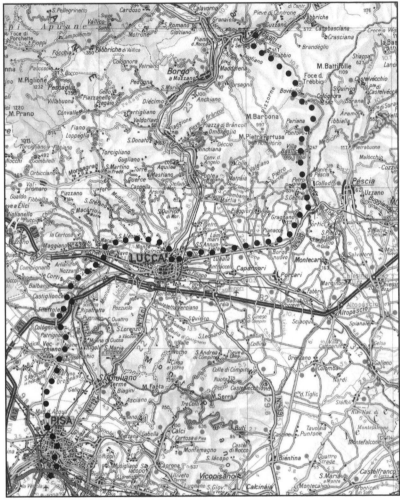

Touring Club Italiano, Auth. 04 November 2002

TOUR 3

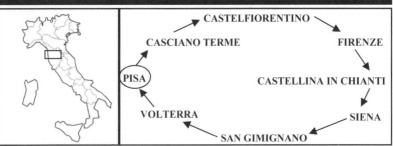

PISA—FIRENZE—PISA
8 Days, 397 km/ 246 mi.

This is a round trip tour from Pisa to Firenze, south to Siena, and back to Pisa. This tour is designed around the Pisa International Airport. You can fly into Pisa with your bike, ride the tour, and fly out again. Each daily stage is short, so you could combine stages and do the entire tour in less than a week, or you can take your time and stretch it to 10 days. The route will take you through classic Tuscan landscape of rolling wheat fields, columnar evergreens, olive groves and vineyards. In addition to Pisa and Firenze you will also visit the sun-lit Piazza del Campo in Siena, the famous towers of San Gimignano, and the ancient walled city of Volterra. Although there is some stiff climbing, there are no mountains to scale and no long days in the saddle. This tour is about scenery and culture combined with a few hours of spectacular riding each day.

Day 1: Pisa—Casciana Terme, 39 km/ 24 mi., PG

Day 2: Casciana Terme—Castelfiorentino, 59 km/ 36.5 mi., PG

Day 3: Castelfiorentino—Firenze, 43 km/ 27 mi., PG-13

Day 4: Firenze—Castellina in Chianti, 55 km/ 34 mi., PG-13

Day 5: Castellina in Chianti—Siena, 52 km/ 32 mi., G

Day 6: Siena—San Gimignano, 42 km/ 26 mi., PG

Day 7: San Gimignano—Volterra, 35 km/ 22 mi., PG

Day 8: Volterra—Pisa, 72 km/ 44.5 mi., G

TOUR 3/ DAY 1

PISA—CASCIANA TERME
39 km/ 24 mi. Degree of Difficulty: PG

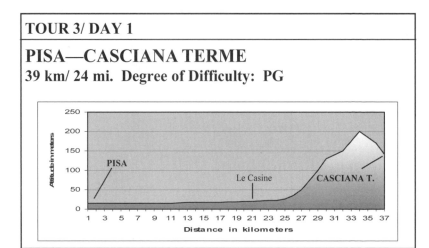

This stage takes you from downtown Pisa out onto the agricultural plain of the Arno River basin. Most of the ride is flat except for about 10 km of climbing near the end. This relatively easy first stage helps you get used to the bike and get over the jet lag.

From the terminal building at Pisa's International Airport follow the "bull's eye" city center signs towards downtown Pisa. These signs will lead you to **Via dell'Aeroporto,** a broad tree-lined avenue. Via dell'Aeroporto will bring you to **Piazza G.Giusti.** Just as you enter the square look for a right turn onto **Via Giuseppe Montanelli.** After several blocks on Via Giuseppe Montanelli you will come to a fork. Here you should go left onto **Cavalcavia S. Ermete Ovest.** After crossing an overpass above railroad tracks you will come to an intersection at **Via Emilia/ N 206.** You should turn right here and head south following signs for **Cecina** and **Grosseto.** If you are departing from downtown Pisa instead of the airport you would also follow signs for Via Emilia and N 206 to Grosseto in order to join this itinerary. See the Airports chapter for additional directions and a map showing this route out of the city.

Via Emilia is a moderately busy road, and the flat agricultural land on either side does little to distract you from the speeding cars. But it is direct and easy to follow. A short distance from Pisa you will pass through the drab but bustling town of **Ospedaletto**. It has many shops, restaurants, and markets and even a hotel. The main road runs straight through it and you need only watch for the signs to Cecina and Grosseto.

After 12 km on Via Emilia you will come to an intersection with signs to Grosseto to the right and **Ponsacco** and **Lari** to the left. You should turn left here and at last get off the busy main road.

You are now on a quiet road that meanders through pleasant farm land. At the town of **Valtriano** you have the choice of riding straight through town or taking a short jog around it. Both roads meet up again on the far side of town. Next is tiny **Cenaia** and then **Quattrostrade**, both unremarkable modern towns. You continue to follow signs for Ponsacco.

Just beyond Quat-
trostrade you will see a huge overhead sign indicating the town of **Perignano** to the left and **Lari** to the right. You should turn right here and enter the small town of **Le Casine.** Pedal straight through town following signs for Lari. Beyond the village you will reach an intersection where you bear left in the

Beware of truck traffic

direction of Lari. Soon the road begins to climb gently as you gradually work your way out of the Arno River valley. Once in the hills you are sur-rounded by olive groves and grape vineyards. Ahead you can see the for-tress of Lari brooding over its walled town.

At the gates of Lari, you have the choice of cycling up through the ancient town or skirting around below its walls following the signs for **Cas-ciana Terme**. Both routes rejoin at the upper end of town. Here the grade steepens for about 1 km until you reach the top of the ridge. There are beautiful views over olive groves and stone farmhouses sprinkled over the hillsides below you. You will shortly reach a turn for the town of **Casci-ana Alta,** which occupies the very top of the hill. Just past this turn you begin a short descent down to a "T" intersection with signs for Pisa and Cecina to the right and Casciana Terme to the left. Going left the road climbs up through wheat fields and olive groves bordered by cypress trees. After a kilometer or so you begin to descend down into Casciana Terme.

Like many spa towns Casciana Terme has a sleepy air, as if every-one is too relaxed to get excited about anything. There are outdoor cafes with linen tablecloths and couples strolling arm in arm browsing shop win-dows. Except perhaps in August when it seems all Europeans go on vaca-tion, you should have no trouble finding a room here; there are more than a dozen hotels to choose from. You can even "take the waters" if you feel you are in need of a little relaxation or perhaps a little sore from your first day in the saddle.

Degree of Difficulty: Despite the appearance of the altitude profile this is actually a relatively easy ride. You gain about 160 meters (528 ft) over 9 km between Le Casine and Casciana Alta, but the grade is gentle and except for a short stretch above Lari, there are no walls to climb. Rating: PG.

Highlights: The walled hilltown of Lari together with the views over the Arno valley will be the highlights of your day. Once you are off N206 the traffic tapers off and you will have the quiet country roads and rolling farm land all to yourselves. This is a beautiful, fairly easy ride that makes for a perfect start to a tour. It is short and easily manageable even with trans-Atlantic jetlag. Rating: PG.

km	Place Name	Cafes	Shops, Mkts	Lodging	Camping	Bank	Bike Shop	Quaintness Rating
4	Ospedaletto	●	●	●		●		
21	Valtriano	●	●					
24	Cenaia	●	●					
27	Quattrostrade	●	●					
28	Le Casine	●	●			●		
32	Lari	●	●	●		●		***
36	Casciana Alta	●	●					*
39	Casciana Terme	●	●	●		●	●	*

Tour 3/ Day 1 Pisa—Casciana Terme

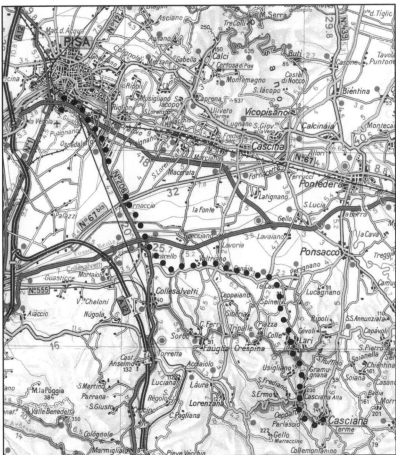

Touring Club Italiano, Auth. 04 November 2002

TOUR 3/ DAY 2

CASCIANA TERME—CASTELFIORENTINO
59 km/ 36 mi. Degree of Difficulty: PG-13

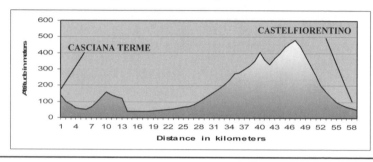

Your day begins with a lovely 6 km descent down into a broad wooded valley that gradually gives way to wheat fields. From Casciana Terme simply follow the main road due north in the direction of **Ponsacco**. As the valley begins to open up look for a right turn with signs for **San Pietro Belvedere** and **Capannoli**. After making the turn you will begin climbing a gentle grade through vineyards and olive groves. After 4 km you pass by the ancient village of San Pietro Belevedere surrounded by centuries-old olive trees. From here the road descends gently to an intersection where the town of Capannoli is to the left. You should continue straight, down a steep hill to the broad valley below.

At the bottom of this descent you will find a 4-way intersection with the main road between **Volterra** and **Ponsacco**. You should go straight in the direction of **Peccioli** across the valley. A long ruler-straight road will lead you to a traffic circle with odd-looking modern sculptures in the middle. Go around the traffic circle and continue straight following the sign for **Montefoscoli**. At the far side of the valley you will hit another intersection where you turn right for Montefoscoli. Just beyond this turn there is another intersection where you bear left again following the sign for Montefoscoli. The road continues for about 2 km up a pleasant valley of pastureland interspersed with trees. There is very little traffic on this portion of the route, and you should have the road to yourself. At the next intersection you should turn left following signs for **Castelfalfi** and **Montaione**.

From here you continue up the valley past a left turn for Montefoscoli and continue towards Castefalfi. After several kilometers of essentially flat riding the road gradually begins to climb. About 30 km into your ride the hills begin. Castelfalfi sits atop the first steep grade. It offers several shops and cafes and a luxury hotel if you feel like splurging. From Castelfalfi the road descends slightly before climbing again. There are wonderful views left and right over rolling farmland, vineyards and olive groves. Four kilometers from Castelfalfi you hit a long steep grade up to **San Vivaldo.** Just before you reach San Vivaldo look for a sharp left turn with a sign for **Montaione**. Turning here you will catapult down a series of steep switchbacks through olive groves. All too soon you will reach the bottom of the narrow valley where, of course, you must climb up the other side.

About 500 meters up from the valley floor you will come to an intersection with a sign marking a right turn for **Gambassi Terme.** There is no sign for the other direction, but it takes you to the bustling modern town of Montaione. For a better ride turn right and follow the narrow lane as it climbs up through a dense shady forest for another 2 km. You will hit two more intersections where you continue to follow the signs for Gambassi Terme. After rolling over the top of the hill you begin a steep dive down towards Gambassi Terme. At this tiny town bear to the left following signs for **Castelfiorentino**. From here the roads descends steeply through olive groves and vineyards with views across the broad Elsa River valley. This is the classic Tuscan landscape you see in postcards: hill tops crowned with columnar evergreens, wheat fields rolling away in every direction, and rambling stone farm houses with red tile roofs.

The long descent rolls to a stop at an intersection with the main road from Montaione. In order to avoid the worst of the traffic you should cross directly over this road and pedal into a modern suburb of Castelfiorentino. You will pass through ranks of modern apartment buildings, shops and restaurants and eventually reach a bridge over the Elsa River. On the far side of the bridge you will enter the old part of town with lovely stone and brick buildings. After the bridge turn left and you will come to a square flanked by important–looking buildings. Here you will find the

Tourist Information Office which can help you find a hotel room. There are several hotels in town, and you should have no difficulty finding a room even in the summer months

Degree of Difficulty: The first climb up to San Pietro Belvedere is an easy G-rated climb. The real work comes later as you climb more than 320 meters (1050 ft.) over 12 km up to San Vivaldo. Then you plunge down to the bottom of a narrow valley only to have to climb your way up the other side. This time you gain 150 meters (492 ft.) in just 5 km. This is serious climbing and steep in places. On a hot, humid day with fully loaded panniers this will be real work. Rated: PG-13

Highlights: The highlight of your day will undoubtedly be the screaming descent down to Castelfiorentino from the top of the climb above Gambassi Terme. You will descend down through olive groves with beautiful views over the Elsa River valley. This is the classic Tuscan landscape you came to see — columnar evergreens, rolling wheat fields, vineyards, olive trees, and crumbling stone farmhouses built like fortresses perched on hilltops. The towns of San Pietro Belvedere, Capannoli, and Peccioli if you care to make the detour are also wonderfully quaint villages well worth exploring.

km	Place Name	Cafes	Shops, Mkts	Lodging	Camping	Bank	Bike Shop	Quaintness Rating
11	San Pietro Belvedere	●	●	●				*
13	Capannoli	●	●	●				**
35	Castelfalfi	●	●	●				**
40	San Vivaldo	●	●	●				*
48	Gambassi Terme	●	●	●		●		*
59	Castelfiorentino	●	●	●		●	●	*

Tour 3/ Day 2 Casciana Terme—Castelfiorentino

Touring Club Italiano, Auth. 04 November 2002

TOUR 3/ DAY 3

CASTELFIORENTINO—FIRENZE
43 km/ 27 mi. Degree of Difficulty: PG-13

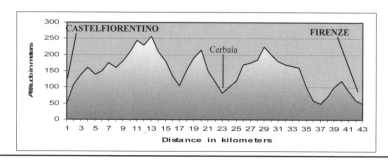

The route from **Castelfiorentino** to **Firenze** rolls through beautiful Tuscan farmland resplendent with vineyards and olive groves. It begins with a short, steep climb out of Castelfiorentino, followed by a short descent, then another climb, then another descent. The road yo-yo's up and down like this all the way to Firenze. Some of the descents and climbs are quite steep but never very long. Fortunately this stage is a short one.

Leaving Castelfiorentino follow signs for **Empoli** north out of the downtown area. After about one kilometer you will see blue signs for Firenze and **Montespertoli** pointing to the right off the main road. A steep 500 meter climb takes you up a ridge overlooking Castelfiorentino and the surrounding countryside. At the top you will find an intersection and signs to the left for Firenze and Montespertoli.

The road continues to climb but at a much more gentle rate. It travels along the top of a ridge with magnificent views down the slopes to the left and right. As you follow the ridge-line there will be frequent shallow descents followed by climbs.

Thirteen kilometers from Castelfiorentino you will reach the town of Montespertoli. This is pleasant more modern town occupying a commanding position atop a hill with views in every direction. It has a pleasant square of lawns and benches shaded by tall evergreens. It makes a nice place for a picnic if you are in need of a break.

From Montespertoli the road drops down a long hill. You should pass by the right turns for Certaldo and Poppiano and keep left for the town of **Baccaiano** at the very bottom of the valley. As promised the road climbs up the other side. The 2 km grade may elicit some gratuitous profanity particularly if you didn't stop for a snack in Montespertoli. The climb tops out at the unremarkable town of **Montagnana,** whereupon you are treated to yet another steep descent down through picturesque olive groves. At the bottom of this descent the road is lined on either side by cypress trees as it crosses the broad Pesa River valley. You cross the river at the town of **Cerbaia.** All along this route you simply follow the signs for Firenze.

After a brief climb above Cerbaia the road meanders through a shady valley of pastureland and trees. A long climb takes you up to the village of **Chiesanuova,** the last of the serious climbs of the day. From Chiesanuova the road drops steeply at first then more gradually before a final plunge down to the Florentine suburb of **Galluzzo.** Except for the traffic which gradually intensifies as you approach Firenze, this is one of the most beautiful stretches of the ride. You will pass the wonderfully picturesque abbey of Sant'Alessandro da Giogoli set slightly above the road and surrounded by olive trees. Beyond the abbey the views take in the whole of the Arno River valley and the domes and spires (and smog) of Firenze. Immediately beyond the abbey the road sails down a series of steep switchbacks through a grassy grove of ancient olive trees. Below you can see the fortress-like edifice of the Certosa del Galluzzo, a Cistercian monastery. At the bottom of the hill, below the walls of the monastery, the road meets an on-coming one-way street out of the town of Galluzzo. You are obliged to make a sharp right turn here which takes you over a rickety bridge to an intersection with **Via Senese.** This is the historic thoroughfare between Firenze and Siena. It will take you all the way to the medieval gates of Firenze — although at a price. As you approach downtown Firenze the traffic can be daunting. On the plus side this route is direct and you are on it for only about 6 km (4 mi.).

Via Senese takes you right through the center of Galluzzo. Unfortunately just beyond Galuzzo the roads signs disappear. Just remember to go straight and stay on the main road. Eventually you will come down a bumpy hill and find yourself before the imposing **Porta Romana** gate at the entrance to the old city of Firenze. Here you can duck through the gate onto **Via Romana** to escape the worst of the traffic. This one- way street will take you to the **Pitti Palace** whereupon you hit a one-way going against you. You have to jog down a few side streets to work your way down to the river.

Degree of Difficulty: This is a fairly short stage, but there is a lot of climbing, and all the ups and downs prevent you from getting into a rhythm. Some of the climbs are steep, but all are relatively short. The real difficulty comes as you try to penetrate the outer defenses of the city of Firenze. Wave after wave of honking, poison gas spewing, steel and rubber assault vehicles will come at you from seemingly every direction. A few kilometers of this, and you will long to be back out in the solitude of a long climb. Rating: PG-13.

Highlights: You will have magnificent views for almost the entire ride, but they become even more magnificent between Chiesanuova to Galluzzo. The abbey of Sant'Alessandro da Giogoli sitting among its olive trees high above the Arno is a spectacular sight. The tight switchbacks down through the olive trees to Galluzzo is another treat you will not forget. But the icing on your cake may be riding through the huge fortified gate at Porta Romana into the old section of Firenze. Narrow cobble-stoned streets take you past the soot-stained facades of Renaissance palaces. You can and should spend days here exploring this exciting city.

km	Place Name	Cafes	Shops, Mkts	Lodging	Camping	Bank	Bike Shop	Quaintness Rating
13	Montespertoli	•	•	•		•		*
17	Baccaiano	•	•	•				
20	Montagnana	•	•					
23	Cerbaia	•	•					*
29	Chiesanuova	•	•	•		•	•	
36	Galluzzo	•	•	•		•	•	*
43	Firenze	•	•	•	•	•	•	*****

Tour 3/ Day 3 Castelfiorentino—Firenze

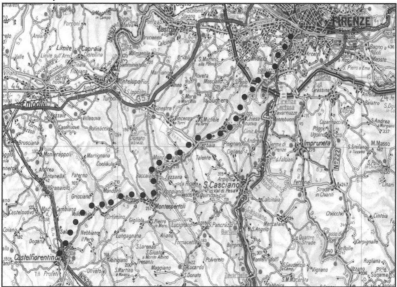

Touring Club Italiano, Auth. 04 November 2002

A gate into the old section of Firenze

TOUR 3/ DAY 4

FIRENZE—CASTELLINA IN CHIANTI
55 km/ 34 mi. Degree of Difficulty: PG-13

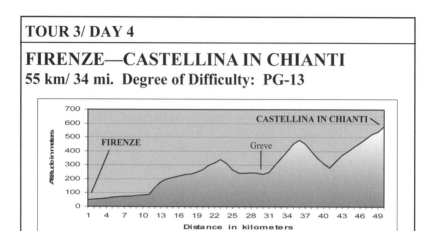

Once you've had your fill of the sybaritic splendors of **Firenze**, this route takes you out of the city and into the verdant hills of the Chianti region. The famous **Via Chiantigiana,** the Chianti Road, will lead you through the hills past vineyards and ancient villages to **Castellina in Chianti**, a spectacular walled hilltown which commands views over the entire region.

The ride begins on the south side of the **Ponte Vecchio** in downtown Firenze. From the bridge turn left and pedal upstream along the broad sidewalk above the river. This parallels the **Lungarno Torrigiana**, which is a one-way street against you. Continue past the next bridge, the **Ponte alla Grazie,** and on to the next bridge upstream. This will be the **Ponte San Niccolo.** Here you reach a busy traffic circle at **Piazza F. Ferrucci.** Dodge your way directly across the square to **Via G. Orsini.** This is a one-way in your direction. After four blocks bear right onto **Via di Ripoli**, another one-way going your way. You stay on Via di Ripoli until you reach a large traffic circle at **Piazza di Badia a Ripoli**.

At the busy Piazza di Badia a Ripoli bear right and look for signs for Via Chiantigiana, **N 222.** You will be following this well-marked route almost all the way to Castellina. The N 222 signs will lead through the suburbs south of Firenze. After several kilometers of riding you will pass under the Autostrada. A short distance beyond the highway you will encounter several traffic circles where you simply follow the N 222 signs. Eventually you will wind up on a long straight tree-lined boulevard which rolls you into the modern town of **Grassina**.

Grassina is not particularly remarkable except as the outer limit of the city suburbs. N 222 leads you through the main square of town and up the hillside behind it. At last you leave most of the traffic behind. At the top of the short climb you begin to roll along the top of a ridge with views over olive groves and manicured rows of grape vines. About 7 km from Grassina you will see a big white sign announcing that you are entering the town of **Strada in Chianti**. Just beyond this white sign you will come to an intersection with a right turn and a sign for **Ferrone**. This brief detour off of N 222 allows you to avoid a few short, steep climbs beyond Strada.

Turning right in the direction of Ferrone you begin a marvelous sweeping descent down into the valley of the Greve River. You will finally roll to a stop at an intersection with the main road through Ferrone. Here you turn left following the signs for **Greve in Chianti** and **Siena**. Ferrone has a few cafes and shops but it is mostly notable for the two huge brick factories at the edge of town.

From Ferrone the road follows the Greve River upstream through a pleasant valley with pastureland and woods on both sides. After a few kilometers you will come to an intersection with a sign for Greve to the left. Turning here the road continues to roll up the shady river valley. As you approach Greve you will pass some modern apartment blocks and commercial buildings. If you bear right at the second traffic light you can find your way to the delightful old section of town. This is about the half-way point of your ride and makes a good place for a break, especially since next up is the first big climb of the day.

From Greve you continue on N 222 towards Siena. The road is mostly flat for about a kilometer out of town and then begins to climb. It starts out gently, working its way up through olive groves and vineyards. About 3 km from Greve it gets steeper and continues that way for another 2 km until you reach the hilltop town of **Panzano**.

The main road cuts right through the central square of Panzano. Just beyond town the road falls away and dives down into the forested Pesa River valley. An exhilarating series of switchbacks takes you down and down. If you can tear your eyes away from the road, there are wonderful views of vineyards and huge villas. As you near the valley floor you will pass a left turn for **Rada in Chianti**. When you finally reach the bottom of the valley you will be only 9 km from your destination. Unfortunately they are all uphill.

The climb out of the valley starts out steeply. The road weaves back and forth up switchbacks through shady forest. The grade lessens the higher you go. Finally you will be able to see the imposing tower of the "Rocca" of Castellina overlooking a jumble of red roof-tops.

Castellina in Chianti has preserved much of its medieval charm. Most of its walls are intact as well as its impressive castle. It is not an unknown destination, and you can expect plenty of fellow visitors during the summer months. It would be advisable to book a room well ahead.

Degree of Difficulty: The riding from Firenze to Greve is easy. The scenery is beautiful, and the few climbs are short. Beyond Greve the scenery remains enchanting, but the riding gets a lot tougher. The climb from Greve to Panzano goes on for 3.5 km, and after the wonderful descent down to the Pesa River you are hit with the 9 km slog up to Castellina. Rating: PG-13.

Highlights: The highlight of your day will be escaping the exhaust and congestion of Firenze for the quiet countryside of the Chianti region. The soothing Tuscan scenery, quiet lanes and cool shady forests will be just what you need after the hot pavement of Firenze. Castellina with its quaint cobblestone streets and photogenic castle awaits you at the top of the final climb.

km	Place Name	Cafes	Shops, Mkts	Lodging	Camping	Bank	Bike Shop	Quaintness Rating
12	Grassina	•	•	•		•		
15	Poggio Ugolino	•	•			•		*
17	Poggio alla Scala	•						
19	Strada in Chianti	•	•	•		•		*
23	Ferrone	•	•			•		
36	Greve in Chianti	•	•	•		•	•	***
40	Panzano in Chianti	•	•	•		•		**
55	Castellina in Chianti	•	•	•		•	•	*****

Tour 3/ Day 4 Firenze—Castellina in Chianti

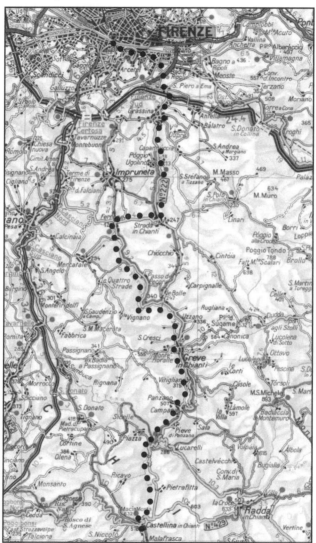

Touring Club Italiano, Auth. 04 November 2002

TOUR 3/ DAY 5

CASTELLINA IN CHIANTI—SIENA
52 km/ 32 mi. Degree of Difficulty: G

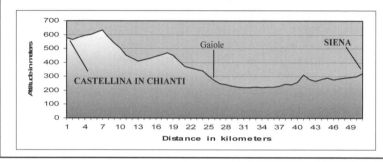

This route is an easy cruise from **Castellina in Chianti** to **Siena.** There is some climbing early in the ride out of Castellina but most of the rest of the day is down hill or flat. The route takes you through **Radda in Chianti,** a gem of a hilltown that rivals Castellina for quaintness and historic preservation. **Gaiole in Chianti** is next, and though not a hilltown it is almost as quaint. From Gaiole you follow a shady river valley almost as far as Siena. Take your time on this route, or it will be over all too soon. This is riding in Tuscany at its best.

From Castellina you should initially retrace your steps back down to the intersection below town where you would turn for **Greve** and **Firenze.** Go straight past this turn following the sign for Radda. The road gradually climbs up into dense forest with occasional views into the valley below. The grade is not steep and coming first thing in the morning the pedals will seem to turn more easily. At about 7 km from Castellina you will crest the top of the climb and begin a steep descent down to Radda. On the way down you will have spectacular views over the town and the rolling wooded hills beyond.

Radda is a wonderful walled village that perches on a ridge overlooking corduroy fields of grape vines. There is a nice circuit you can do around the outside of the walls, but be sure to explore the narrow cobblestone streets inside the gates.

From Radda you should continue downhill following the signs for Siena and **Montevarchi.** After going over a brick overpass and past signs for Firenze, the road climbs gently for a few hundred meters to another intersection where there is a right turn for Siena. You can take this turn; it is a short-cut to Siena, but if you do you will miss some great riding and an opportunity to see the town of Gaiole. Bearing left in the direction of Montivarchi only adds about 8 km to your ride and half of that is downhill.

From this intersection the road climbs gently up through dense forest with occasional views back towards Radda. There is little traffic on this road and it should be quiet and cool. After about 6 km you will reach a right turn onto **N 408** with signs for Gaiole and Siena. Turning here takes you down an broad sweeping descent that eventually rolls you into Gaiole. As you approach the old section town be sure to bear left off the main road and down the main street of town. The quaint old stone buildings of Gaiole are built on either side of a creek which runs through the middle of town. You can rejoin the main road just below town.

From Gaiole the road continues to descend but more gently. You will pass by huge villas at the end of cypress-lined driveways. Manicured vineyards gradually give way to olive groves and finally pastures and forest as you reach the bottom of the valley. About 3 km below Gaiole you will pass a right turn which climbs back up to Radda. This is the short-cut you passed earlier.

For the next 13 km you follow a shady river valley through woods. There is little traffic; it is quiet, cool, and beautiful. You will pass several intersections where you need only follow the signs for Siena. The road is flat or gently rolling. Eventually you will find yourself climbing up one side of the valley. This takes you up out of the trees into cultivated farm land. You will pass a left turn for **Castelnuovo Berardenga.** Just beyond this turn you will reach the town of **Pianella**.

Beyond Pianella the road begins a steep climb which winds up to the hamlet of **San Giovanni**. From here you get your first glimpse of the towers and spires of Siena. A switchbacking descent takes you down through a dense forest. Emerging from the woods you roll into **Ponte Bozzone**, mostly a wide spot in the road, but it does have a restaurant and some shops.

From here the road rolls up and down several short hills. You soon find yourself on the outskirts of Siena. You will descend down a hill to a large traffic circle where you bear right following the bulls-eye sign to the city center. At the next traffic circle you again follow the city center sign. This will lead you below the walls of the old section of Siena to the **Porta Ovile**. You can enter the city here, but you will be pushing your bike up the steep, narrow **Via di Vallerozzi.** Another option is to continue past Porta Ovile a short distance uphill to **Via Giuseppe Mazzini.** This is a busy main road which runs along outside the walls on the north side of the city. If you turn left on Via Mazzini you will see another entrance into the old city at the **Barriera San Lorenzo**. Then you can ride along **Via Garibaldi** to **Via dei Montanini** which is the main street running through Siena, although it changes name a few times. A left off of Via dei Montanini will lead you to the famous **Piazza Il Campo**. There are a few cars inside the city walls, but most of it is more or less a pedestrian zone.

Siena is one of the most famous tourist destinations in Italy. It goes without saying that if you want to stay anywhere near the city center, you must book months in advance. Another option for those living dangerously is to apply at the Tourist Information Office just off the Piazza Il Campo for an "affittacamera," a private room for rent in someone's home. This is big business in Siena, and the Tourist Office has a long list of rooms that may be available. Siena is a fascinating place, and most enjoyable if you stay in the old section of the city.

Degree of Difficulty: There are a few short stretches that will have you standing on the pedals, but overall this is an easy ride. You can get up late, linger over breakfast, and still have plenty of time to explore Siena. Fun for the whole family. Rating: G.

Highlights: In terms of places, Radda, Gaiole, and of course Siena will be the highlights of your day, and perhaps your whole tour. But this is also some of the most pleasant riding you will find anywhere. Quiet roads take you through cool forests with occasional vineyards and olive groves for variety. There are no killer climbs; it is all grins all the way.

km	Place Name	Cafes	Shops, Mkts	Lodging	Camping	Bank	Bike Shop	Quaintness Rating
10	Radda in Chianti	●	●	●		●		*****
24	Gaiole in Chianti	●	●	●		●		***
40	Pianella	●	●					
46	Ponte Bozzone	●	●					
52	Siena	●	●	●	●	●	●	*****

Tour 3/ Day 5 Castellina in Chianti—Siena

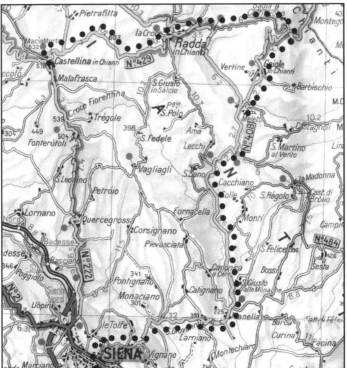

Touring Club Italiano, Auth. 04 November 2002

TOUR 3/ DAY 6

SIENA—SAN GIMIGNANO
42 km/ 26 mi. Degree of Difficulty: PG

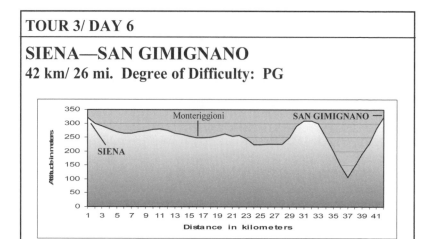

This is the easy way from **Siena** to **San Gimignano**. This route is only 42 km (26 mi) and shouldn't take you more than two hours of pedaling door to door. What you trade for the ease of approach is a bit more traffic. For something quieter and more challenging see the route from Siena to San Gimignano via Casole d'Elsa described in Tour 1/ Day 3.

This ride begins at the **Porta Camollia** gate at the northwest end of the old section of Siena. Immediately upon leaving the safety of Siena's medieval walls you will be assaulted by modern traffic. Following the signs for **Firenze** you must run the gauntlet of traffic down a long hill to a busy traffic circle. Here follow the sign for **Monteriggioni** and the **Via Cassia, N 2**. The directions are well-marked and you should have no trouble escaping the busy suburbs of modern Siena.

The road climbs gently away from this intersection. At all succeeding intersections simply follow the Monteriggioni signs. After about 2 km the traffic will diminish and you will begin a long descent into open agricultural lands. You are still on the Via Cassia which ordinarily is a busy secondary highway, but here the nearby Autostrada seems to attract most of the traffic.

The long descent rolls you into a shallow valley with fields on both sides of the road. There are a few slight rises to pedal over, but generally the road trends down. About 15 km from Siena as you coast down a gentle hill through some trees you will pass a sewage treatment plant on the left (you can't miss it!). Just beyond this you will see the walls and towers of Monteriggioni crowning the hillside to the right. A dirt road marked by a number of hotel and restaurant signs takes you off the main road and winds up past a parking area to the main gate in the walls. Monteriggioni is a wonderful place to explore and absolutely worth the short detour.

Back on the main road you continue north towards **Poggibonsi.** About 1 km down the road from the Monteriggioni turn you will reach a left turn with signs for **Colle Val d'Elsa** and **Volterra.** Turning here you get off N 2 and strike out across a broad flat valley of wheat fields and sunflowers. After about 1.5 km you will come to another left turn with a sign for **Strove.** Turning here a ruler-straight road lined by cypress trees takes further into the lovely countryside. After a few kilometers you will pass through the quaint village of **Abbadia Isola.** Most of the past millennium seems to have passed this town by giving it a forgotten, slightly threadbare air.

From Abbadia Isola the road climbs gently into rolling fields of sunflowers. This is the classic Tuscan landscape you see in paintings in the museums of Firenze and Siena. In a grove of trees off the left side of the road you will see the crenulated towers of **Castel Petraio.** This fortified manor has been converted into a luxury hotel, but its towers and walls add a dramatic flare to the landscape. Beyond Castel Petraio you will see the delightful walled town of Strove. This is a tiny circular town with narrow alleys for streets. It is well worth a quick detour to explore or for a cup of cappuccino in its single café.

A few kilometers from Strove the road abruptly descends down to an intersection with signs for **Scorgiano** to the left and Colle Val d'Elsa to the right. You should turn right. After a short distance you will reach another intersection where you again bear right. After a few kilometers of pedaling you enter the modern town of **Gracciano d'Elsa.** The traffic picks up here as you pass apartment blocks and shops. You will eventually come to a traffic circle where you bear left following the sign for San Gimignano.

A steep hill grinds out of town. At the top of the climb you will reach the suburb of **La Grazie** and a right turn for San Gimignano. The road crosses over a high plateau past the village of **Borgatello.** Here you get a wonderful view of the famous towers of San Gimignano crowning the next hilltop. If you don't find yourself stopping repeatedly to admire the sight and snap pictures you will have more discipline than most. Unfortunately in order to reach the fabled city you must plunge down a steep descent and then climb up the other side.

At the bottom of the winding descent you will reach an intersection where you turn left following the sign for San Gimignano. You now begin a 5 km slog up to the city walls. It is steep going and you may be accompanied by speeding cars making for the same destination. If the cars bother you, remember that it could be worse. I once labored up this climb on a hot day with a garbage truck for company. Unfortunately neither of us had the strength or stamina to pull away and so arrived at last at the top together.

The approach to San Gimignano.

In mid-summer San Gimignano can be a busy place. If you do not have advance reservations you can try applying at the Tourist Information Office. They can probably find you a room, but it may not be near town.

Degree of Difficulty: This is not a difficult ride. There are two climbs, but only one of them, the last one up to the city gates, is hard. It is not especially steep, but it goes on for 5 km. That last long grunt bumps a G ride up a notch. Rating: PG.

Highlights: This is one of those rides you come to Tuscany for: easy riding, beautiful scenery, historic castles. The down side is that it's tough to get a rythym going because you will be constantly stopping to take photographs. Monteriggioni and San Gimignano are on everyone's hit parade, but Abbadia Isola and Strove are little jems you will have all to yourself.

km	Place Name	Cafes	Shops, Mkts	Lodging	Camping	Bank	Bike Shop	Quaintness Ratting
15	Monteriggioni	●	●	●		●		*****
18	Abbadia Isola	●	●					***
20	Strove	●	●	●				****
28	Gracciano d'Elsa	●	●			●		
31	La Grazie	●	●					
33	Borgatello	●						
42	San Gimignano	●	●	●	●	●	●	*****

Tour 3/ Day 6 Siena—San Gimignano

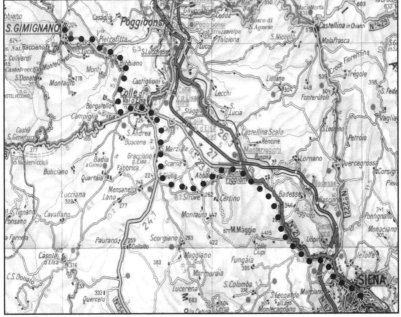

Touring Club Italiano, Auth. 04 November 2002

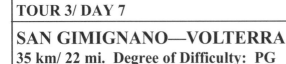

TOUR 3/ DAY 7

SAN GIMIGNANO—VOLTERRA
35 km/ 22 mi. Degree of Difficulty: PG

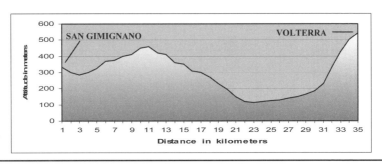

This is another relatively easy day in the saddle — short and sweet but with one leg-crushing climb at the end of the day to give you a sense of accomplishment. This route takes the back way to **Volterra** in an effort to avoid most of the traffic. The road travels along the spine of a ridge with magnificent views off to the north and south. The scenery on this route is as beautiful as you could find anywhere in Tuscany.

From the main gates of **San Gimignano** you follow the signs for **Pisa** and **Certaldo**. This takes you downhill for about a kilometer to an intersection in front of a beautiful old abbey surrounded by vineyards. Here you should turn left at the sign for Volterra.

From this intersection the road climbs steadily but not steeply for several kilometers. There are spectacular views across sloped vineyards back towards the towers of San Gimignano. After about 6 km of more or less continuous climbing you will hit the top of the ridge. From here you roll up and down several short steep climbs along the ridgeline. The scenery off to both sides of the road is more than enough to distract you from the effort of climbing. About 10 km from San Gimignano you will pass a left turn with a sign for Volterra. You want to continue straight. About a kilometer beyond this you will reach the village **il Castagno** and a right turn for **Castelfiorentino**; again you continue straight.

Beyond il Castagno the road begins to descend. There are a few short rises to pedal over but now you are mostly coasting downhill. Ahead across rolling hills and golden wheat fields you can see the ancient walled city of Volterra perched on top of its hill.

About 22 km from San Gimignano after a particularly steep descent you will reach a bridge and an intersection with a left turn for **N 439d** (the "d" stands for diretto (direct)) and signs for Volterra. There is another left turn on the other side of the bridge which also leads to Volterra. This is a shorter and more scenic route but is much steeper than taking the first left.

N 439d follows a river valley far below the walls of Volterra. It starts out basically flat and then gradually begins to climb.   The road finally veers away from the valley bottom and charges up a steep hill to an intersection with **N 68,** the main road between Volterra and **Colle di Val d'Elsa**. At this intersection you turn right and climb the final kilometers up to the city. As you crest the hill the road weaves around beneath the city walls and the impressive towers of its citadel. Follow the bulls-eye city center signs; they will lead you through the gates into the city.

Volterra is one of the most fascinating hilltowns in Tuscany. Its history dates back thousands of years. You can see the successive periods of history like tree rings in the construction of its outer walls. The foundations are giant blocks laid by the Etruscans. The more elegant stone work above was added by the Romans. Finally there is a jumble of styles above that reflecting the turbulence of relatively recent times. Inside these walls there is a rabbit warren of narrow streets and alleys. Like the other well-known hilltowns of Tuscany and Umbria these streets can be crowded with tourists during the summer months. There are plenty of hotels and even a rare campsite, but if you want to stay in the city center, it is best to book ahead.

Degree of Difficulty: The hard part of your day will be the final climb up to Volterra. No matter how you approach this ancient city, it will involve a long steep climb. On the plus side it comes after a relatively short day in the saddle. Rating: PG.

Highlights: San Gimignano and Volterra are two of the most fascinating hilltowns in all of Italy. They are worth every pedal stroke to visit. Nevertheless it is the beautiful landscape and the quiet roads along this route that will leave you in awe. Five star scenery, five star riding, this is cycling at its best.

km	Place Name	Cafes	Shops, Mkts	Lodging	Camping	Bank	Bike Shop	Quaintness Rating
11	Il Castagno	●	●	●				**
25	Molino d'Era	●	●	●				
35	Volterra	●	●	●	●	●	●	*****

Tour 3/ Day 7 San Gimignano—Volterra

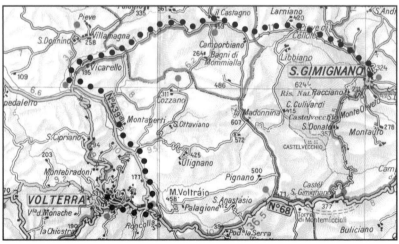

Touring Club Italiano, Auth. 04 November 2002

TOUR 3/ DAY 8

VOLTERRA—PISA
72 km/ 45 mi. Degree of Difficulty: G

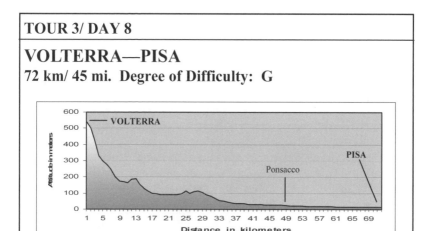

This is the longest stage of this tour, but with the exception of a few short hops it is downhill or flat the whole way. It takes you from the heights of **Volterra** down the Era River valley to the town of **Ponsacco** where you turn left and retrace your steps from the first day back into **Pisa.** It should be an easy day of pedaling through beautiful landscape.

To leave Volterra find you way back to N 68, the main road in and out of town, and follow the signs in the direction of **Cecina.** You will be going in the opposite direction from which you entered town down the eastern slope of the hill. The road makes a few tight switchbacks as it drops down below the city walls. About 1 km down the hill look for a right turn with signs for Pisa and **Pontedera.** Point the handlebars downhill and kick off as you will soon be flying down the steep grade. Ahead of you the flanks of the hill roll into golden wheat fields. Every knoll is occupied by a formidable-looking stone farm house. Nine kilometers of uninterrupted descent bring you to an intersection with **N 439.** Here you turn right again following the sign for Pontedera.

From here the road rolls along through wheat fields. There is a short climb or two as it contours along the side of the river valley. Twenty kilometers from your starting point you will reach an intersection with **N 439d.** Here you turn left continuing to follow the Pontedera signs. This being one of the main roads to Volterra there is apt to be more traffic, but the road is wide and flat, and the riding is easy. After another 5 km you will roll down a short hill into **La Sterza**, a modern town at a cross-roads. It has a few shops and a hotel.

You continue on N 439 towards Pontedera and Ponsacco. Beyond La Sterza the road rolls a bit with a few short climbs. After about 6 km you will see the medieval-looking town of **Peccioli** perched on a wooded hilltop on the opposite side of the valley. A few kilometers beyond the turn for Peccioli you will pass through the hamlet of **Selvetelli**. You are now in the broad, flat Era River valley. The road is wide and straight, and the cars take advantage of it. There are not many but they go by fast.

The road passes below the town of **Capannoli** which climbs the ridge to the left. This quaint town makes a good lunch stop as it has several cafes and markets. There is also a good view over the valley from the square at the top of the town.

From Capannoli you roll out onto the plain of the Arno River. Six kilometers of flat riding bring you to the busy town of Ponsacco. Here things get a little complicated. As you enter town you have to watch for signs to **Perignano** and **Lari**. This will put you on **Via Sauro** which leads you out of town. At the edge of town you bear right onto **Via delle Colline** following the signs for Perignano and Lari.

You are now on the main road that cuts due east along the base of the hills south of the Arno. This was your outbound track from Pisa on Day 1 and should look familiar. You will pass by **Le Casine** and **Cenaia** and eventually reach the intersection with **N 206,** which leads you back into Pisa. The scenic part of your ride is behind you; you are now just making time. About 10 km on N 206 brings you to busy downtown Pisa and the end of your tour of the lovely hills of Tuscany.

This tour was conceived around the idea of flying in and out of the Pisa International Airport. Most trans-Atlantic flights leave in the morning. You would probably not have time to do the ride, pack the bikes and gear, and still make a morning flight. This means you should plan spending your last night in Pisa and flying out the next morning. There are plenty of hotels in the city, and you probably would not need advance reservations except perhaps in August.

Degree of Difficulty: This is the longest stage of this tour, but it is almost entirely flat or downhill. And after seven days in the saddle climbing Tuscan hills, it should be cake the whole way. The most difficult part will be negotiating the traffic in downtown Pisa. Rating: G.

Highlights: Without question the highlight of your day will be the exhilarating descent out of Volterra. As you negotiate the steep winding turns a beautiful tableau of Tuscan landscape spreads out below you. This 9 km descent could be the highlight of your entire tour. Rolling down the Era River valley is also pleasant. The gentle downhill will make the pedaling feel effortless.

km	Place Name	Cafes	Shops, Mkts	Lodging	Camping	Bank	Bike Shop	Quaintness Rating
26	La Sterza	•	•	•				
33	Selvatelle	•	•					
35	Capannoli	•	•	•				**
42	Ponsacco	•	•	•		•	•	
46	Perignano	•	•					
49	Cenaia	•	•					
52	Valtriano	•	•					
69	Ospedaltto	•	•	•		•		
72	Pisa	•	•	•	11 km	•	•	*****

Tour 3/ Day 8 Volterra—Pisa

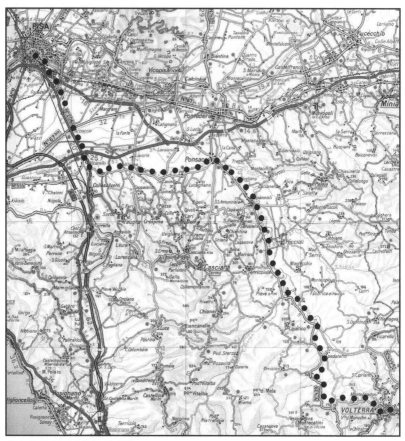

Touring Club Italiano, Auth. 04 November 2002

TOUR 4

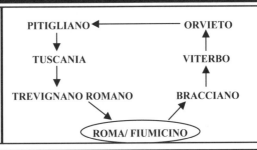

PITIGLIANO ◄——————— ORVIETO
↓
TUSCANIA   VITERBO
↓   ↑
TREVIGNANO ROMANO   BRACCIANO

ROMA/ FIUMICINO

ROMA/ FIUMICINO—ORVIETO—ROMA/ FIUMICINO
8 Days, 476 km/ 295 mi.

This is a tour of the "Lost Corner of Tuscany." Few of the destinations are likely to appear in most guide books. Except in the vicinity of Orvieto you are unlikely to see a single tour bus. This tour is about quiet country roads through lovely landscape, spectacular fortified villages, and ancient tombs which pre-date the Romans. It begins at Rome's international airport at Fiumicino and wanders into the rolling hills of the Etruscan heartland for 8 days before circling back to the airport. This tour will take you far off the beaten path. In many places you are unlikely to find English spoken. If taking the path less traveled appeals to you, then this could be the tour for you.

Day 1: Roma/ Fiumicino—Bracciano, 63 km/ 39 mi., PG

Day 2: Bracciano—Viterbo, 55 km/ 34 mi., PG-13

Day 3: Viterbo—Orvieto, 55 km/ 34 mi., PG

Day 4: Orvieto—Pitigliano, 72 km/ 44.5 mi., PG-13

Day 5: Pitigliano—Saturnia—Pitigliano, 64 km/ 40 mi., PG

Day 6: Pitigliano—Tuscania, 55 km/ 34 mi., G

Day 7: Tuscania—Trevignano Romano, 52 km/ 32 mi., G

Day 8: Trevignano R.—Roma/ Fiumicino, 60 km/ 37 mi., G

TOUR 4/ DAY 1

ROMA/ FIUMICINO—BRACCIANO
63 km/ 39 mi. Degree of Difficulty: PG

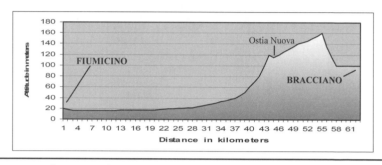

If you are flying into Rome, you will most likely be landing at Leonardo Da Vinci International Airport in the sea-side town of **Fiumicino.** For a detailed description of how to ride away from the airport see the **Airports** section above.

The suggested route out of the airport takes you past the pleasant beach resort of **Fregene,** about 16 km (10 mi.) from the airport. From Fregene follow signs to **Maccarese.** The road heads north and gradually curves around to the east. Five kilometers of flat, tree-lined road bring you bustling Maccarese. Go past the shops and markets and up over a railroad overpass. Coming down the other side turn left following signs for **Via Auralia.** This road parallels the railroad tracks for about 2 km until you come to a fork. Straight ahead there are signs for **Torrimpietra.** You should bear right following signs for Via Auralia.

After this turn the road narrows and goes through a stand of trees and over a curious wooden bridge that creaks under your wheels. It would be great riding except for the traffic which can be heavy, particularly on summer weekends as Romans flock to the beaches. After about 1 km you will come to the Autostrada. Signs to the left point to **Civitavecchia** and to the right for **Roma.** You want to go straight following signs for **Santa Maria di Galaria** and **Anguillara.** Once past the Autostrada the traffic diminishes and soon you are in quiet, rolling farmland.

About 7 km from the Autostrada you will reach a 4-way intersection. You should go straight ahead on **Via di Santa Maria di Galaria** and continue up the Arrone River valley. After about 4 km of flat riding the road gradually begins to climb. The climb continues for 3.5 km and gets steeper as you go. You finally top out on a ridge with wheat fields and vineyards dropping away on all sides. Santa Maria di Galaria, a collection of forlorn stucco buildings, is there to greet you. The road continues along the ridge line for about 2 km and then descends down to a 4-way intersection where you turn left in the direction of **Bracciano** and **Ostia Nuova.**

You are now on the busy **Via Claudia Braccianese**. About 200 meters from this turn you will pass a right turn for Ostia Nuova and Anguillara. Continuing straight the road rolls past fields of wheat and corn and sunflowers bordered by trees. After about 4 km you will reach a right turn for **Vigna di Valle** and **Lago di Bracciano**. Turning here gets you off the main road, and after a short climb a wonderful view of the lake opens up before you. About 1 km from the main road you will pass a right turn for Anguillara. You continue straight as the road descends down through woods to the lake shore. As you pedal along the lake shore you can see ahead the forbidding fortress of Bracciano overlooking the lake.

The town of Bracciano is built up above the lake. To reach it you will have to climb a short but steep hill up to the castle walls. The medieval section of town offers cobblestone streets, cafes, as well as many shops. There are eight hotels in the vicinity of Bracciano. Many of them are down on the lake shore. You should have no trouble finding a room except perhaps in August when it would be wise to book ahead.

Degree of Difficulty: At 63 km (39 mi.) this is a do-able first day on the bike even after a trans-Atlantic flight. There is a pretty good climb up to Santa Maria di Galaria, but it is not particularly steep. The effects of jet lag, dodging speeding cars on the way out of the airport, and getting used to your fully-loaded bike will be the main difficulties of the day. The route itself is not hard. Rating: PG.

Highlights: The long blissfully quiet stretch up the Arrone River valley is just the antidote you need after escaping the airport traffic. The view over Lago di Bracciano as you crest the ridge above the lake is unforgettable. And sunset over the lake from the table in the outdoor café is the perfect way to end your first day in the saddle.

km	Place Name	Cafes	Shops, Mkts	Lodging	Camping	Bank	Bike Shop	Quaintness Rating
9	Focene	●	●					
16	Fregene	●	●	●				
22	Maccarese	●	●	●		●		
45	Ostia Nuova	●	●					
63	Bracciano	●	●	●	●	●	●	****

Tour 4/ Day 1 Roma/ Fiumicino—Bracciano

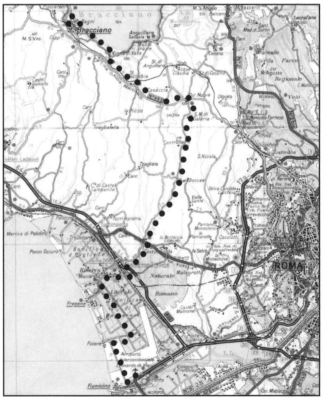

Touring Club Italiano, Auth. 04 November 2002

TOUR 4/ DAY 2

BRACCIANO—VITERBO
55 km/ 34 mi. Degree of Difficulty: PG-13

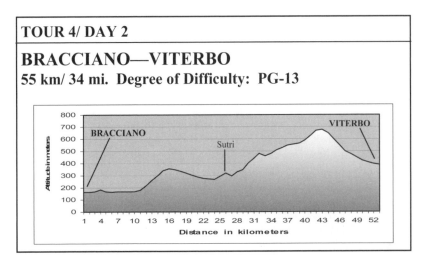

     This is a relatively short route but with a lot of sustained climbing. It begins down on the lake shore below **Bracciano** and continues around the lake in a clockwise direction towards **Trevignano Romano.** This is a beautiful stretch of road with magnificent views over the lake. And contrary to what you might expect, it is not all flat. There are a couple of short, steep climbs and descents as the road weaves its way through the olive groves marching up the slopes of the extinct volcano crater.

     Ten kilometers from Bracciano you will see a left turn with signs for **Sutri.** Turning here the road immediately begins to climb steeply. As you wind your way up the mountainside there are spectacular views over Lago di Bracciano and the lake-front town of Trevignano. After about 3.5 km of sustained climbing the grade gradually lessens as you reach the summit. If you happen to do this ride on a clear day, the views back into the lake will be unforgettable. Two kilometers of more or less flat riding over the top of the ridge bring you to the descent down the other side. At 25 km from Bracciano you will hit an intersection with **N 2,** the **Via Cassia.**

     Turn left here following signs for Sutri. The road descends very gently for about 1 km into a cliff bound river valley. On the left side of the road you will pass a series of impressive Etruscan tombs carved into the sheer rock walls of the valley. On the other side of the narrow valley you will see the medieval town of Sutri perched on top of a cliff. A short steep climb brings you up to its fortified gate and curtain wall. Do not miss the chance to pull off the road and cycle through its quaint cobblestone alleys and squares. Sutri is a forgotten gem of medieval architecture that has largely escaped the march of time and tourists.

From the main gate of Sutri follow signs for **Ronciglione**. The road rolls through rural farm land for about 2 km before hitting the long climb up to Ronciglione. About 4.5 km from Sutri you will reach an intersection with signs for **Roma** to the right and **Viterbo** to the left. If you go left here the main road skirts around below Ronciglione, or you can turn right towards Roma, and then take an immediate left to go up into the town of Ronciglione. It is a prosperous town with a wonderful medieval quarter complete with brooding castle. There are also many cafes and markets in case you want to fortify yourself for the next long climb up above **Lago di Vico**.

Ronciglione.

From Ronciglione follow the signs for Viterbo. The road will climb briefly before descending down through thick woods towards Lago di Vico. At the bottom of the decent there is an intersection with signs to the right for Viterbo, and from here the road begins to climb more or less continuously for the next 11 km. The grade varies from steep to gentle and throughout you will be treated to dramatic views down into the narrow crater of Lago di Vico. There are also magnificent views in the other direction down the slopes of the mountainside and across rolling agricultural land as far as the Tevere River valley.

About 45 km from Bracciano the descent down to Viterbo begins. The road plunges down into a broad valley that you see below you. After 10 km of downhill the road meets the medieval walls of Viterbo and the impressive Porta Romana gate into the old part of the city.

Viterbo is a large town with the associated modern sprawl, but inside its medieval walls it has preserved much of its historic charm. It is a university town, so there are many hotels. You should have no trouble finding a place to stay. Just follow the blue " i " signs for the Tourist Information Office, and they can help you find a room.

Degree of Difficulty: As mentioned above, this is a relatively short stage, but there is a significant amount of climbing. The grade up from Lago di Bracciano is sustained for 3.5 km before it moderates, and the 11 km climb around the rim of Lago di Vico includes several short steep pitches. In sum, you will be very happy to see the long descent down into Viterbo. Rating: PG-13.

Highlights: This is a beautiful ride. The circuit around the north shore of Lago di Bracciano takes you through olive groves and past ancient stone farm houses. The views back over the lake as you labor up the climb out of the ancient volcano crater can easily eat through half a roll of film. Sutri is one of those charming, forgotten towns refreshingly free of tour buses and plastic statues of "David." Don't let yourself pass by in the interest of making time. This is the kind of town you come to Italy to see. Ronciglione, while not as quaint as Sutri, is at least as interesting as some of the more well-known hilltowns farther north in Tuscany. The circuit around Lago di Vico is also beautiful with views down into the lake on one side and across the broad plain below on the other. Finally there is Viterbo which in addition to its well-preserved medieval character offers a taste of the vibrant Italian café culture which is so wonderfully distinct from the shopping malls of home.

km	Place Name	Cafes	Shops, Mkts	Lodging	Camping	Bank	Bike Shop	Quaintness Rating
26	Sutri	•	•	•		•		*****
32	Ronciglione	•	•	•		•	•	***
38	San Rocco	•						
55	Viterbo	•	•	•		•	•	***

Tour 4/ Day 2 Bracciano—Viterbo

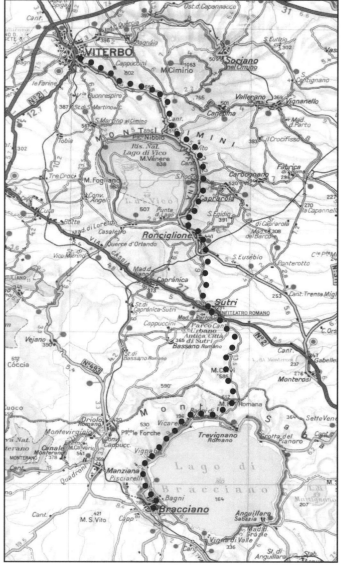

Touring Club Italiano, Auth. 04 November 2002

TOUR 4/ DAY 3

VITERBO—ORVIETO
55 km/ 34 mi. Degree of Difficulty: PG

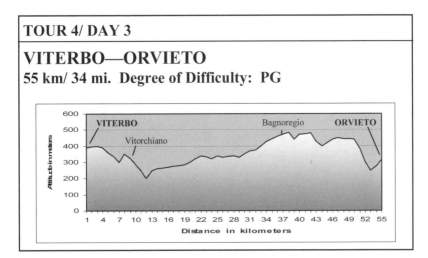

This route involves a lot of short up and downs. It takes you through beautiful, quiet countryside past unforgettable medieval hilltowns and winds up at **Orvieto,** which is perhaps the quintessential Italian hilltown.

Starting from the **Porta Romana** gate where you entered Viterbo, turn left and follow the walls north to where they make an abrupt left turn. Here you will find a major intersection with signs to the right for **Bagnaia, La Quercia,** and **Orte.** You can also reach this intersection by leaving the old part of the city by the **Porta Fiorentina** gate and turning right. After a short distance you will reach the same intersection. From this intersection the road climbs gently up a tree-lined boulevard for 2 km to the town of La Quercia. As you enter the main square of town look for a left turn with a sign to **Vitorchiano.** Upon making this turn you will leave most of the traffic behind for the rest of the day.

The road to Vitorchiano plunges down a steep descent through overgrown pastures and fields. This is immediately followed by an equally steep climb up to an overpass over the Autostrada and the modern town of **Paparano.** From Paparano the road descends for about 2 km to the gates of the medieval village of Vitorchiano.

Whatever you may have thought of Sutri, Vitorchiano is better. This is the kind of forgotten treasure that makes exploring Italy on your own so rewarding. You will find no tour buses here, no trinket shops; you will have to search hard to find even a postcard. Instead you will find a burly fortified gate concealing delightful twisting alleys with laundry strung overhead. Tiny markets and shops are squeezed into narrow doorways. The village is built out on a tongue of crumbling rock which falls away into a brushy ravine below. Its houses cling precariously to each other as if to keep from losing their balance. This is a gem; don't miss the opportunity to explore it.

From Vitorchiano you continue down hill into a narrow valley. On the way down there are great views back up at the jumble of stone house perched on the cliffs. After about 2 km of descent the road crosses a bridge over a soupy green stream and then climbs steeply up the other side. You will soon pass a right turn with a sign for **Sippicciano**; you should continue straight. The road rolls along through open fields and occasional stands of trees. About 7 km from Vitorchiano you will reach the town of **Magugnano.** Navigate your way through town following the signs for **Montefiascone** and **Bagnoregio**. The road continues more or less flat for about 5 km until you reach an intersection with a larger road. Here you turn right following the signs for Bagnoregio.

At about 38 km from Viterbo you will begin to see a remarkable stone village built on a high point of rock with sweeping views down over the valley to the east. This is the village of **Civita di Bagnoregio**. It is the site of the original medieval town which was abandoned over time in favor of the present location. What remains is a wonderfully preserved medieval village. At the bottom of the gentle descent into the modern town of Bagnoregio you will see a parking area on the right. If you bear right here, you will come to a modern causeway which crosses a ravine to Civita di Bagnoregio. This is another medieval jewel that is well worth a short detour to explore.

Continuing on from Bagnoregio the road descends steeply from town, only to climb up the ridge opposite. After about 4 km you will come to a traffic circle where you should follow the signs for **Orvieto**. The road descends at first and then rolls up and down along the top of a ridge-line with magnificent views down into the river valley below.

At about 50 km from Viterbo you will pass through the pleasant village of **Canale.** At this point a magnificent view of Orvieto opens up before you. The city sits atop sheer sandstone cliffs, the edges crowded with rambling stone houses. Church spires and towers rise over the red tile roofs. Velvet green vineyards spread down the slopes below the city. If you happen to reach this point in the late afternoon with the golden rays of sunshine lighting up the cliffs and walls of the city, you could have a near-religious experience.

From Canale the road sails down a long series of broad switchbacks, and the view towards Orvieto seems only to improve as you approach the city. Unfortunately you will be wrenched out of your reverie when you reach the bottom of the descent and face the steep 3 km climb up to the city gates. Hopefully the dramatic sight of the cliffs above, pock-marked with ancient Etruscan tombs, will be enough to distract you from the pain of lactic acid build-up in your legs.

At the top of the climb you will pass through the massive city gates into a labyrinth of cobblestone streets. You are unlikely to find that you have the place to yourself. In fact, in the summer months it may be too crowded to ride your bike down the main street. Nevertheless, Orvieto is a treasure to be explored and savored. There is no shortage of accommodations for the legions of visitors who tramp through here each day, but in the peak season you may want to book ahead. In a pinch you should be able to find a room in one of the many hotels down below the city at the train station.

Degree of Difficulty: This is not an especially long ride, but there are a lot of short, steep climbs to tackle including the last one up to the gates of Orvieto. Rating: PG.

Highlights: Vitorchiano, Civita di Bagnoregio, and Orvieto are three of the most spectacular hilltowns you can find in all of Italy, and that's saying a lot! The riding between these towns is quiet and blissfully traffic-free. And the view as you descend down towards the foot of Orvieto rates a full five stars.

km	Place Name	Cafes	Shops, Mkts	Lodging	Camping	Bank	Bike Shop	Quaintness Rating
2	La Quercia	●	●					
8	Paparano	●						
10	Vitorchiano	●	●	●				*****
18	Magugnano	●	●					
38	Bagnoregio	●	●	●		●		*****
55	Orvieto	●	●	●		●		*****

Tour 4/ Day 3 Viterbo—Orvieto

Touring Club Italiano, Auth. 04 November 2002

TOUR 4/ DAY 4

ORVIETO—PITIGLIANO
72 km/ 45 mi. Degree of Difficulty: PG-13

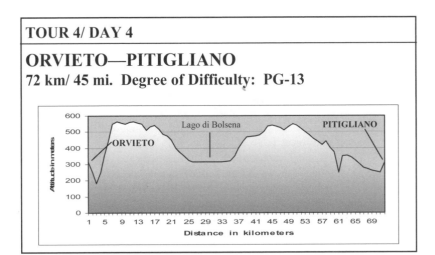

This route takes you up above **Orvieto** and then down into the volcanic basin that forms **Lago di Bolsena**. Bring extra film, because this one will be spectacular. The views across the lake as you speed down switchbacks into the town of **Bolsena** are unforgettable. After a short ride around the lake you must climb up out of the basin again, but the views are almost as good. Once over the top the route leads you the fortified medieval towns of **Onano** and **Sorano**. These are both 5-star attractions but are just far enough off the beaten path to have maintained their genuine charm. After a steep descent down below Sorano and an equally steep climb up the other side, you roll to the foot of spectacular **Pitigliano**. A last climb up long switchbacks beneath the sheer cliffs of this ancient Etruscan city ends a wonderful day on the bike.

You begin at the gates of Orvieto. Following the signs for Bolsena you dive down an all-too-quick descent to a 4-way intersection. You go straight across and immediately begin to climb. The road cuts back and forth up a hillside in long switchbacks giving you great views back at the city. This can be a busy road, and you should expect heavy traffic, but because of the steep grade most of it is going slowly. About 4 km of sustained climbing brings you to a left turn with signs for **Porano** and **Bagnoregio.** Turning off the busy main road here you go about 100 meters to a right turn with a sign for **Torre San Severo.** This quiet country road parallels the main road and spares you the excitement of cars speeding by your elbow.

From this turn the road meanders through pleasant rural farm land. In the summer months the fields will be filled with sunflowers. After about 4 km you will reach the village of Torre San Severo, a shady unremarkable spot. Beyond town the road begins to descend down through huge fields of sunflowers to the intersection with **N71**. Go straight across the highway and continue towards Bolsena. The road climbs away from the main road for about 1 km and rolls through fields of wheat and sunflowers. About 3 km from the highway the road begins a long easy descent down into the volcanic crater that forms Lago di Bolsena.

This is a spectacular stretch of road. It drops down through olive groves with marvelous views out over the lake. As you get lower down the towers of the town of Bolsena come into view. The road zig-zags down through town to a central square ringed with cafes. This is roughly the half-way point of the ride and makes a good place to stop for lunch or a snack.

From Bolsena you follow signs for **Acquapendente** and **Siena** around the north side of the lake. You will pass several commercial campgrounds along the lake shore. After about 7 km on this fairly busy road you will reach an intersection with **N489** and signs for **Latera** and **Pitigliano**. Turning left off of the main road you continue along the flat lake shore. About 1.5 kilometers from this intersection you will see a right turn with a sign for **Grotte di Castro**. Turning here a stiff 4 km climb takes you up out of the lake basin to this charming medieval village. At the top of the climb turn left into town and follow the signs for **Viterbo** through the cobblestone streets. Just outside of town you will see a right turn with a sign for **Onano**. The road climbs steeply from here but only for a short distance. Once over the top you begin a gradual descent down to Onano. You can see its castle towers looming above the jumble of stone houses. Following the bulls-eye signs for the town center turn right off the main road and pedal up its narrow streets. From the central square below the castle follow the signs for **Sorano** out of town.

From Onano the road drops precipitously down into a ravine below the cliffs on which the town is perched. And of course you have to immediately climb your way out. As you wind up the switchbacks on the other side of the valley, there are tremendous views back towards the town. All along this route you will pass Etruscan tombs hewn into the soft rock of pretty much any available cliff-side. Some are no more bigger than coffins; others can be a series of elaborate chambers.

After climbing for about 2 km the road begins to roll along through patches of trees and pasture land. Gradually you begin the descent down to Sorano. You can see the twin castles of this town through the trees. The road spills you out into the main square just above the old section. It is well worth a short detour to explore the narrow twisting alleys behind its brooding medieval gate.

Pitigliano

From the main square of Sorano you sail down a series of tight switchbacks into the narrow valley below and begin to work your way up the other side. The sheer cliffs on both sides are marked by ever more Etruscan tombs. Once you top out on the climb the road meanders gently down through pasture land. About 8 km from Sorano there will be a left turn for **Pitigliano**. Straight ahead is **Sovana.** Turning left here the road descends down into a shady wooded valley below Pitigliano. You are treated to a breath-taking view up at the city walls as you approach. A long set of switchbacks winds up to the gate into the old section of town.

Pitigliano is a spectacular example of medieval architecture. You may blow through a roll of film at sunset when the city ramparts are lit up in golden light, so be sure to bring extra. There are four hotels in Pitigliano. The inexpensive Hotel Guastini is just at the top of the climb next to the city gates. There are also a number of private rooms for rent in the old part of the city. Check with the Tourist Information Office.

Degree of Difficulty: There is some serious climbing out of Orvieto and out of the Lago di Bolsena basin. There are also short steep pitches leaving both Onano and Sorano. Luckily none of them are very long. Nevertheless, on a hot, humid day in mid-summer they will be a challenge. Rating: PG-13.

Highlights: The scenery on this ride is a solid 5-stars. The view back to Orvieto as you labor up the climb even with all the traffic will uplift your soul. And if that doesn't do it, then surely the sweeping descent into Bolsena will have you singing like Maria von Trapp. Onano and Sorano are the quaint unspoiled hilltowns you came to see. And at sunset the walls of Pitigliano are unforgettable.

km	Place Name	Cafes	Shops, Mkts	Lodging	Camping	Bank	Bike Shop	Quaintness Rating
11	Torre San Severo	●	●					*
26	Bolsena	●	●	●	●	●		****
39	Grotte di Castro	●	●					***
48	Onano	●	●					****
60	Sorano	●	●	●		●		****
72	Pitigliano	●	●	●		●	●	*****

Tour 4/ Day 4 Orvieto—Pitigliano

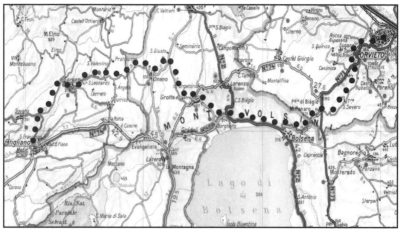

Touring Club Italiano, Auth. 04 November 2002

TOUR 4/ DAY 5

PITIGLIANO—SATURNIA—PITIGLIANO
64 km/ 40 mi. Degree of Difficulty: PG

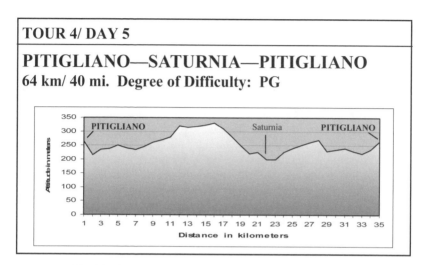

This is a beautiful route through the "outback" of Tuscany. It takes you on a loop from **Pitigliano** to the hot springs at **Saturnia** and back to Pitigliano. You will be touring through lovely rural countryside with hardly a passing car to spoil the effect. Leave the panniers in your room; today you are sight-seeing, not traveling.

From Pitigliano glide back down the switchbacks on the way to **Sorano**. Five kilometers from town at the top of a long gentle grade turn left at the intersection following the signs for **Sovana** and Saturnia. The road rolls through pasture land and stands of trees. About 3 km from the turn the road begins to descend followed by a gentle climb up to the ruined castle of Sovana. This is a beautiful village with a main street lined with stone houses and sidewalk cafes.

From Sovana the road descends around below town. The road cuts down through the soft rock, and it feels like you are in a deep bob-sled run. About 1 km below town you will enter a 100 meter tunnel. There are ancient Etruscan tombs carved into the rock all along here. Its worth pulling over to scramble up and explore them. Many have remarkable carvings of faces and geometric patterns. The most elaborate of these tombs is the **Tomba Ildebranda** which you will pass a few kilometers from Sovana. It has an interesting network of caves with pillared entrances and base-relief carvings. Unfortunately you must pay to visit them.

About 14 km from Pitigliano the road begins to climb. The grade starts out gently and gradually steepens as you approach **San Martino sul**

Fiora. The view opens up below as you climb through rolling wheat fields and olive groves, each bordered by rows of trees. At 18 km from Pitigliano you will pass through quiet San Martino. Beyond the town the road descends briefly before resuming a gentle uphill grade. It meanders through stands of trees with intermittent views across the valley below. Just before the village of **Catabbio** you will pass a road-side fountain where you can refill waterbottles. A short steep climb brings you to the main square of Catabio where there is another fountain. At the far end of town there is an intersection where you turn left at the signs for Saturnia and **Manciano**.

From this intersection you begin a 7 km descent through some of the most lovely country you will find anywhere in Tuscany. Olive groves and hay fields roll away below you to forested mountains to the south. You sail down switchbacks lined with ancient, gnarled olive trees. The stone houses of **Poggio Capane** flash by. The road eventually levels out at an intersection with a right turn for the towns of **Usi** and **Murci**. Continuing straight the road climbs a gentle grade through shady trees for about 1 km to a right turn for the town of Saturnia. You should continue straight following the signs for Manciano.

From the turn for the town of Saturnia the road descends for another 2 km into a broad flat valley. Off to the left as you will see the steaming baths of **Termi di Saturnia,** a huge modern hotel spa. If you continue straight across the valley for another 2 km to where the road begins to curve to the left you will see a dirt road bearing off to the right. You may see cars parked along the dirt road. About 200 meters down this road you will find the free baths of Saturnia. The steaming, turquoise waters spill down a series of bone-white pools. It would be an idyllic scene if not for the strong sulfur aroma of the mineral baths. There is a café here with an ivy-covered patio that serves pizza, drinks, and ice cream. In the summer months you can expect to find the pools and the café pretty crowded. It is an interesting scene and worth seeing even if you decide to pass on "taking the waters."

From the hot springs the road climbs up out of the valley. There is a great view down over the cascading pools. Once you crest out on top of the climb the road rolls along through pasture land. Ahead you can see the town of **Montemerano** crowning a hilltop. Just below this town you will reach an intersection with signs to the left for Manciano, or you can go straight across the road and climb up to Montemerano. It is worth the climb up to this quaint old hilltown. Down its narrow cobblestone main street you will find a few bars and cafes that offer a quiet lunch stop. There is also a large round fountain at the edge of town with benches and shade trees for a picnic lunch or just a rest.

From Montermerano follow the signs for Manciano. The road is busier now and you will see some traffic as you approach this large town. A long climb up a series of switchbacks with wonderful views over rolling forested ridges brings you to an intersection just below town. Turn left here following the signs for Pitigliano. You will instantly plunge down a steep winding descent through pasture land and woods for about 4.5 km. The remaining 15 km back to Pitigliano roll along through the hills with lovely views over the countryside to the left and right. You will be able to see

The Saturnia hot springs.

Pitigliano ahead, and a last steep series of switchbacks brings you up to the town.

Degree of Difficulty: There is a fair amount of climbing on this route, some of it steep, but without panniers you will feel like you're flying up the grades. Rating: PG.

Highlights: Easy climbs, great views, no traffic, this is 5-star riding. The thermal springs at Saturnia will ease any tired muscles. Sovana with its Etruscan tombs and Montemerano with its shady streets are icing on the cake.

km	Place Name	Cafes	Shops, Mkts	Lodging	Camping	Bank	Bike Shop	Quaintness Rating
8	Sovana	•	•	•		•		****
18	San Martino	•	•					*
24	Catabbio	•	•					*
32	Satrunia	•	•	•		•		**
39	Montemerano	•	•	•				***
46	Manciano	•	•	•		•	•	*
64	Pitigliano	•	•	•		•	•	*****

Tour 4/ Day 5 Pitigliano—Saturnia—Pitigliano

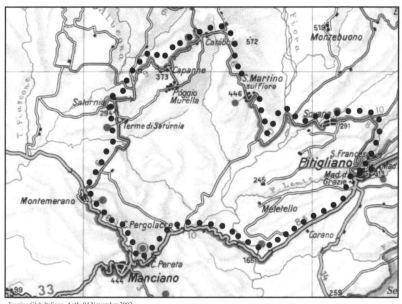

Touring Club Italiano, Auth. 04 November 2002

TOUR 4/ DAY 6

PITIGLIANO—TUSCANIA
55 km/ 34 mi. Degree of Difficulty: G

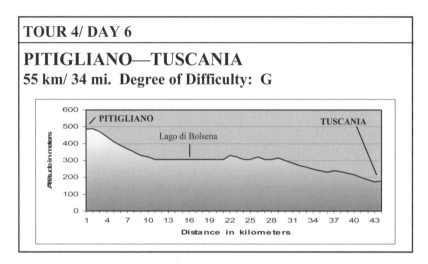

This route marks where you turn the corner and begin your trek back to the airport. First you will return to the shores of **Lago di Bolsena** and then south to ancient **Tuscania**.

From Pitigliano you follow signs for **Orvieto** and **Bolsena.** This puts you on **N74** heading due east. After a short steep descent out of Pitigliano you begin a long gradual climb that takes you up to the volcanic rim above Lago di Bolsena. The views are of course spectacular. Just below the crest you will come to an intersection where you bear left onto **N489** and continue down towards the lake. Just down the hill from this turn the road forks again with the left turn going to **Grotte di Castro** and the right to **Gradoli.** You should turn right here and continue down the steep incline into the lake basin.

You can see the village of Gradoli below you. It has a pleasant medieval section and fantastic views over the lake. As the hill begins to roll out onto the flat plain on the north shore of the lake, watch for an unmarked right turn which heads down to the lake shore. If you come to a left turn with a sign for Grotte di Castro, you have gone too far.

Once you reach the lake, the road turns into hard-packed dirt and follows closely along the shoreline. Although it is dirt, the road is perfectly rideable even for skinny road tires. This is a beautiful, quiet stretch of road. There are any number of cool grassy spots under shade trees where you can lean up your bike and plunge into the water for a swim. The road meanders along the lake shore for about 10 km. It then veers away from the water and climbs a steep hill. Dropping down the other side it meets the main road to **Montefiascone**.

Turn left here following the signs for **Capodimonte.** After about 2 km there is a left turn with a sign for Capodimonte which takes you off the main road and along the lake again. Capodimonte has a yachty air with lots of boats moored along the shore. The town is built up on a headland with a castle overlooking the lake. The road skirts along the base of the town and returns to the main road, where after about 1 km you can get off the main road again and ride into the quaint town of **Marta.**

Like Capodimonte, Marta is also built up on a rocky headland overlooking the lake. Entering by this side road takes you through the narrow streets of the town. At the main square below the impressive clock tower turn right following the signs for **Tuscania.** This leads you back to the main road. Cross directly over and continue south on a quiet narrow road through wheat fields and vineyards. It follows the course of the Marta River and trends down hill for several kilometers. After crossing over the river a few times it climbs gently away from the river valley and winds its way over rolling hills. Soon the walls and towers of Tuscania come into view.

Tuscania is one of those towns that ooze charm. It is not on the way to anywhere and so managed to escape notice during much of the past century. Most of its medieval curtain wall is intact, and its narrow streets weave between shaky-looking stone houses. It is honey-combed with Roman and Etruscan ruins and is famous for its necropolis. There are only two hotels in town and during the summer months you may wish to book ahead. But there are also a number of private rooms for rent, as well as agriturismos nearby. Inquire at the Tourist Information Office.

Degree of Difficulty: This is not a difficult ride. The one long climb of the day - after leaving Pitigliano - comes first thing in the morning when you are fresh and the temperature is cool. Once you reach the crest of the ridge above Lago di Bolsena the ride is pretty much cake all the way to Tuscania. Rating: G.

Highlights: The steep descent down to Lago di Bolsena is bound to be a highlight, as will be the quiet ride along the edge of the lake with its shimmering views across the water. But the timeless, almost other-worldly atmosphere of Tuscania may be the most memorable.

km	Place Name	Cafes	Shops, Mkts	Lodging	Camping	Bank	Bike Shop	Quaintness Rating
19	Gradoli	●	●	●		●		**
37	Capodimonte	●	●	●	●	●	●	***
40	Marta	●	●	●		●		***
55	Tuscania	●	●	●		●	●	*****

Tour 4/ Day 6 Pitigliano—Tuscania

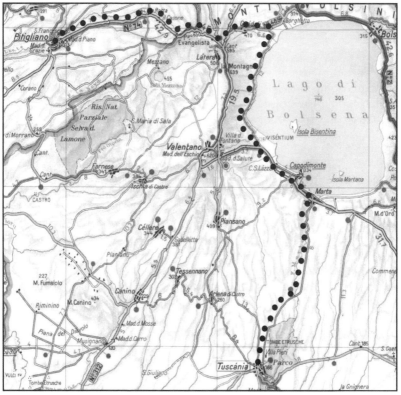

Touring Club Italiano, Auth. 04 November 2002

TOUR 4/ DAY 7

TUSCANIA—TREVIGNANO ROMANO
52 km/ 32 mi. Degree of Difficulty: G

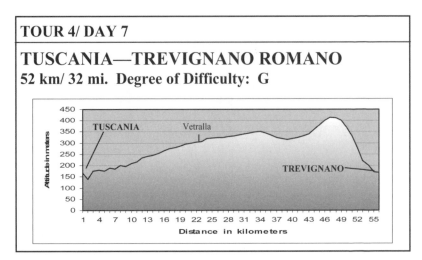

This route takes you back to the shores of **Lago di Bracciano**. But instead of returning to the town of Bracciano, you will go to **Trevignano Romano** on the opposite shore of the lake. It sits on a rocky headland below a ruined castle with wonderful views across the lake. This is a relatively easy ride with only one major climb up the flanks of Monti Sabatini above the lake. For most of the rest of the ride you will be pedaling through wheat fields and olive groves on the gentle slopes of Monti Cimini.

The ride starts at the gates of **Tuscania**. Following the signs for Viterbo you drop down below the town and cross the Marta River. All the way down you will see Etruscan and Roman ruins littering the slope. Once across the bridge there is a short steep climb up to the plateau above. At the top of the climb you will reach a fork where you bear right for **Vetralla.**

After making this turn the road rolls through miles of wheat fields. You can see the bulk of Monte Cimini looming ahead. About 14 km from Tuscania you will pass the Autostrada leading to Viterbo. The wheat fields begin to give way to olive groves, and you can see the trees dotting the landscape ahead on the slopes of Monti Cimini. At 20 km from Tuscania you will hit the main road from Viterbo to Vetralla, **N 2**, the **Via Cassia**. The traffic picks up here and for the next 8 km or so you will have to share the road with cars and trucks.

Vetralla is a busy place. It has a quaint medieval section up above the modern sprawl, but the suburban congestion extends for more than 3 km along the Via Cassia — all the way through **Cura**, the next town down the road. The traffic gradually diminishes as you leave Cura behind.

About 34 km into the ride you will pass through the town of **Capranica.** It has a wonderful medieval section reminiscent of Pitigliano built out on cliffs overlooking a narrow valley. The road sails down a tight set of switchbacks with wonderful views up at the city walls.

From Capranica to **Sutri** the road travels down a wooded valley hemmed in by cliffs on either side. It is beautiful and shady, and despite the frequent cars it is great riding. At Sutri you will cross your outbound route. On the right side of the road you will pass the complex of Etruscan tombs carved into the rock face. About 2 km beyond these you will reach the right turn for Trevignano Romano. Here you encounter the only real climb of the day. About 5 km of sustained climbing takes you up to the brink of Monti Sabatini above Lago di Bracciano. If you didn't notice the view on the way from Bracciano to Viterbo you won't be able to ignore it on the way back. This is 5-star scenery, and best of all it's all down hill.

About 4 km straight down takes you to the intersection with the road that circles the lake. You turn left here and pedal about 1 km into Trevignano Romano. This delightful lake-front town has a boardwalk and outdoor cafes along the water. Most of the hotels are at the far end of town. You should have no trouble finding a room here except perhaps in August. There are also a number of commercial campgrounds farther along the east shore of the lake in the direction of **Anguillara.**

Degree of Difficulty: There are a lot of short climbs and descents between Tuscania and Capranica, but none of then are long or particularly steep. The only obstacle in your way is the climb up Monti Sabatini above Lago di Bracciano. While long and steep it will be less than a half hour out of your day. Rating: G.

Highlights: The rolling quiet roads from Tuscania to Vetralla in the shadow of Monti Cimini is wonderful riding. The section from Capranica to Sutri is also beautiful. But the view across Lago di Bracciano from the top of the climb will be the pinnacle of your day. After a relatively easy day on the bike you get to relax in an outdoor café along the waterfront of Trevignano Romano.

km	Place Name	Cafes	Shops, Mkts	Lodging	Camping	Bank	Bike Shop	Quaintness Rating
21	Vetralla	●	●	●		●	●	
24	Cura	●	●	●		●		
34	Capranica	●	●	●		●		**
39	Sutri	●	●	●				*****
52	Trevignano R.	●	●	●	●	●		***

Tour 4/ Day 7 Tuscania—Trevignano Romano

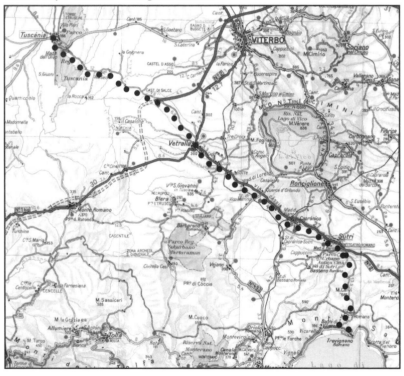

Touring Club Italiano, Auth. 04 November 2002

TOUR 4/ DAY 8

TREVIGNANO ROMANO—ROMA/ FIUMICINO
60 km/ 37 mi. Degree of Difficulty: G

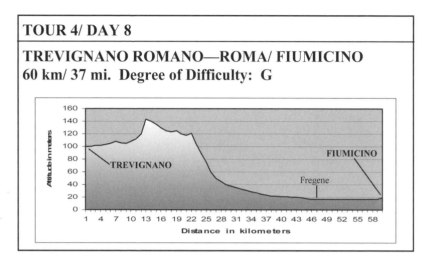

This route takes you back to the airport. Bear in mind that flights back to the U.S. depart in the morning or early afternoon. While it is possible to complete this ride, pack your gear, and break down your bike in time to make a flight, it would make for a very stressful day. You will be much better off staying one more night in **Fregene**, and then riding the last 17 km (10 mi.) to the airport the next morning. The entire route to **Fiumicino** is described here, and you can decide whether you wish to stop at Fregene.

From **Trevignano Romano** you continue clockwise around **Lago di Bracciano**. The road is flat and shady. You will pass several commercial campgrounds and hotels. Five kilometers from Trevignano you will pass a left turn with signs for **Roma**; continue straight following the signs for **Anguillara Sabazia**. About 12 km from Trevignano you will come to a left turn up a steep hill with signs for Anguillara and Roma. At the top of the short, steep climb you will hit an intersection on a busy street at the edge of downtown Anguillara. You turn left here following the signs for Roma. A busy road past gas stations and car dealerships takes you out of Anguillara and through mostly flat farmland to **Ostia Nuova**.

At Ostia Nuova you rejoin your out-bound track from the airport, and things should look familiar. You will reach an intersection with **N 493**, the **Via Claudia Braccianese**. Signs point to Roma to the left and **Bracciano** to the right. You want to turn left and pedal about 100 meters to another intersection with a right turn for **Fregene**. Turning here you get off the main road and away from the traffic.

The road climbs briefly along a ridgeline with wheat fields stretching away in every direction. At 20 km from Trevignano you will pass **Santa Maria di Galeria,** and here the road dips and begins the long descent down to the coast. You are unlikely to see any cars at all along this pleasant country road.

The descent goes for 3.5 km before it levels out. At 27.7 km from Trevignano you will hit an intersection with a large white sign welcoming you to **Fiumicino,** even though it is still 32 km away. This is a 4-way intersection, and you go straight following the sign for **Via Auralia.** The road continues through quiet farm land for another 7 km to the Autostrada interchange. Here traffic picks up. You go under the highway overpass and follow signs for Fregene. The road narrows and crosses the weird wooden bridge. After another kilometer or so you will hit an intersection with **Torrimpietra** to the right and Fregene to the left. Turning left you will reach **Maccarese** after about 2 km. Go up over the railroad overpass and turn right towards Fregene. Five kilometers from this overpass you will come to a blinking yellow light and a right turn for Fregene. If you intend to lay over one more night before your flight home, turn here and go about 100 meters to a left turn at another blinking yellow light. This takes you down the main street of Fregene past shops and cafes. As mentioned under the Airports section, there are three hotels in Fregene, and it is the most convenient overnight stop near the airport. During July and August, it may be prudent to make a reservation for your last night.

To continue on to the airport from the turn for Fregene you simply go straight past the first blinking yellow light. The road continues straight and flat for about 5 km to an abrupt 90 degree right turn. After 2 km it makes another 90 degree left turn around the end of the airport runways. You then parallel the runways for 7 km until you reach a 4-way intersection. Here you turn left following the "Aeroporto" sign. Continue straight on this road to your second left where there is a green sign for Roma. This takes you up a ramp onto the big boulevard that rolls into the airport. See the Airports section for a more detailed description of the approach to the terminal buildings.

Degree of Difficulty: Except for the short climb up to Anguillara this ride is flat or down hill. You greatest difficulty will be dodging traffic on the way into the airport. Rating: G.

Highlights: The ride around Lago di Bracciano between Trevignano Romano and Anguillara is quiet and shady. The long descent below Santa Maria di Galeria which takes you past olive groves and vineyards, your last of the trip, is also wonderful. Although probably not the highlights of the whole tour, they nevertheless make for a pleasant ride.

km	Place Name	Cafes	Shops, Mkts	Lodging	Camping	Bank	Bike Shop	Quaintness Rating
13	Anguillara	•	•	•	•	•	•	**
21	Ostia Nuova	•	•					
35	Maccarese	•	•	•		•		
43	Fregene	•	•	•		•		*
50	Focene	•	•					
60	Aeroporto Leonardo da Vinci	•	•	•		•		

Fregene.

Tour 4/ Day 8 Trevignano Romano—Roma/ Fiumicino

Touring Club Italiano, Auth. 04 November 2002

TOUR 5

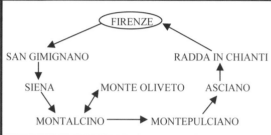

FIRENZE—MONTALCINO—FIRENZE
8 Days, 458 km/ 284 mi.

This is *the* classic bicycle tour of Tuscany. Virtually all commercial bike tour companies offer some variation of this route. It takes you through the gorgeous scenery that has made this region a popular destination since the time of Hannibal and his elephants. For the touring cyclist this route offers the perfect combination of scenery, culture, quiet and sometimes challenging riding. If you have never visited Tuscany and want to find out what all the hullabaloo is about, this is the ride for you.

Day 1: Firenze—San Gimignano, 71 km/ 44 mi., PG-13

Day 2: San Gimignano—Siena, 62 km/ 38 mi., PG

Day 3: Siena—Montalcino, 60 km/ 37 mi., PG

Day 4: Montalcino—Monte Oliveto, 50 km/ 31 mi., PG

Day 5: Montalcino—Montepulciano, 55 km/ 34 mi., PG-13

Day 6: Montepulciano—Asciano, 48 km/ 30 mi., PG

Day 7: Asciano—Radda in Chianti, 52 km/ 32 mi., PG

Day 8: Radda in Chainti—Firenze, 60 km/ 37 mi., PG

TOUR 5/ DAY 1

FIRENZE—SAN GIMIGNANO
71 km/ 44 mi. Degree of Difficulty: PG-13

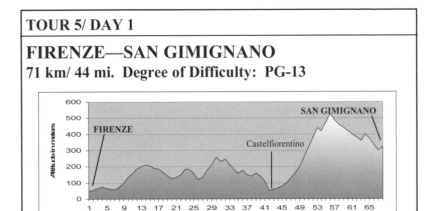

This route begins at the **Ponte Vecchio** in downtown **Firenze**. It is designed to take you out of the city with a minimum of unpleasantness and set you free into the rolling green hills of Tuscany. There is a fair amount of climbing on this route, some of it steep, but the total distance is relatively short.

From the Ponte Vecchio you cross to the south bank of the Arno River. Follow **Via De Guicciardini** past the Pitti Palace. At the far end of **Piazza de Pitti** the street becomes one-way against you and the name changes to **Via Romana.** The easiest course is to go Italian style and ride against the traffic for the four blocks to the **Porta Romana.** The safer alternative is to turn right on **Via Mazzetta** where Via Romana enters Piazza de Pitti and go about four blocks to Via Serragli where you can turn left for Porta Romana. Once at the Porta Romana you must forge your way straight across the large traffic circle to **Via Senese.** Follow the direction signs for **Siena.**

Via Senese is one of the main boulevards in and out of Firenze, and you can expect heavy traffic. It pulls up a long hill past apartment blocks and shops. Once over the top you get to speed down hill, but so do the cars. After about 7 km of fairly unpleasant riding you enter the suburb of **Galluzzo.** As you enter the main part of town keep your eye out for a right turn onto **Via Volterrana** and signs to the towns of **Chiesanuova** and **Castelfiorentino.** If you enter the main square of Galluzzo, the **Piazza Niccolo Acciaioli,** you have gone too far.

Via Volterrana veers away from the center of town and passes under the walls of the fortress-like **Certosa di Galluzzo,** a Cistercian monastery. After crossing a rickety wooden bridge over the Greve River the road begins to climb. The grade gets steep as the road winds back and forth up serpentine switchbacks up through olive groves, but the views back down over Firenze are worth every pedal stroke.

After about 2 km of steep climbing the grade moderates. You pass the delightful church of **Sant'Alessandro da Giogoli** just above the road on the right. Olive trees march down the slopes below you into the haze of Firenze. After a short flat stretch the road begins to climb again. At 14 km from Firenze you pass through nondescript Chiesanuova. The next 6 km descends down a beautiful valley of vineyards and wheat fields bordered by trees. At the bottom of the descent you spill out into the main square of the town of **Cerbaia.**

Go straight through Cerbaia following signs for **Castelfiorentino.** The tree-lined road strikes across the broad Pesa River valley and climbs up the slope on the far side. A short series of switchbacks whip back and forth up through ancient olive groves. There are wonderful views off to both sides of the road over the agricultural valleys below.

After passing through the unremarkable town of **Montagnana** the road drops steeply down to modern **Baccaiano.** The road then immediately begins to climb again up a broad sweeping curve. A the top of the hill sits **Montespertoli**, a pleasant but not particularly picturesque town. The main road skirts below the town and continues along the top of the ridge towards Castelfiorentino.

At about 40 km from Firenze the large town of Castelfiorentino will appear below you. A very steep descent takes you down from the ridge top to the main street through town. At the intersection at the foot to the descent you should turn left in the direction of **Certaldo.**

The main road through Castelfiorentino can be busy. After passing through the main square look for a right turn which crosses the Elsa River to the modern suburbs on the far bank. Once across the river bear left. A busy street will take you past shops and markets and out of the city. You will soon reach an intersection with a busy road which climbs up to the town of **Montaione** to the right. You want to go straight across this intersection and continue up the valley in the direction of **Gambassi Terme**.

You will now be on a quiet country road that angles up out of the river valley into the hills. After about 6 km you will reach the sleepy spa town of Gambassi. The road continues to climb up through shady woods above town to an intersection where you turn left in the direction of **San Gimignano.**   From here the road descends briefly before climbing at a fairly gentle rate up to the village of **Il Castagno.** As you enter town bear left and follow the signs for San Gimignano.

It is about 10 km from Il Castagno to San Gimignano. After a few short climbs you will come upon one of the most magnificent views in Tuscany. The famous towers of San Gimignano appear ahead across a rolling patch-work of vineyards. From here a lovely 3 km descent takes you down to an intersection where you turn right for the final climb up to the town gate. San Gimignano can be a busy place during the summer months. Although there are no fewer than 15 hotels in the area, you will want to book ahead.

Degree of Difficulty: This is a challenging ride with a lot of short, steep climbs.   On a hot, humid day in mid-summer, those towers of San Gimignano will be a welcome sight. Rating: PG-13.

Highlights: Once you have escaped the congestion of Firenze you will be treated to classic Tuscan landscapes: rolling hills, vineyards, and olive trees. Although the climbs will be tough, the views should keep you entertained. San Gimigano, one of the jewels of Italy, will be your reward.

km	Place Name	Cafes	Shops, Mkts	Lodging	Camping	Bank	Bike Shop	Quaintness Rating
7	Galluzzo	•	•	•		•		
14	Chiesanuova	•	•					
20	Cerbaia	•	•					*
23	Montagnana	•	•					*
26	Baccaiano	•	•	•				
30	Montespertoli	•	•	•		•		*
43	Castelfiorentino	•	•	•		•	•	*
62	Il Castagno	•	•	•				**
72	San Gimignano	•	•	•	•	•	•	*****

Tour 5/ Day 1 Firenze—San Gimignano

Touring Club Italiano, Auth. 04 November 2002

TOUR 5/ DAY 2

SAN GIMIGNANO—SIENA
62 km/ 38.5 mi. Degree of Difficulty: PG

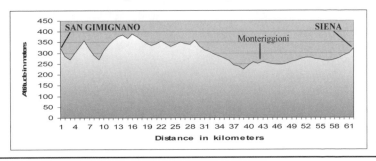

This route takes you through the beautiful, rolling Tuscan country-side you see in tourist brochures and coffee table books. It tees off at **San Gimignano** and takes you off the fairway to **Casole d'Elsa, Strove,** and **Monteriggioni**, and finally to the pin at **Siena**. There are a few short steep climbs but the cypress-lined hills and vineyards should be enough to distract you. Except for the last pull into Siena, the route should be mostly free of traffic.

From the gates of San Gimignano follow the signs for **Castel San Gimignano** and **Volterra.** This takes you down through vineyards and olive groves for about 2 km before climbing steeply up to the village of **San Donato.** Then it's down again on long curving switchbacks. You will pass a modern high-security prison which looks quite out of place in the lovely landscape. After 3 km of wonderful down-hill you will cross a bridge over a muddy creek and begin a steep 3 km climb up to **N 68**, the main road to Volterra. Turn right here in the direction of Volterra. Castel San Gimignano is just ahead. It has a quaint medieval section and wonderful views from its hilltop location. Beyond Castel San Gimignano the road begins to roll along the top of a ridge. There are several steep descents followed by short climbs. You may encounter traffic whizzing by at high speed, but there is a wide shoulder on this portion of N68.

Four kilometers from Castel San Gimignano on N 68 you will reach a left turn with a sign for **Casole d'Elsa.** Turning off the main road you begin a long twisting descent through rolling wheat fields and stands of trees. After several kilometers you will pass a turn for **Posano**; continue straight. About 8 km from the main road you will come to another inter-

section marked by a huge abandoned factory building. You turn right here
following the sign for Casole d'Elsa.

A short distance from this turn you will pass the hamlet of **Il
Murlo.** It has a restaurant and little else. It also marks the beginning of the
steep climb up to the walls of Casole, which you can see on the hilltop
ahead. Casole d'Elsa has all the charm of San Gimignano but none of the
crowds. It is definitely worth a detour to explore. And as the half-way
point of your ride it makes a good lunch stop.

Piazza il Campo, Siena

From Casole you follow the signs for **Colle di Val d'Elsa.** The
roads drops like a rock from the town gate. About 2 km down look for a
right turn with signs for **Lano** and **Mensanello.** From here the road follows the ridge line down to the valley of the River Elsa. After 10 km of
more or less uninterrupted descent you meet the main road with signs for
Colle di Val d'Elsa to the left and **Grosseto** to the right. You turn left here
and go about 100 meters and then turn right onto the road with signs for
Scorgiano. After another 100 meters look for a left turn with a sign for
Strove.

The road climbs steeply out of the valley up onto a rolling plateau
of farm land. This is the classic Tuscan scenery you see in paintings and
postcards: a quiet road meandering through wheat fields and vineyards
bordered by cypress trees, rambling stone farm houses with red tile roofs
perched on every hilltop. This is 5-star riding. You may find that it's
tough to keep a rhythm because you are constantly stopping to snap photographs.

After about 4 km you come to the walled village of Strove. It is a
tiny place and worth a quick tour inside its walls. It is one of those gems
that has managed to stay off the tour bus circuit. Just beyond Strove you
will see the crenulated towers of **Castel Pietraio**, a luxury hotel.

The cypress-lined road lays out straight ahead of you through a broad valley of wheat fields and sunflowers. After a few kilometers you pass through the quaint, crumbling stone village of **Abbadia Isola.** And eventually you will reach an intersection with the main road to Siena. You should turn right here following the signs for Siena.

About a kilometer from this turn you will see the walls and towers of Monteriggioni up on a hillside to the left. This is a magical place and worth the short ride up the hill to its gates. Leave your bike in the main square and prowl its back alleys and walls. It offers a fascinating perspective on medieval life.

Back on the road to Siena you will begin to climb gently. At the top of the grade the road continues mostly flat for a few kilometers. It passes through pleasant farm land of wheat, sunflowers, and vineyards. At about 8 km from Monteriggioni the grade will suddenly steepen and for the next 3 km or so you will be pumping hard. At the top of the long hill you will reach a traffic circle. You are now in the suburbs of Siena and the traffic will become heavy. Follow the signs for the city center and **Porta Camollia.** You will have to run a gauntlet of heavy traffic for about 3 km until you reach the old city gate at Porta Camollia; once through it you are safe. There is little or no traffic inside the city walls, although there can be heavy pedestrian traffic.

Siena is one of the primary tourist draws in Italy, and if you arrive in mid-summer, it is wise to have advance reservations. Because of the chronic housing shortage, there is a thriving business among city residents renting out spare rooms. You can check at the Tourist Information Office for a list of what's available. Siena richly deserves it popularity and is particularly well-suited to exploring on a bike.

Degree of Difficulty: There is fair amount of climbing on this route, but if you want to see the famous "hilltowns" that pretty much comes with the territory. Most of the climbs on this route are short, and the beautiful scenery will distract you from all the work. Rating: PG.

Highlights: This is a great ride. You will be on quiet roads in beautiful Tuscan landscape, and you will pass through some of the most beautiful towns in Italy: Casole d'Elsa, Strove, Abbadia Isola, Monteriggioni, and finally Siena. This is a ride to savor.

km	Place Name	Cafes	Shops, Mkts	Lodging	Camping	Bank	Bike Shop	Quaintness Rating
6	San Donato	●	●	●				*
13	Castel San Gimignano	●	●	●				**
27	Il Murlo	●						
29	Casole d'Elsa	●	●	●		●		*****
37	Mensanello	●	●					*
43	Strove	●	●	●				****
45	Abbadia Isola	●	●					***
48	Monteriggioni	●	●	●		●		*****
62	Siena	●	●	●	●	●	●	*****

Tour 5/ Day 2 San Gimignano—Siena

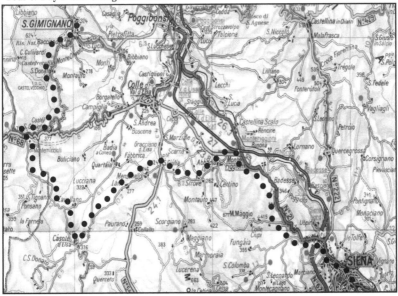

Touring Club Italiano, Auth. 04 November 2002

TOUR 5/ DAY 3

SIENA—MONTALCINO
60 km/ 37 mi. Degree of Difficulty: PG

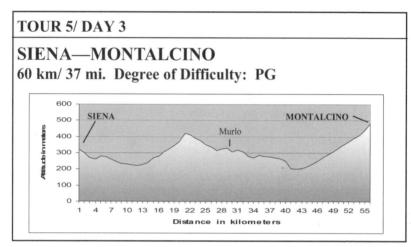

This route takes you into the rolling hills south of **Siena**. You will visit the quaint medieval towns of **Murlo** and **Buonconvento** en route to spectacular **Montalcino**, but this ride is mostly about beautiful, quiet, rolling countryside.

The ride begins at the **Porta San Marco gate** at the south end of the old section of Siena. Point your bike down hill and push off; you will careen down a series of switchbacks below the city walls. You will encounter several confusing traffic circles, but keep following the signs for **Costafabbri, Roccastrada,** and route N 73. There will also be signs for **Grosseto,** but ignore them because they will lead you to the Autostrada.

After reaching the valley floor below Siena the road climbs briefly before descending down to the suburb of Costafabbri. The road then goes up a short, steep climb, and just as you reach the top you must look for a left turn with a sign for **Casciano di Murlo.**

This turn takes you off the busy main road and leads you down a quiet lane walled on both sides. Soon you break out into the countryside and a long gentle descent takes you down through olive groves into a broad valley of wheat fields bordered by cypress trees. This is classic Tuscan scenery, and you get to soak it in undisturbed except perhaps by the occasional tractor. About 13 km from Siena the road begins to work its way up out of the valley. At the village of **Ville di Corsano** the grade increases dramatically. It is heavy going for about a kilometer. You get a brief reprieve as the road skirts around the village of **Grotti,** then you are back out of the saddle for another 2 km of steep going. On the way up there are magnificent views back towards the towers of Siena.

At the top of the climb you will reach an intersection with signs for Casciano di Murlo and Grosseto to the right and **Vescovado** and **Murlo** to the left. Going left the road continues to climb for a short distance before beginning a long twisting descent. Above you on the right as you go down you will see the ruins of an impressive fortress, the **Torre di Cervoli**. At the bottom of the decent you cross a bridge and begin a gentle climb up to the tiny stone village of **Lupompesi**. Just beyond it you will descend down into Vescovado di Murlo. The road passes above Vescovado and continues to descend for about a kilometer. Ahead you will see the ancient walled village of Murlo perched up on a small hill. There is a short, steep climb up to its gate, but it is well worth the effort to explore. There is a café for lunch and a museum of Etruscan artifacts.

From Murlo you follow signs for **Buonconvento.** The road rolls along through hills of pasture land, wheat, and sunflowers. There are occasional villas on hilltops at the end of long tree-lined driveways. With no traffic, beautiful scenery, and a gentle downhill, this is 5-star riding.

About 9 km from Murlo (40 km from Siena) you will reach an intersection with a sign for **Bibbiano** and Montalcino to the right. Bibbiano is an intriguing-looking castle just down the road, and you can see Montalcino crowning a hill in the distance. But don't be tempted by this road; after about 2 km, including a steep downhill, it turns to dirt. If you turn left at this intersection following the sign for Buonconvento a short steep descent takes you down to the valley floor. A flat tree-lined lane brings you to the interesting brick fortifications of Buonconvento. Take a spin around the narrow cobblestones streets of the old section. The walls are soot-stained and laundry hangs across the space above you. It has a wonderful time-worn feel. There are several restaurants, and if you can't find a place to stay in Montalcino, this makes a good alternative. There are three hotels in town.

From Buonconvento you follow signs for Montalcino out the south end of town. You soon merge onto **N 2** , the **Via Cassia**. Cars tend to speed along this secondary highway, and there is no shoulder, but you are not on it for long. After about 1 km there is a right turn off the main road with a sign for Montalcino. This is also where the last long climb of the day starts.

The grade starts out gently, but it gradually ramps up as you approach Montalcino. Wheat fields give way to vineyards which in turn give way to olive groves as you climb. The view is magnificent and stretches across the valley as far as **Montepulciano.** When you finally reach the gates of the town you enter a labyrinth of tiny streets that lead ever up. At the very top is the "Fortenza," the fortress, overlooking it all.

Montalcino is one of the most charming hilltowns in Tuscany. As such it is a popular destination. There are several hotels in town and a number of Agriturismos nearby. Nevertheless in the summer months you should book ahead.

Degree of Difficulty: There are two climbs that will get your undivided attention on this ride. The first begins at Ville di Corsano. It is about 3.5 km long and steep. The second is the final climb up to Montalcino. This one is about 10 km long, but not as steep. The rest of the ride is mostly rolling ups and downs. Rating: PG.

Highlights: The highlight of this ride is the classic Tuscan countryside. The rolling hills and columnar evergreens, tiny walled villages, and spectacular Montalcino high on its hill, this is why you bicycle tour in Tuscany.

km	Place Name	Cafes	Shops, Mkts	Lodging	Camping	Bank	Bike Shop	Quaintness Rating
5	Costafabbri	•	•					
13	Ville di Corsano	•	•					*
15	Grotti	•	•					*
28	Lupompesi	•						**
29	Vescovado	•	•	•		•		
31	Murlo	•	•	•				****
45	Buonconvento	•	•	•		•	•	****
60	Montalcino	•	•	•		•		*****

Tour 5/ Day 3 Siena—Montalcino

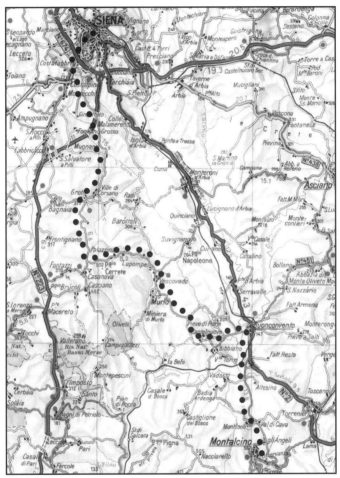

Touring Club Italiano, Auth. 04 November 2002

TOUR 5/ DAY 4

MONTALCINO—MONTE OLIVETO— MONTALCINO
50 km/ 31 mi. Degree of Difficulty: PG

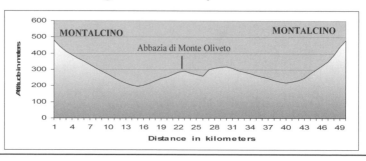

This route is a out-and-back loop from **Montalcino**. It is fairly short, and without panniers it should be pure fun. Bring extra film as this is a very picturesque route. It is also a popular route with commercial bike tour companies, and you may encounter other parties of cyclists.

From Montalcino you sail back down to **Buonconvento**. If you passed on exploring its medieval section on the route from Siena, take the time now. The main street through the old section leads to a fortified gate at the north end of town. Once through the gate bear right. At the main road, the **Via Cassia**, turn right back towards Montalcino. After about 100 meters you will see a left turn for **Asciano** and **Abbazia di Monte Oliveto Maggiore**.

Turning here you climb up a pleasant valley away from the main road. This is the classic Sienese landscape of murals and paintings. Golden wheat fields roll away to stands of cypress trees. Crumbling stone farm houses crown each hilltop. Six kilometers of gentle but sustained climbing brings you to the village of **Bollano**, a cluster of brick religious buildings. You are pedaling along the top of a ridge that falls away steeply on either side. The views are spectacular. Ahead you will see the spires of the Abbazia di Monte Oliveto Maggiore hiddened among tall cypress trees. At 8 km from Buonconvento (22 km from Montalcino) you reach the monastery gates. The abbey grounds and cloisters are well worth visiting. It is a functioning monastery of the Olivetan order of Benedictine monks and is famous for its frescoes of the life of St. Benedict.

From the gates of Monte Oliveto the road descends for about 1.5 km to an intersection where you turn right following the signs for **Arezzo** and **San Giovanni d'Asso**. From here the road climbs briefly before beginning a 2 km descent down through the famous clay hills of the Sienese "Crete." At the bottom of the descent there is another short steep climb to the top of a ridge where you will find wonderful views across rolling fields of wheat and olive trees. This is 5-star riding: no traffic, easy riding, and wonderful scenery.

About 8 km from Monte Oliveto (30 km from Montalcino) you will come to the town of San Giovanni d'Asso. It's medieval section is built on a point of rock above the main road which skirts around the town to the valley below. At the intersection below the town you should continue straight following the river valley in the direction of **Torrenieri.** The next 9 km are an easy gentle downhill past vineyards climbing the slopes of a shallow valley. Soon you roll to a stop at a 4-way intersection on the main street of Torrenieri. You should continue straight across the intersection following the signs for **Via Cassia** and **Montalcino.** This street loops around and merges onto the Via Cassia. The traffic goes by pretty fast here, but there is a wide shoulder. The shoulder gives way just as you reach the right turn for Montalcino. From this turn you begin the long climb back up to Montalcino.

It starts out gently, rolling through wheat fields and vineyards. This relatively easy grade continues for about 3 km. By 4 km, however, you are out of the saddle, and by 6 km you are checking to see if your brakes are rubbing. By 7 km you can see the walls of Montalcino and know you are almost home. An ice-cold sparkling mineral water in one of the outdoor cafés on the main square will taste especially good after this climb!

Degree of Difficulty: This is not a difficult ride. There is some climbing, but it is on mostly gentle grades. Only the last long climb back up to Montalcino bumps it up from G to PG.

Highlight: This ride is a tour of the Sienese "Crete" country. The steep eroded clay hills and rolling wheat fields bordered by cypress trees have made this region famous for centuries. Monte Oliveto is renowned for its medieval architecture and its glimpse of monastic life. But the 9 km coast down the valley from San Giovanni to Torrenieri and that ice-cold beverage on the main square in Montalcino could be the highlights of your day.

km	Place Name	Cafes	Shops, Mkts	Lodging	Camping	Bank	Bike Shop	Quaintness Rating
14	Buonconvento	●	●	●		●	●	****
22	Abbazia di Monte Oliveto	●	●	●				*****
31	San Giovanni d'Asso	●	●	●		●		***
40	Torrenieri	●	●	●				
50	Montalcino	●	●	●		●		*****

Tour 5/ Day 4 Montalcino—Monte Oliveto—Montalcino

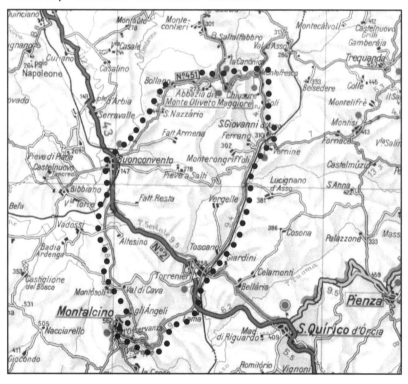

TOUR 5/ DAY 5

MONTALCINO—MONTEPULCIANO
55 km/ 34 mi. Degree of Difficulty: PG-13

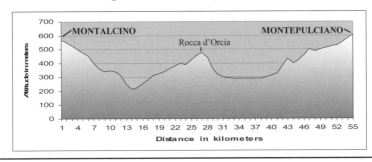

This is perhaps *the* classic ride in Tuscany. With little traffic, spectacular scenery, and challenging riding, you haven't "done" Tuscany until you've done this ride. Almost every postcard stand in Tuscany has two or three shots taken along this route.

It begins at the walls of the Fortenza at the top of Montalcino. Follow the signs for **Sant'Antimo.** The road swings down below the walls of the fortress. At the fork in the road at the edge of town bear left. The road descends gradually through olive groves and vineyards. You can see the massive bulk of the mountain of Monte Amiata directly ahead and off to the left the Rocca d'Orcia castle standing guard on its hilltop. Sooner than you think you will be standing on that same distant hilltop.

For 8 km you coast down the narrow road. Your only distractions are the spectacular views and several rough sections of pavement. The long descent finally bottoms out in a valley. Off to the right you can see the famous abbey of Sant'Antimo which dates from 781. It is neither huge nor ornate, but with its pale brick and groves of olive trees, it is a beautiful setting. Just ahead overlooking the abbey from a low hill is **Castelnuovo dell'Abate,** a pleasant town with several shops and cafes.

From Castelnuovo the road continues more or less flat for about 2 km. Then just as the view opens up the road drops down through terraced olive groves into the Orcia River valley. The steep 3.5 km descent rolls to a stop at the village of **Monte Amiata.** Here you cross a bridge over the river, and then begin to climb up the other side.

About 4.5 km above the village of Monte Amiata you will reach an intersection with signs to **Siena** and **Castiglione d'Orcia** to the left. Turning here you climb for another 3 km past the hamlet of **Poggio Rosa,** which has a café and a market. A little beyond this village you will reach another intersection where again you go left following the signs for Siena and Castiglione d'Orcia.

From this intersection the road descends for about a kilometer and then climbs again more steeply. After 9.5 km of climbing from the bridge over the Orcia River you will finally reach the top. Five star views stretch away in every direction. Montalcino is plainly visible with its vineyards spread neatly across the slopes below it.

From here the road plunges down steeply to Castglione d'Orcia. This pretty village is perched on a high ridge overlooking the Val d'Orcia. It has a quaint medieval section just above the road and a park with a fountain on the right as you enter town where you can fill water bottles. Just beyond the town sits the impressive Rocca d'Orcia fortress. It has a formidable, no-nonsense air and an incredible view over the Orcia valley which it has guarded for centuries. From here big switchbacks take you down through olive groves with great views back up at the castle. At the very bottom of the long descent you will reach the **Via Cassia, N 2**.

At this intersection you should turn left following the signs for Siena and **San Quirico.** After about 1 km you will see a right turn with signs for **Pienza, Chianciano**, and **Monticchiello.** Turning here the road strikes off flat and straight across the valley.

About 3 km from this turn you will come to a spectacular crenulated castle sitting among a stand of trees. This is **Spedaletto,** a fortified haven for travelers on the ancient pilgrim's road to Rome. Now it operates as an Agriturismo and has a fountain where thirsty cyclists can refill water bottles.

From Spedaletto the road continues straight and flat for another 3 km to a 4-way intersection with signs for to Pienza to the left. Turning here you go about 2 km until you see a right turn with a sign for Monticchiello. From this turn the road gradually begins to climb. It is a fairly gentle grade at first but gets steeper. Ahead you can see the walls and towers of Montic-chiello, a wonderfully preserved medieval town that seems to have missed out on the past 500 years. From a saddle below town there is a short, steep tree-lined lane that leads up to a massive fortified gate. Inside there are shops and cafes and tiny narrow alleys for streets. This is a good spot for a break before you power up the last 12 km to **Montepulciano.**

When you've had your fill of atmosphere and espresso at Montichiello ride back down to the saddle below town. There is a right turn here with signs for Chianciano and Montepulciano. The road descends steeply from the saddle before climbing the opposite hillside. Pause a moment here before you start down. This is one of those scenes you will see on postcards all over Tuscany. The tree-lined road climbs in serpentine switchbacks up the opposite slope. It is a beautiful sight, and on the postcards you send home you can tell all your friends you rode up that very hill.

Unfortunately that hill is pretty steep and goes for about 5 km. At the top you will break out of shady woods and descend a short distance down through hay fields. At the next intersection turn left following the signs for Montepulciano.

From here the road gradually climbs for about 2.5 km to an intersection with the main road between Chaincino and Montepulciano. You turn left here for the final pull up to Montepulciano. After about 2 km you will come to an intersection at the base of town. Montepulciano is built up on a narrow spur of rock like the prow of a sunken ship. You can reach the old section by climbing up the steep side from this intersection, or you can circle around to the north side of town where the grade is easier. To find the easier route follow the signs in the direction of **Arezzo**.

Montepulciano is one of the most famous hilltowns in Tuscany and deservedly so. Most of its medieval architecture and fortifications are intact, and it produces the renowned Vino Nobile red wine. In the summer months you will need to book ahead to get a hotel room in the old section of town. But if you arrive without reservations and can't find a room, you can roll down the hill about 10 km to **Chianciano Terme**. This is an old spa town with dozens of hotels.

Degree of Difficulty: There are some big climbs on this ride. From the bridge at the village of Monte Amiata to the summit above Castiglione d'Orcia it is 9.5 km of continuous climbing. From the valley below Monticchiello it is about 15 km to Montepulciano of which 12 km are uphill. With panniers and mid-summer heat this can be heavy going. As such it may not be suitable for out-of-shape-riders. Rating: PG-13.

Highlights: The serpentine descents down through the olive groves from Montalcino to Castiglione dell'Abate and then down to Monte Amiata are spectacular. But it is outdone by the even more spectacular descent down from Castiglione d'Orcia. These will not only be the highlights of your day, but of your entire trip. The quintessentially Tuscan scenery combined with the medieval quaintness of Sant'Antimo, Castiglione d'Orcia, Spedaletto, and Monticchiello will only add to your day. No traffic, beautiful scenery, great riding, this is why you came to Tuscany.

km	Place Name	Cafes	Shops, Mkts	Lodging	Camping	Bank	Bike Shop	Quaintness Rating
10	Castelnuovo dell'Abate	•	•	•		•		**
15	Monte Amiata	•						
21	Poggio Rosa	•	•					**
27	Castiglione d'Orcia	•	•	•		•		****
39	Monticchiello	•	•	•				*****
55	Montepulciano	•	•	•		•	•	*****

Tour 5/ Day 5 Montalcino—Montepulciano

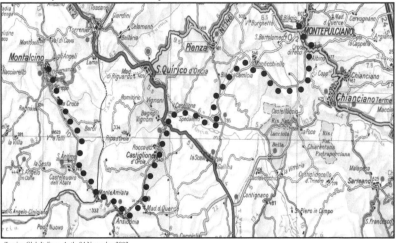

Touring Club Italiano, Auth. 04 November 2002

TOUR 5/ DAY 6

MONTEPULCIANO—ASCIANO
48 km/ 30 mi. Degree of Difficulty: PG

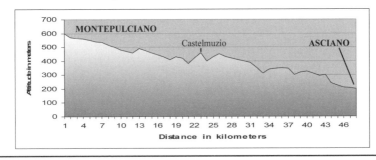

This is a beautiful route through classic Tuscan countryside that is, perhaps uniquely, more down than up. In fact there are only two serious but short climbs on the entire route. This is a day for coasting and soaking up the scenery.

From the main square of **Montepulciano** follow the signs in the direction of **Pienza**. These will take you to the same intersection below the south end of town where you came in from **Monticchiello**. From here the road sails down a long gentle descent with wonderful views over corduroy fields of grape vines. It is 13 km from Montepulciano to Pienza and almost all but the last kilometer are downhill. While the route is not traffic-free, the easy riding and spectacular views are more than enough to compensate. The pull up the last kilometer to Pienza is fairly steep. About half-way up you will pass a statuary plant on the left with some rather unusual specimens on display.

Pienza is a beautiful spot and well worth a stop. As you enter town there is a park in front of the main gate with an outdoor café. This is a great stop for a cappuccino and a "dolci." Pienza also seems to be on every commercial bike tour company's itinerary. You may encounter other groups of cyclists here—all on identical bikes. Inside the gates a long central street divides the town. There are lots of touristy shops, a pretty piazza, a museum, the duomo, etc. After a spin through town get back on the main road past the park and follow signs for **San Quirico** and **Siena.**

The main road descends gently out of Pienza. About 1.5 km from town look for a right turn with signs for **Castelmuzio.** You turn here and get off the main road. You are now on a quiet country lane. It descends for about 2 km. At the bottom where you cross a small stream look to the left and you will see an interesting, slightly down-at-the-heels fortified farm-house.

At the top of the next climb you can see Castelmuzio ahead perched high on its hill. A steep descent takes you down to the foot of the climb up to town. A very steep 2 km climb takes you up through olive groves to the walls. Castelmuzio is tiny walled village. Don't miss the chance to explore its few twisting streets. You will need the rest after that last climb anyway.

Castelmuzio

From the gate of Castelmuzio turn left following the sign for **Montisi.** A short distance from town the road suddenly nose-dives into a 15% grade. You plummet to the bottom of a narrow ravine separating Cas-telmuzio from its neighbor, Montisi. The grade up the other side isn't quite as steep, but it is a leg-breaker nevertheless. As you crawl to the top of the climb, you will see the walls of Montisi above you and signs for **Sinalunga** to the right and **San Giovanni d'Asso** to the left. Montisi is also a pretty town with more shops and cafes than Castelmuzio, and would make a good lunch stop.

From Montisi it is 7 km down hill all the way to the intersection below San Giovanni. This is beautiful country. Rolling fields fall away in every direction. There is little or no traffic. This is 5-star riding. As you near San Giovanni the descent gets gradually steeper. The last pitch is quite steep. At the intersection at the bottom of the descent you turn right following the signs for **Asciano.**

The road climbs up past the walls of San Giovanni and rolls along the top of a ridge. Once again the views are spectacular and you should see very little traffic. There is a steep descent down to an intersection with a left turn for **Monte Oliveto** and **Buonconvento**. You should continue straight for Asciano. The road climbs briefly then rolls along through pretty agricultural land. About 5 km from San Giovanni you hit a downhill which will take you the last kilometers into Asciano.

Asciano is a fairly large town, but it has only 3 hotels. If you plan to arrive during July and August you may want to book ahead. Although not built on a hill, it is an ancient site. There is an interesting museum with Etruscan artifacts found in the area. There are also many shops and restaurants to poke through as you explore town.

Degree of Difficulty: Even though you descend 400 meters over the course of the day, this route is not as easy as it looks. The climbs up to Castelmuzio and Montisi are adults-only venues. At 2 km each they are survivable, if just barely. The rest of the ride is pretty much cake. Rating: PG.

Highlights: This route offers spectacular scenery, quaint medieval hill-towns, and fantastic, mostly traffic-free riding. The descent from Montepulciano to Pienza is a classic. This is postcard country and your greatest challenge will be not stopping every few minutes to snap more pictures. Castelmuzio and Montisi are diamonds in the rough far from the fumes of tourist buses. The descent from Montisi to San Giovanni is as beautiful as any in Tuscany.

km	Place Name	Cafes	Shops, Mkts	Lodging	Camping	Bank	Bike Shop	Quaintness Rating
13	Pienza	●	●	●		●		****
20	Castelmuzio	●	●	●				*****
23	Montisi	●	●	●		●		***
30	San Giovanni d'Asso	●	●					**
48	Asciano	●	●	●		●	●	***

Tour 5/ Day 6 Montepulciano—Asciano

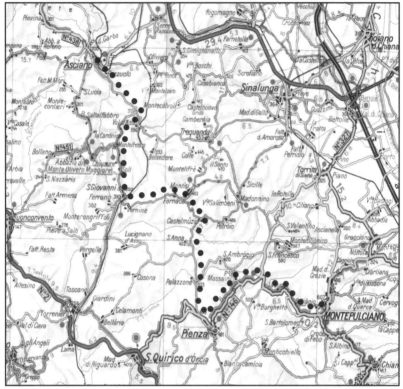

Touring Club Italiano, Auth. 04 November 2002

TOUR 5/ DAY 7

ASCIANO—RADDA IN CHIANTI
52 km/ 32.5 mi. Degree of Difficulty: PG

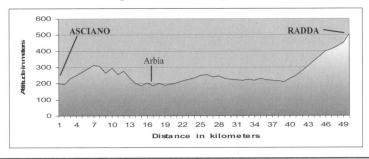

This route takes you through the dramatic clay hills south of **Siena** and into the lush forested valleys of the Chianti region. It starts hard and ends hard, but in between is some of the most sublime riding you will find anywhere.

From **Asciano** you follow the signs for Siena. The first 2 km or so are a gentle downhill, then you begin to work. A long climb of about 3 km winds up you the hills above Asciano. At the top you pass through tiny **Pievina,** which has a restaurant/ bar in case you missed breakfast. From here the road rolls along the top of a high ridge with views over rolling wheat fields that drop away on both sides. About 8 km from Asciano the ups and downs become more pronounced, but as you crest each short, steep climb you catch glimpses of the towers of Siena in the distance. Finally a long descent takes you down to a bridge over a murky stream. A short hop over another low hill and you drop down to the modern suburb of **Arbia**.

Just as you enter town look for a right turn with green Autostrada signs for **Roma** and **Arezzo** together with signs for **Sinalunga** and **Santa Maria a Dofana.** If you cross a set of railroad tracks you've gone too far. This side road leads you away from the congestion of Siena traffic and its dreary suburbs. After about 1 km you will reach a fork where you bear left. After crossing a set of railroad tracks you will meet the busy highway **N 326**. Dash straight across and you are home free; the rest of the ride is on quiet back roads.

From where you crossed the highway follow signs to the **Monteaperti** battlefield monument. This is where the Sienese whipped the Florentines in 1260.

Beyond Monteaperti you will pass a right turn for **Castelnuovo Berardenga;** continue straight. The road climbs at a gentle rate through olive groves and vineyards. About 7 km from the highway you will come to another intersection with signs for Siena to the left. Turning here you will climb for another kilometer before dropping down to an intersection with **N 408**. Siena is to the left and **Gaiole in Chianti** to the right. Turning right the road climbs briefly, then you descend into a wooded valley, and for the next 13 km you cruise down through a shady chestnut forest. It is absolutely beautiful, mostly downhill, and largely traffic-free.

After about 10 km on N 408 you will pass a right turn for **Roma** and **San Regolo;** continue straight. After another 2 km you will come to a left turn with signs for **Radda in Chianti.** From this intersection you begin to climb and long switch-backed ascent. Vineyards climb the ridges on either side. Finally you reach a saddle with signs for Radda to the left. After a brief flat there is a very steep last climb up to the town walls, but it will be worth the effort. Radda is is one of the most charming hilltowns in Tuscany. Its medieval walls and fortified gates are intact, and its narrow cobblestoned streets wind past quaint shops and cafes. The views over the walls extend over rolling vineyards and forested valleys. This is a beautiful spot.

There are 8 or 9 hotels in the vicinity of Radda as well as Agriturismos and private rooms for rent. Nevertheless in July and August you should book ahead.

Degree of Difficulty: This is a pretty easy route except for the first 10 and the last 5 km. The first 10 km out of Asciano involve several steep climbs followed by steep descents. Luckily it comes early in the day when you are fresh and the weather is cooler. The last 5 km are all up, but it is so beautiful you probably won't notice. Rating: PG.

Highlights: The road from Asciano towards Siena goes through the classic "Crete" area: rolling clay hills with deeply eroded ravines. This is the landscape that you see in the background of all those paintings in Siena and Firenze. Once you reach N 408 you enter a very different landscape. This is cool, shady woodland. A green mossy brook parallels the road. The gentle downgrade makes for effortless riding. And even though it is at the top of a stiff climb, the quaint medieval town of Radda will be ample reward for your efforts.

km	Place Name	Cafes	Shops, Mkts	Lodging	Camping	Bank	Bike Shop	Quaintness Rating
5	Pievina	●						*
18	Arbia	●	●					
23	Monteaperti	●	●					**
52	Radda in Chainti	●	●	●		●	●	*****

Tour 5/ Day 7 Asciano—Radda in Chianti

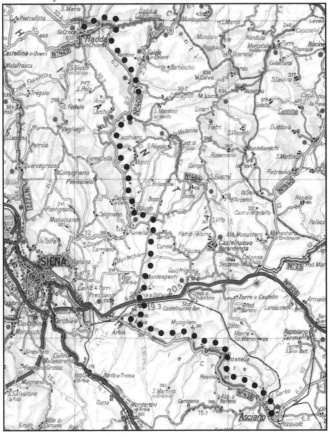

Touring Club Italiano, Auth. 04 November 2002

TOUR 5/ DAY 8

RADDA IN CHIANTI—FIRENZE
60 km/ 37 mi. Degree of Difficulty: PG

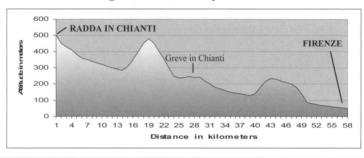

This route traces the famous Chianti road, N 222. It leads you from the blissful solitude of the Chianti vineyards back to the maddening crowds of **Firenze**. Except for two steep climbs it is an easy ride.

The route begins at the gates of Radda. It starts with a plunge down to the saddle below town. Just past the curious brick overpass turn right following the signs for **Greve in Chianti** and **Firenze**. The road circles around under the brick overpass, then drops down through rows of grape vines to the valley below. Once down in the valley the road descends very gently through shady woods and pasture land. Ten kilometers of lovely, gentle descent bring you to shady **Lucarelli,** which consists of a restaurant/ bar. You may want to stop here for a shot of espresso because from here you have a 3.5 km climb straight up to **Panzano.** About 1 km into the climb you hit an intersection where you go right—uphill. The road switchbacks back and forth and there a wonderful views over the forested valley, but it is pretty heavy going.

Finally the climb tops out at the pleasant central square of Panzano. Almost immediately it nosedives down the other side in the direction of Greve and Firenze. Your reward for all the climbing is a 4.7 km downhill sleigh ride into Greve. The views over the olive groves and vineyards below are spectacular. The road slides into Greve along a tree-lined boulevard. At the stop light as you enter town turn left to reach the pretty main square. Here the outdoor cafes offering tall glasses of sparkling mineral water and soft drinks are hard to pass up.

Back out on the road you continue to follow the signs for Firenze. After a few flat kilometers down the shady valley you come to a fork where you can turn right to go to **Strada in Chianti** or left to **Ferrone.** If you turn right here, you will have to climb an extra 100 meters or so in elevation. The easier route is to bear left and continue down the Greve River valley for about 9 km to Ferrone. When you reach Ferrone look for a right turn off the main road and a sign for Strada in Chianti. Turning here you still have to climb up to Strada but it is shorter and on a more gentle grade.

At the top of the climb up from Ferrone you will reach an intersection with N 222 just as it leaves Strada. There are lots of restaurants and shops to the right in case you skipped lunch in Greve. To continue on to Firenze you turn left.

Photo by Doug Knisley

The road rolls along the top of a ridge with wonderful views over the vineyards of the Chianti hills. After about 5 km of little ups and downs you hit a steep descent down to the town of **Grassina**, a modern suburb of Firenze. A pleasant tree-line boulevard leads out of town to a busy traffic circle. You continue to follow signs for N 222 into Firenze. After you pass under the Autostrada, you will reach a traffic circle where N 222 veers off to the right. This will take you down town, but a more direct route is to bear left across the traffic circle onto **Via Benedetto Fortini.** This busy boulevard will take you all the way down to the river at the **Ponte San Niccolo** bridge. From here the **Ponte Vecchio,** where this tour began 8 days ago is downstream to the left.

Degree of Difficulty: This ride would be cake except for the two climbs up to Panzano and Strada. These are steep and long enough to ruin even the sunniest disposition. Rating: PG.

Highlights: You will likely see other cyclists on this route. This is one of the classic rides of Tuscany. The rolling vine-covered hills of the Chianti region alternate with quiet wooded valleys to give you almost perfect riding conditions.

km	Place Name	Cafes	Shops, Mkts	Lodging	Camping	Bank	Bike Shop	Quaintness Rating
13	Lucarelli	•						*
19	Panzano in Chianti	•	•	•		•		**
25	Greve in Chianti	•	•	•		•	•	***
38	Ferrone	•	•					
42	Strada in Chianti	•	•	•		•		*
44	Poggio alla Scala	•						
48	Poggio Ugolino	•	•					*
52	Grassina	•	•	•		•		
60	Firenze	•	•	•	•	•	•	*****

Photo by Geri Walsh

Tour 5/ Day 8 Radda in Chianti—Firenze

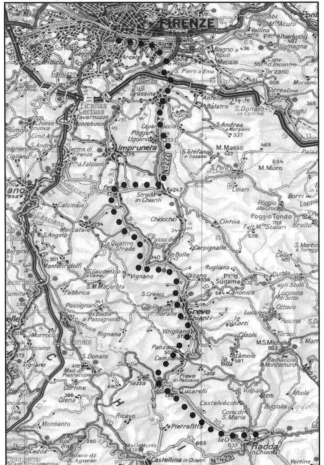

Touring Club Italiano, Auth. 04 November 2002

Assisi

TOUR 6

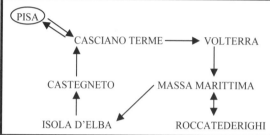

PISA—ELBA—PISA
9 Days, 490 km/ 304 mi.

This tour combines spectacular scenery, dramatic walled hill-towns with white sand beaches and the turquoise waters of the island of Elba. From the international airport in Pisa it leads you south to the ancient Etruscan stronghold of Volterra. From there you strike off into the unusual countryside of the Lardenello region to Massa Marittima. A day trip takes you to one of the most picturesque hilltowns in Tuscany, Roccatederighi. Then you catch a ferry over to the island of Elba where you can combine great riding with great beaches. The return trip to Pisa weaves through olive groves and forgotten towns along the coastal range of hills above the sea. This is a great ride.

Day 1: Pisa—Casciana Terme, 39 km/ 24 mi., PG

Day 2: Casciana Terme—Volterra, 41 km/ 25 mi., PG

Day 3: Volterra—Massa Marittima, 66 km/ 41 mi., R

Day 4: Massa—Roccatederighi, 63 km/ 39 mi., PG

Day 5: Massa—Isola d'Elba, 52 km/ 32 mi., G

Day 6: Isola d'Elba—Western Circuit, 54 km/ 33.5 mi., PG

Day 7: Isola d'Elba—Castagneto Carducci, 57 km/ 37 mi., PG

Day 8: Castagneto C.—Casciano Terme, 79 km/ 49 mi., R

Day 9: Casciana Terme—Pisa, 39 km/ 24 mi., G

TOUR 6/ DAY 1

PISA—CASCIANA TERME
39 km/ 24 mi. Degree of Difficulty: PG

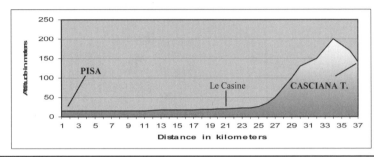

This is a relatively easy first day. It allows you to get over the jet lag and get used to riding a loaded bike. The route is designed to get you out of the city of Pisa and into the countryside as painlessly as possible. Most of the ride is flat except for the last 10 km. There is just enough climbing to give you a taste of what's to come.

The tour begins at the international airport at the edge of downtown Pisa. See the Airports chapter for a more detailed description and map of how to get out of Pisa's airport. An abbreviated version follows here.

From the terminal building at the airport follow the "bull's-eye" signs to the city center. These will lead you under a highway overpass and onto **Via dell'Aeroporto.** Follow this broad tree-lined boulevard to a square, the **Piazza G.Giustini.** Just as you enter the square look for a sharp right turn onto **Via Giuseppe Montanelli.** Follow this street for several blocks until you reach a fork. Here you should bear left onto **Cavalcavia S. Ermete Ovest.** This street leads you over a railroad overpass to an intersection with **N 206**, the **Via Emilia.** You turn right here and pedal out of town following the signs for **Cecina** and **Grosseto.**

You should follow the signs for Cecina and Grosseto for 12 km to an intersection with a left turn for **Ponsacco** and **Lari.** Turning here you at last get off the main road. A quiet country road leads you through the towns of **Valtriano, Cenaia,** and **Quattrostrade.** Just beyond Quattrostrade you will see a giant overhead sign indicating a right turn for Lari. Turning here you will enter the village of **Le Casine.** Pedal right through town following the signs for Lari.

A short distance from Le Casine you will begin to climb away from the flat farm land of the Arno River valley. As you wind your way up into the hills the fields of corn and sunflowers give way to olive trees and grape vines. Soon you will see the walls and towers of Lari ahead.

At the fortified gates of Lari you can pedal up through this interesting town past its impressive castle, or bear left and skirt around below the town. Both routes rejoin above the town. You should now follow signs for **Casciana Terme**. The grade gets steeper as you reach the top of the ridge, and there are spectacular views back down into the valley.

At the top of the climb you pass a turn for **Casciana Alta**, an interesting-looking medieval village built on the very top of the hill. The road skirts around below it and descends down to an intersection where you turn left for Casciana Terme. After another short climb you will roll over the top of a ridge and the town itself appears below you.

Casciana Terme is a modern spa town. It does not have the medieval charm of historic hilltowns, but it is a convenient distance from Pisa, and like most spa towns in Italy it has a lot of hotels to choose from. There is a pretty main square at the center of town lined with outdoor cafes. And if the first day in the saddle leaves you a little sore, you can "take the waters" in the municipal thermal spring.

Degree of Difficulty: Although this is a relatively short stage, there is 9 km of continuous climbing from Le Casine up to Casciana Alte. The grade is not steep, but it does seem to go on and on. Rating: PG.

Highlights: The castle town of Lari will give you your first taste of a genuine Italian hilltown. As you climb past its walls the view back into the Arno river valley is spectacular.

Photo by Geri Walsh

km	Place Name	Cafes	Shops, Mkts	Lodging	Camping	Bank	Bike Shop	Quaintness Rating
4	Ospedaletto	●	●	●		●		
21	Valtriano	●	●					
24	Cenaia	●	●					
27	Quattrostrade	●	●					
28	Le Casine	●	●			●		
32	Lari	●	●	●		●		***
36	Casciana Alta	●	●					*
39	Casciana Terme	●	●	●		●	●	*

Tour 6/ Day 1 Pisa—Casciana Terme

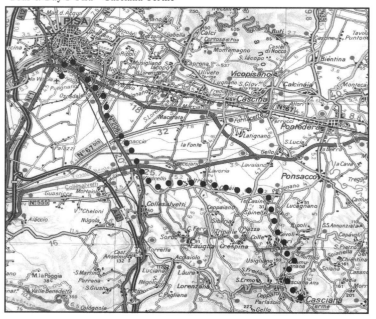

Touring Club Italiano, Auth. 04 November 2002

TOUR 6/ DAY 2

CASCIANA TERME—VOLTERRA
41 km/ 25 mi. Degree of Difficulty: PG

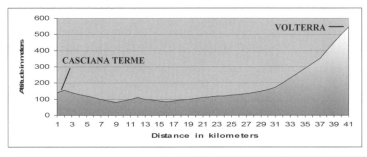

This is another relatively short day that ends with a long climb. It will be easy pedaling up the valley of the Era River. You will be able to see the ancient walls of **Volterra** crowning the hilltop ahead. Finally you will come to the foot of the climb and there is no alternative but to grind your way up. It is a tough slog but well worth it. Volterra is one of the most fascinating hilltowns in Tuscany.

Starting in **Casciana Terme** follow the signs for **Chianni**. The road climbs away from Casciana Terme up a manageable hill. You will then sail down through olive groves for the next 4 km. Another short steep climb takes you up to an intersection where you turn left following the sign for **Terricciola**. You can see medieval Chianni high up on a hill to the right, and if you have the legs it may be worth exploring. You avoid this hill but miss seeing the town by turning left.

From this turn the road descends for about 2 km to another intersection with a right turn and a sign for **La Sterza**. The next 6 km roll through pasture land and wheat fields. Eventually you will reach another intersection where you turn left. Three kilometers of flat riding bring you to the village of La Sterza, where you meet **N 439** to Volterra.

From La Sterza the road continues flat for about 5 km to an intersection with signs for Volterra and **Saline di Volterra** via N 439 to the right and Volterra via **N 439d** (direct) to the left. You can go either way, but the route to the left via N 439d is slightly shorter.

Route N 439d follows a river valley for about 6 km. You will then come to another intersection at a bridge over the river where you can continue straight for Volterra or cross the bridge and continue on N 439d. Going straight is shorter but quite steep. It also has less traffic. By crossing the bridge and following N 439d the climb is not quite as steep, but it leads you to an intersection with **N 68,** which is the busy main road into Volterra. The trade-off for this easier route is that you may be subjected to the roaring engines of cars and trucks on the last pitch up to the walls of the city. As soon as you get inside one of the city's massive gates you will leave the traffic behind.

Volterra is a great destination on a bike. You will get a wonderful sense of accomplishment after struggling up the steep slope to its gates. There are a variety of hotels to choose from and even a rare campground. Nevertheless in July and August you may need to book ahead.

Degree of Difficulty: This second day on the bike will be similar to the first. Most of the day is relatively flat riding which serves as warm-up for the big climb at the end. The climb up to Volterra is steep but well worth the effort. Rating: PG.

Highlights: The highlight of your day will unquestionably be your arrival in Volterra. As you make your way up the final grade you will be treated to 5-star views in every direction. This is the classic Tuscan landscape of postcards and paintings — rolling wheat fields, crumbling stone farmhouses, and columnar cypress trees marching single-file over hilltops. Volterra is perhaps the most dramatic of Tuscan hilltowns. It has retained its medieval walls and its huge brooding fortress, its maze of alleys and twisting cobble stone streets. It is a wonderful destination for any trip to Italy, but you will savor it all the more by getting there by bike.

km	Place Name	Cafes	Shops, Mkts	Lodging	Camping	Bank	Bike Shop	Quaintness Rating
15	La Sterza	•	•	•				
31	Molino d'Era	•	•	•				
41	Volterra	•	•	•	•	•		*****

Tour 6/ Day 2   Casciana Terme—Volterra

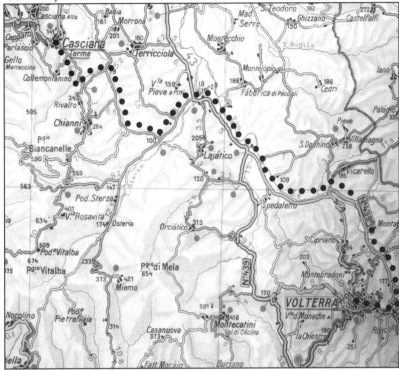

Touring Club Italiano, Auth. 04 November 2002

TOUR 6/ DAY 3

VOLTERRA—MASSA MARITTIMA
66 km/ 41 mi. Degree of Difficulty: R

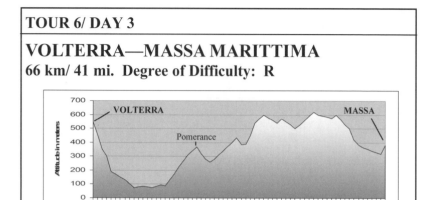

   This route is up and down all day, but fortunately it begins with a down. From **Volterra** a series of steep, winding switchbacks drop you down 475 meters (1,558 vertical feet) in just 9 km (5.6 mi.) to the railroad town of **Saline di Volterra.** The views on the way down are some of the most spectacular in Tuscany. Wheat fields roll away in every direction; stone farmhouses crown every hill. This is the way to start your day.

   At Saline di Volterra you take a left off the main road following signs for **Pomerance.** You can see this town high on a distant hill to the south. Luckily you have several kilometers of mostly flat riding to warm up for the long climb.

   Pomerance is a pleasant town. It has many cafes and shops where you can re-energize before plunging into the hilly country to the south. Leaving Pomerance you continue on the main road following signs for **Larderello.** The road descends steeply followed by a more gradual climb. This sets the pattern for the rest of the ride.

   At 34 km from Volterra you climb over a ridge and drop down to the town of **Montecerboli.** Here the scenery changes from the classic Tuscan wheat fields and olive groves to more heavily forested hills. You also enter a bazaar landscape of giant cooling towers. Larderello is a center of thermal energy production. Steel pipes run in complicated patterns all over the landscape and concrete cooling towers rise like creatures from a B-grade monster movie. It is such a contrast to the lovely landscape you just passed through that it is somehow impressive.

The main road passes above the interesting medieval section of Montecerboli. Just beyond it there is a left turn with signs for Larderello. You should continue straight following signs for **Castelnuovo di Val di Cecina** and **Massa Marittima.**

At 36 km you will pass the tragi-comical thermal spa of **Bagno la Perla.** The forlorn old hotel sits like a stranded ship below a giant thermal power plant. It is a wonder that it could have enough customers to remain open.

From Bagno la Perla a steep climb brings you up above the bustling town of Castelnuovo. The main road goes right through the middle of town. Follow signs for "Massa M." and **Grosseto.** Beyond Castelnuovo you gradually leave the thermal energy plants behind and enter a more wild, forested countryside. A long pleasant descent followed by an equally long ascent brings you to an intersection where you continue straight following signs for Massa and Grosseto. The next 12 km take you through rolling forest with some short climbs and descents. At length you will reach an intersection with **N 441**. Here you turn right following signs for Massa. A 4 km descent takes you down to one last short but steep climb up to lovely, medieval Massa Marittima.

Massa is set just above the flat coastal plain that rolls away to the Tirrenian Sea. The views from its ramparts at sunset are not to be missed. For such a large town Massa has relatively few hotels (just three). There are, however, dozens of Agriturismos in the area. The local tourist office can help you line up accommodations.

Degree of Difficulty: This is a relatively long ride with lot of hills, some of them steep. The frequent downhills give you a bit of a rest, but they also make it difficult to find a rhythm. You will appreciate the unique landscape of this ride much more if you are in shape. Rating: R.

Highlights: The smooth, winding descent from Volterra with its spectacular views rates as one of the best in Tuscany. The view back towards Volterra from Pomerance is equally impressive. The sci-fi landscape of the Larderello region is also remarkable by virtue of its strangeness. Finally sunset from the walls of Massa Marittima will be unforgettable.

km	Place Name	Cafes	Shops, Mkts	Lodging	Camping	Bank	Bike Shop	Quaintness Rating
9	Saline di Volterra	●	●	●		●		
24	Pomerance	●	●	●		●		**
34	Montecerboli	●	●			●		*
36	Bagno la Perla	●						
40	Castelnuovo	●	●	●		●	●	
66	Massa Marittima	●	●	●		●	●	*****

Tour 6/ Day 3 Volterra—Massa Marittima

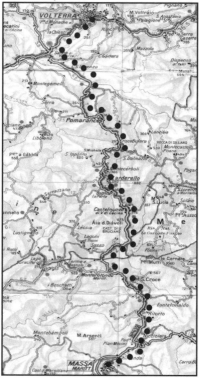

Touring Club Italiano, Auth. 04 November 2002

TOUR 6/ DAY 4

MASSA—ROCCATEDERIGHI—MASSA
63 km/ 39 mi. Degree of Difficulty: PG

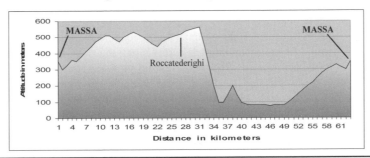

This is an out-and-back loop from **Massa Marittima**. Leave the panniers in your room and head out on those suddenly ultra-light bikes. This is a spectacular ride which will take you through several undiscovered hilltowns. The most difficult part of your day will be deciding whether to eat lunch in a cafe in one of those picturesque towns or picnic along the way in an olive grove with postcard views over the Marema plain.

The route begins with a gentle but sustained climb back in the direction of **Volterra**. Go past the turn for Volterra and continue in the direction of **Siena**. About 8 km from Massa you will cross an elevated section of road at the end of which is a left turn for the town of **Prata**. This ancient village is built up above the main road. Its stone houses are arranged in a defensive ring like a circle of wagons. Just beyond the turn for Prata you will come to a right turn with a sign for the village of **Tatti.**

The road to Tatti climbs very gently up through pastures and low forest. You are unlikely to encounter any traffic. At 17 km from Massa you will climb over the top of a rise and coast down to the village. Tatti is a stack of stone houses built up on a spur of rock with magnificent views of the Marema plain below. Terraced olive groves march down hill on three sides. It's a sleepy place with narrow cobble-stoned alleys and a ruined fortress above it. If you bear to the right coming into town you will find a few cafes, a pizzeria, and a some shops in the lower section of town.

To continue on from Tatti you should bear left above the town following signs for **Roccatederighi.** The road continues to climb gently and then rolls along the side of a ridge offering 5-star views back over Tatti and into the valley below. At length you will see Roccatederighi through the trees. It is one of the more spectacular sites for a hilltown you will find anywhere in Italy. It is built out on a long the spine of rock. A forbidding castle perches on a pinnacle at one end of the ridge. The enchanting aroma of baking bread wafts down its narrow streets. Tiny markets hidden in doorways bulge with fresh produce. Sunny cafes beckon you to their tables. There is even an excellent bike shop in case that annoying mystery noise is finally getting to you.

From Roccatederighi continue on the main road in the direction of **Sassofortino.** As the road climbs leisurely along the ridge there are spectacular views back towards Roccatederighi on its rocky spur. About 3 km from Roccatederighi and just before you reach Sassofortino watch for a right turn with a sign for **Grosetto** and a 20% grade warning sign. This is a bona-fide XXX-rated climb that thankfully you get to go down rather than up. It drops like an elevator shaft straight down. If you can drag your eyes away from the road as you plummet downwards you will get yet more 5-star views of Roccatederighi as well as the ruined fortress in the village of **Montemassi** below you.

In a startlingly short period of time you will find yourself 464 meters (1,531 ft) lower and out on the flat plain. The road ends at a "T" intersection where you turn right following signs for **Ribolla.** Just ahead you can see Montemassi and its picturesque ruined fortress sitting atop its own hill. If you have the legs for it, it is definitely worth puffing up through the olive groves to explore. Otherwise you can continue past it on the road to Ribolla.

Ribolla is an unremarkable place and shouldn't even slow you down unless you need a bite to eat in its cafe. Two kilometers beyond Ribolla you will pass a right turn for Tatti. You should continue straight for another few kilometers until the road reaches an intersection with a right turn for Massa.

From here the road climbs gradually through the hills. After a few kilometers the riding becomes easier and you are soon coasting gently downhill. You will be able to see Massa on top of a ridge to your left. You will hit the main road at **Ghirlanda** where you turn left for the final climb up to Massa.

Degree of Difficulty: This is not a particularly hard ride. There is a fair amount of climbing, but it is all on gentle grades. And without panniers to hold you back, you will be dancing up those hills. Rating: PG.

Highlights: The wonderfully picturesque towns of Tatti, Roccatederighi, and Montemassi are clearly the highlights of this ride. Coming in a close second are the spectacular views over the Marema plain to the sea. Genuine, un-touristy hilltowns, great views, and virtually no traffic make this a 5-star ride almost from start to finish. If you could do only one ride in Tuscany, this might be it.

km	Place Name	Cafes	Shops, Mkts	Lodging	Camping	Bank	Bike Shop	Quaintness Rating
11	Prata	●	●					***
22	Tatti	●	●					****
28	Roccatederighi	●	●	●		●	●	*****
38	Montemassi	●	●	●				*****
43	Ribolla	●	●			●		
62	Ghirlanda	●	●	●				
63	Massa Marittima	●	●	●		●	●	*****

Tour 6/ Day 4 Massa—Roccatederighi—Massa

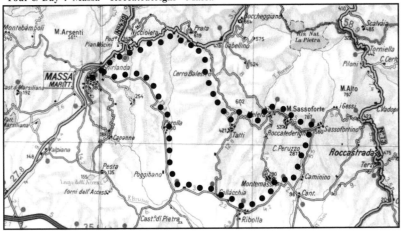

Touring Club Italiano, Auth. 04 November 2002

TOUR 6/ DAY 5

MASSA MARITTIMA—ISOLA D'ELBA
52 km/ 32 mi. Degree of Difficulty: G

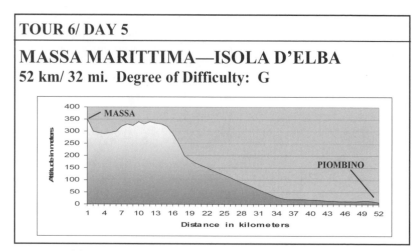

This stage takes you from **Massa Marittima** to the ferry docks at **Piombino** where you catch the boat to the island of Elba. Except for a few short, steep climbs early on, it is an easy downhill ride most of the way. The only real difficulty of this ride is negotiating the traffic into the city of Piombino.

From the main square of Massa follow signs for **Follonica.** This will lead down to a 4-way intersection with the main road below town. Go straight across the main road onto a quiet country lane. This road hooks back around below Massa passing through vineyards and wheat fields. At the next intersection marked by a wonderful fortified mill go straight. At each successive intersection where there is a choice between taking a dirt road or the paved road, stick to the pavement. After a few pleasant kilometers of flat riding you will come to a "T" intersection on the corner of which is the Agriturismo "**Colmbaia.**" It is a distinctive large stone building which you can see for some distance before reaching the intersection. Turn left here following the sign for **Montebamboli**.

The road continues flat for several kilometers, but the pavement is in bad shape, and you will have to watch for deep potholes. You will also pass several Agriturismos on this stretch. About 8 km from Massa you will hit a very steep but thankfully short climb. At the top you descend a short way to another short, steep climb. This pattern continues for two or three kilometers. At the top of each hill you are rewarded with splendid views over the rolling countryside.

At about 13 km from Massa you will reach the hamlet of Montebamboli. This entire town has been turned into an Agriturismo. There are great views from top of this hill across vineyards, olive groves, pasture land, and rolling forest. A few kilometers from Montebamboli the road plunges down a steep grade and before you know it you are spilled out onto the flat coastal plain which stretches away to the sea.

At 21 kilometers from Massa you will reach a 4-way intersection with a sign for **San Lorenzo** straight ahead. Going straight you enter a long, leafy green tunnel where the tree branches grow across the road above your head. The town of San Lorenzo is unremarkable except for a bazaar, monster-sized modern building called "Petra." A few kilometers beyond San Lorenzo you will pass **Casalappi**, another entire village turned into a Agriturismo.

Beyond Casalappi you will reach another 4-way intersection where there is a sign for **Riotorto** to the left. However, you go straight in the direction of the two huge red and white stripped smoke stacks that you can see in the distance. These stacks rise above a power plant near Piombino and make a good point of reference. A few kilometers beyond this intersection you will reach **N 439** which parallels the Autostrada. Again you go straight in the direction of the twin stacks following the sign for **Piombino**.

You are now on a narrow farm lane which parallels the Autostrada before crossing over the top of it. About 3 km from the Autostrada overpass you will come to a crossroads named **La Sdriscia**. You should turn left here and head for the twin stacks. By going left here and weaving through agricultural fields, you will spare yourself a few kilometers of heavy traffic on the main road into Piombino. At the next intersection you should go right, away from the power plant and towards gritty, industrial Piombino which you can now see clearly.

You will finally meet **N 398,** the main truck route into Piombino, at the town of **Fiorentina.** Here you enter the fray and for the next 5 km you have to share the road with trucks, buses, and cars. Piombino could be the ugliest city in Italy, certainly in Tuscany, and the fume-belching traffic does little to improve the effect. This will be awful riding, but it is only for a relatively short distance. Just follow the signs for **Isola d'Elba.** If you need a break from the excitement or are hankering for a taste of home, you can pull in under the golden arches of a MacDonalds. It's right there on the side of the road just like one you might find in downtown Newark, New Jersey.

A short distance beyond the MacDonalds the road goes down a gentle hill and you have to negotiate your way across two lanes of traffic and get into a left turn lane. From here the Isola d'Elba signs lead you into the bowels of industrial Piombino. Once you cross a set of railroad tracks you will find yourself on a pleasant pine tree-lined boulevard that winds around to the ferry docks for Elba.

There are four different ferry lines servicing the island of Elba from Piombino. Car ferries depart for **Portoferraio** every 15 minutes during the summer months. There is no need to stand in a long line to catch the very next ferry as one of the other companies will be sending another one over within 15 minutes. The round trip fare is about $15.00 per person and there is an extra charge for the bike. You purchase tickets at a building on the right before you reach the docks. The ferry docks are downhill past the ticket agency building; just follow the signs for "**Porto.**"

Once on the waterfront you can ride your bike past the lines of cars, wave your ticket at the guys standing on the boarding ramp, and they will usher you aboard. Just make sure the ferry is going to Elba and not Corsica or some where else. One important tip: do NOT ride your bike onto the car ferry. The deck is slick with oil and very slippery.

The trip over to Elba takes about an hour. The ferry ties up below the Medici fortress in Portoferraio. The steamy port exudes all the exotic charm of the Mediterranean. The smell of salt water and drying fish mix with that of outdoor vegetable markets and sun tan oil. Add ever-present exhaust fumes and you have a very heady mix. This is the very essence of a Mediterranean holiday.

A word about accommodations: In July and August reservations are a must. You can throw yourself on the mercy of the Tourist Office, but there's no telling where they will find a room or for how much. Even the campgrounds get booked up months in advance. The other problem is that hotels and campgrounds are reluctant to accept reservations for less than a week. So unless you want to spend a week on Elba, finding a room may take some hunting. The place to start is on the internet at http:// new.elbalink.it. It offers a wealth of information about the island as well as a list of all or most of the accommodations available.

Don't be put off by smelly Piombino and all that traffic. The awful, ugly part of Piombino will take no more than a half hour of your day. The island of Elba is very much worth the effort.

Degree of Difficulty: There are several short, steep climbs at the beginning of this ride. Otherwise from Montebamboli to Piombino it is flat or downhill all the way. Except for negotiating the traffic into Piombino this is an easy, pleasant ride. The riding on Elba, however, can be challenging. Don't forget that you will have to pedal to wherever you intend to stay after getting off the ferry in Portoferraio. Rating (Massa to Piombino): G.

Highlights: The long downhill from Montebamboli almost as far as Piombino is easy and effortless, but the real highlight of your day will be stepping off the ferry onto the exotic island of Elba. Crystal clear water, white sand beaches, and magnificent riding await you.

km	Place Name	Cafes	Shops, Mkts	Lodging	Camping	Bank	Bike Shop	Quaintness Rating
23	San Lorenzo	●	●					
46	Fiorentina	●	●					
52	Piombino	●	●	●	●	●		
†	Isola d'Elba	●	●	●	●	●	●	*****

† via car ferry

Tour 6/ Day 5 Massa Marittima—Piombino

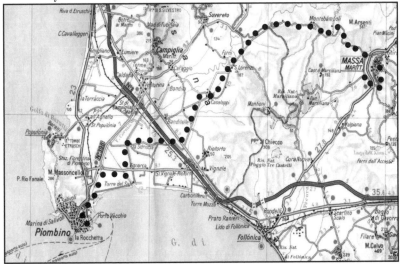

Touring Club Italiano, Auth. 04 November 2002

TOUR 6/ DAY 6

ISOLA D'ELBA—WESTERN CIRCUIT
54 km/ 33.5 mi. Degree of Difficulty: PG

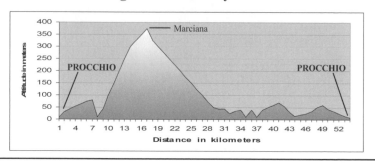

This stage arbitrarily starts in the seaside town of **Procchio**. It is a loop around the western end of the island, and you could pick it up anywhere along the route depending on where you are staying. You would of course leave the panniers in your room which will make the day all the more enjoyable. The route is described in a counter-clockwise direction. This gets the big climb out of the way early. The prevailing wind is also out of the northwest which gives you a tail-wind for much of the ride. The drawback is that on hot days you may want this breeze to cool you down. It is a beautiful ride in either direction, and you can choose which way you want to do it based on the weather and where you are staying.

Starting from Procchio you head west following the road along the beach and the signs for **Marciana Marina**. At the end of the beach the road climbs the headland forming the bay. The views are partially obscured by pine trees, but you may welcome the shade. Occasionally you will catch a glimpse over the cliff-side of a narrow path leading down to a stretch of white sand among the rocks. The road meanders along above the rocky shore for about 7 km whereupon you round a headland and Marciana Marina appears below you. The road drops steeply down to this festive sea-side resort. Turning right off the main road takes you down to the waterfront. During the high season its stony beach is crowded with sunbathers.

Back on the main road you continue in the same direction following signs for **Poggio** and **Marciana**. The road veers away from the coast and begins to climb up towards the high rocky peaks which surround

Marciana Marina. As soon as you leave the holiday villas and condos behind you begin climbing steeply. After about 3 km of sustained climbing the grade moderates and you begin to get wonderful views down over Marciana Marina and the rocky coastline. At 14 km from Procchio you hit a series of tight switchbacks which bring you up to the pretty hillside town of Poggio. Here you will find a breathtaking view across the rocky coast of Elba to the mountains of Tuscany on the mainland. It is worth all the sweat and grinding to get up here just for the view.

Looking northeast from Poggio, Isola d'Elba

Three kilometers of more gentle climbing from Poggio bring you to the town of Marciana. It too has magnificent views down to the sea. And better yet this is the top of the long climb. From here you coast down to the sea on a gentle grade past the tiny holiday resorts of **Sant'Andrea** and **Patresi.** The road is quite rough in places, and you will have to hang on to your handlebars. Practically every shallow cove has a small hotel or two but this does not detract from the grandeur of the rocky coast. On clear days you can see as far as the high mountains of Corsica and closer-by the smaller islands of Pianosa and Montecristo.

At the far western tip of the island you descend down to the village of **Chiessi**, a gem set among the rocks and azure water. Climbing up the headland the other side you turn the corner and begin to cruise along the southern shore of the island. You soon pass elegant **Fetovaia** with its beautiful cove, tennis courts, and row upon row of beach umbrellas. Between Fetovaia and the next town, **Seccheto,** there are rocks you can climb down to if you are looking for a more secluded bathing experience. Seccheto has a few shops and restaurants and of course a beach. **Cavoli** is the next down the coast. It has a stunning beach but is down a steep hill off the main road. From Cavoli the road climbs higher up on the cliff-side and soon turns inland towards **Marina di Campo.**

A quick descent brings you into this busy resort town. Turning right off the main road takes you into the old section of town. There are narrow streets, sidewalk cafes, and all kinds of touristy shops. This is definitely where the action is on this side of the island. To return to Procchio you follow the main road out of Marina di Campo following the signs for **Portoferraio.** The road very gradually climbs up a low hill and drops back down to the intersection where this ride began at the center of Procchio.

Degree of Difficulty: The climb from Marciana Marina up to Poggio is steep and long. On the positive side this is the only really difficult climb of the day. Once you reach the top at the town of Marciana it is easy cruising for the rest of the day. This would be a G-rated ride without the big climb; that obstacle bumps it up one notch. Rating: PG.

Highlights: The views from Poggio and Marciana are nothing short of spectacular. The downhill rush from Marciana to Colle d'Orano where you finally have to pedal again is pure joy. Rounding the southwest corner of the island you are high up on the cliff-side watching the pounding deep blue waves below. Once on the south shore you pass by the beautiful turquoise coves at Fetovaia and Cavoli. This is the best ride on the island.

km	Place Name	Cafes	Shops, Mkts	Lodging	Camping	Bank	Bike Shop	Quaintness Rating
8	Marciana Marina	●	●	●	●	●		**
14	Poggio	●	●	●				**
17	Marciana	●	●	●		●		**
29	Chiessi	●	●	●		●		***
35	Fetovaia	●	●	●	●			*****
37	Seccheto	●	●	●				****
39	Cavoli	●	●	●				*****
44	Marina di Campo	●	●	●	●	●	●	*
54	Procchio	●	●	●				**

Tour 6/ Day 6 Isola d'Elba—Western Circuit

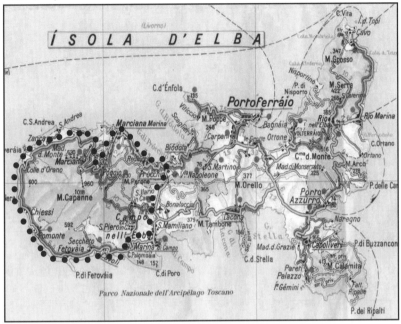

Touring Club Italiano, Auth. 04 November 2002

TOUR 6/ DAY 7

ISOLA D'ELBA—CASTAGNETO CARDUCCI
57 km/ 37 mi. Degree of Difficulty: PG

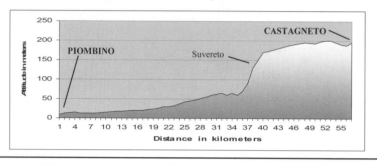

When you've had your fill of sun and sand or more likely when the date on your return ticket begins to loom, this route gets you back on the road to **Pisa**. Catch a morning ferry back to the mainland, and prepare yourself for running the gauntlet of traffic out of **Piombino**. You will be retracing your steps from the ferry docks; simply follow the signs for **Roma** through scenic downtown Piombino. At about 5 km from the ferry dock you will reach **Fiorentina.** Here you should bear right at the busy intersection following the sign for Roma. At the next intersection bear right again following the sign for **Follonica**. This at last gets you off the busy main road onto the quiet lane that takes you east past the Autostrada. Follow this road towards the twin stacks of the power plant. You will come to a detour which forces you to turn left. At the cross-roads of La Sdrisca you turn right and pedal due east towards the hills.

After crossing over the Autostrada you continue east back towards **Casalappi** and **San Lorenzo** (See Tour 6/ Day 5). About 1.5 km beyond San Lorenzo and 32 km from Piombino you will come to a 4-way intersection with a sign for **Venturina** to the left. Turning here you will pedal across a pleasant agricultural valley. After about 1 km you will reach **N 398**, a larger main road with signs for Venturina and **Suvereto** to the left. From this intersection you can see the medieval town of Suvereto perched on its hill ahead of you. About 3 km of flat riding brings you to the base of the steep climb up to the town.

Suvereto is a great stop. You should definitely pull off the road and explore the narrow twisting streets inside its ancient gate. There is a ruined fort at the very top of the village with great views across the coastal plain to the sea. Suvereto is also a good place to refill water bottles and get a snack before the next climb.

From Suvereto you continue uphill following the sign for **Castagneto Carducci.** Although it is quite steep, the climb only goes for a kilometer or so. Soon you top out on the ridge and are treated to a vast panorama across the plain to the sea. On clear days you can see all the way to Elba. The road rolls along the top of the ridge then slips down the eastern side. Here it is blissfully shady as the road meanders through low forest. The road generally trends uphill but there are no climbs that will have you out of the saddle for long. It is shady and quiet and a wonderful contrast to your escape from Piombino.

Suvereto

At about 51 km from Piombino you will pass the village of **Sassetta.** This is a quaint village with a wonderfully forgotten air to it. It has a few shops and markets and even a hotel. It also has a roadside fountain where you can fill water bottles. Another six shady kilometers take you back over to the western slope of the coastal range.

Castagneto Carducci sits high on its hill behind medieval walls and surveys all below it. Olive groves march down the terraced slopes towards the flat plain below. There are only one or two hotels in Castagneto itself, but there are several in the immediate area. Check with the local Tourist Office for accommodations. Luckily everything from here is down hill.

Degree of Difficulty: Once again the hardest part of your ride will probably be fighting your way out of Piombino. The climb up above Suvereto is steep but relatively short. From there the remaining 20 km will be shady and cool and almost flat. Looking at the map you may notice that you could avoid the Suvereto climb by taking the coastal road through San Vincenzo, but be forewarned: the coastal road can be choked with heavy traffic. Rating: PG.

Highlights: The villages of Suvereto, Sassetta, and Castagneto Carducci are far off the beaten track and every bit as quaint as the more popular hilltowns of Tuscany. The quiet, shady riding may be just what you need after the sometimes maddening crowds of Elba.

km	Place Name	Cafes	Shops, Mkts	Lodging	Camping	Bank	Bike Shop	Quaintness Rating
1	Piombino	●	●	●	●	●		
6	Fiorentina	●	●					
29	San Lorenzo	●	●					
37	Suvereto	●	●	●		●		*****
50	Sassetta	●	●	●		●		****
57	Castagneto C.	●	●	●	●	●	●	*****

Tour 6/ Day 7 Isola d'Elba—Castagneto Carducci

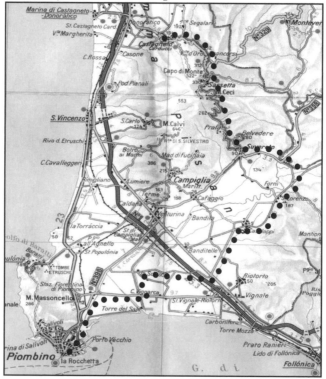

Touring Club Italiano, Auth. 04 November 2002

TOUR 6/ DAY 8

CASTAGNETO C.—CASCIANA TERME
79 km/ 49 mi. Degree of Difficulty: R

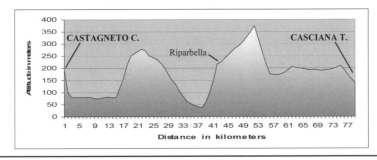

This challenging up-and-down route travels along the range of coastal hills. You could avoid these hills by riding along the highway down on the coastal plain, but you would have to endure sometimes heavy, high speed traffic most of the day. Riding along the hills, while more arduous, is much more scenic and keeps you away from the traffic.

The route begins at the 4-way intersection below **Castagneto Carducci.** As you come down the hill from town turn right (north) following the signs for **Bolgheri** and **Bibbona.**   The road passes through flat open farm land for about 5 km before entering a tree-lined section that affords some welcome shade. After about 9 km you hit an intersection with signs for Bolgheri to the right. Turning here you go about 500 meters to a left turn with a sign for Bibbona. For the next 5 km the road rolls along past vineyards and olive groves. After a short descent it begins to climb up to the town of Bibbona.

The road cuts quickly through Bibbona. At each intersection through town follow signs for **Cecina** and **Casale Marittima.** This will lead you down a short hill to an intersection with the main road. You turn right here in the direction of Casale. From this turn you pedal up a long fairly gentle hill through rolling wheat fields and vineyards. At length you will be able to see medieval Casale ahead on its hill. Follow the bulls-eye sign for the town center. The road will wind through the narrow twisting streets of the old section of town. This is an interesting place to pause and take in the ambiance. You can fill your water bottles at the fountain in the shady town square at the top of the climb.

From Casale you continue uphill following signs for **Guardistallo.** About 3 km of sometimes steep climbing will bring you up almost to the top of the coastal mountain range and the town of Guardistallo. On clear days you can see over the plain below to the congested resort-town of Cecina. The road skirts around below Guardistallo and descends gently towards **Montescudaio.** About 5 km of easy descent brings you past Montescudaio and down into a valley where you meet **N 68**, the busy main road between Cecina and **Volterra.** As you reach the bottom of the descent you will come to a traffic circle where you bear right following the sign for Volterra. After about 100 meters you will join N 68 itself. You pedal in the direction of Volterra for about 500 meters until you see a left turn for the town of **Riparbella.**

Casale Marittima

From N 68 the road towards Riparbella gives you about 1.5 km to warm up, then the real climbing starts. For the next 12 km you will be slugging away uphill. The steepest section is up to Riparbella, then the grade moderates to the point that you can begin to enjoy the view again. The road contours along the steep ridge and offers 5-star views down towards the sea.

At 52 km from Castagneto you will reach the town of **Castellina Marittima.** This marks the end of the serious climbing. A quick descent takes you past the villages of **Pomaia** and **Pastina,** then a short climb winds up to **Santa Luce**. The next 10 km roll easily along the slopes of the ridge.

At 71 km from Castagneto you will come to an intersection with signs for **Pisa** to the left and **Casciana Terme** to the right. From here about 4 km of easy climbing takes you up to the ridge above Casciana Terme. A short descent takes you down to town. If you skipped it on your first visit, you might try the municipal pool/ mineral bath at the center of town to soak away the effects of your long day in the saddle.

Degree of Difficulty: This is a relatively long stage with some stiff climbing, particularly up to Riparbella. The absence of traffic and the wonderful views will help to distract you, but you will still be spinning low gears for long stretches. Rating: R.

Highlights: Of the several towns you pedal through Casale Marittima is perhaps the prettiest. Guardistallo, Montescudaio and Reparbella don't have quite the medieval feel, but each offers spectacular views down towards the sea. This is a scenic, quiet ride with just enough climbing to be challenging but not humbling.

km	Place Name	Cafes	Shops, Mkts	Lodging	Camping	Bank	Bike Shop	Quaintness Rating
13	Bibbona	●	●	●		●		
18	Casale Marittima	●	●	●		●		****
22	Guardistello	●	●	●		●		***
25	Montescudaio	●	●	●	●	●		***
42	Riparbella	●	●					***
52	Castellina Marittima	●	●					**
64	Santa Luce	●	●	●		●		****
79	Casciana Terme	●	●	●		●	●	*

Tour 6/ Day 8 Castagneto Carducci—Casciana Terme

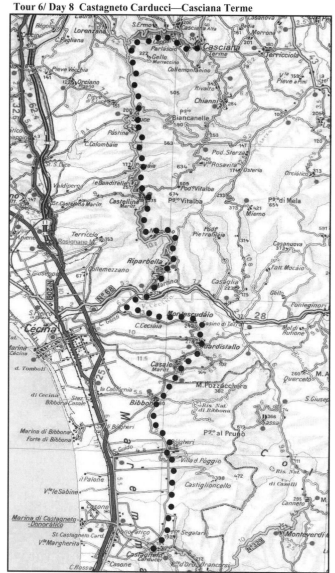

Touring Club Italiano, Auth. 04 November 2002

TOUR 6/ DAY 9

CASCIANA TERME—PISA
39 km/ 24 mi. Degree of Difficulty: G

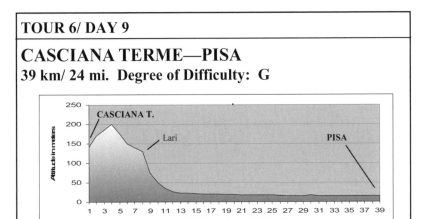

This is a short, easy ride that retraces the opening day route back into Pisa. From **Casciana Terme** you need to climb back up the hill above town in the direction of **Casciana Alte**. Once you crest the ridge you drop down a short distance to the right turn with the signs for Casciana Alte and **Lari**. A short climb brings you past the turn for Casciana Alte. If you did not stop to explore this town on your first day, it may be worth doing it this time. This is the highest point of your ride; everything from here to Pisa is downhill.

From the turn for Caciana Alte the road rolls along the top of the ridge overlooking the Arno River valley. After a short distance you will come to a right turn for Lari. The map indicates that you can continue straight on this road to **Crispina**, **Faulia**, and **Collesalvetti** en route to Pisa. Unfortunately the section beyond **Usigliano** is a rough dirt road. It is ride-able if you don't mind the bumps, but it involves a few short, steep climbs. Retracing your route past Lari has the benefit of being all downhill and familiar. That is the route described here.

From the intersection below Casciana Alte you sail downhill past Lari. At each intersection follow signs for **Le Casine**, **Perignano** and **Ponsacco**. Once you reach Le Casine, you turn left on the main road following the signs for **Pisa.** This quiet, flat road takes you along the base of the hills through the towns of **Cenaia** and **Valtriano**. After about 12 km you will reach the intersection with **N 206,** the main road back to Pisa.

At N 206 you turn right following the sign for Pisa. Twelve kilometers of board-flat road lead you through the suburb of **Ospedaletto** and into the city. If you are making for the airport, you will want to turn left onto **Cavalcavia San Ermete Ovest.** The turn is several blocks past the Autostrada overpass as you enter the city limits. This will bring you to **Piazza G. Giusti,** where you turn left on **Via dell'Aeroporto** to reach the terminal building.

If you wish to continue into downtown Pisa, you simply follow the bulls–eye city center signs on N 206, the **Via Emilia.** Remember that you will be pedaling into a city. The traffic will get worse the closer you get to downtown. Just after you cross over a wide set of railroad tracks the Via  Emilia jogs right and becomes one-way. Eventually it will lead you to a busy traffic circle at **Piazza Guerazzi.** If you dash straight across the square past the imposing **Bastione Sangallo** fortress, you will reach **Via San Martino,** a narrow one-way street that curves around following the river to the **Corso Italia.** This is a pedestrian street that cuts though the city between **Piazza Vittorio Emanuele II,** the central downtown square, and **Ponte di Mezzo,** the bridge which leads to the **Piazza dei Miracoli** and the Leaning Tower. The Corso Italia is the best way to navigate downtown Pisa on your bike.

Degree of Difficulty: Except for the short climb out of Casciana Terme to Casciana Alta this ride is either down hill or flat. The only difficulty you will encounter is dodging traffic as you enter Pisa. Rating: G.

Highlights: If you skipped Casciana Alte and Lari on the way out, it's worth exploring these ancient towns on the way back. Likewise if you skipped Pisa on your arrival, it is worth taking the time to see it now. Most people who visit Pisa seem to rush straight to the Leaning Tower and ignore the rest of the city. During medieval times Pisa was one of Italy's principal city-states. It's architecture and culture rivaled Firenze and Siena. It is definitely worth taking the time to explore.

km	Place Name	Cafes	Shops, Mkts	Lodging	Camping	Bank	Bike Shop	Quaintness Rating
3	Casciana Alte	●	●					***
7	Lari	●	●	●		●		***
11	La Casine	●	●			●		
12	Quattrostrade	●	●					
15	Cenaia	●	●					
18	Valtriano	●	●					
35	Ospedaletto	●	●	●		●		
39	Pisa	●	●	●	11 km	●	●	*****

Tour 6/ Day 9 Casciana Terme—Pisa

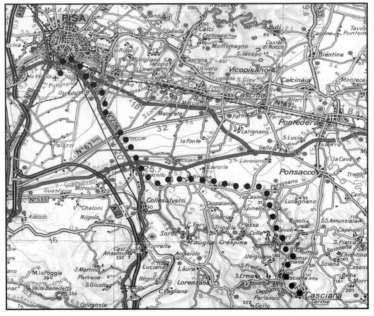

Touring Club Italiano, Auth. 04 November 2002

TOUR 7

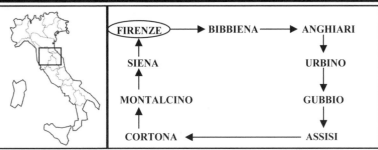

FIRENZE—URBINO—FIRENZE
9 Days, 700 km/ 434mi.

This is a challenging tour. With the exception of one long stage from Assisi to Cortona, every daily route features at least one epic climb. This tour is about both culture and riding. It takes you to some of Italy's most famous medieval cities such as Urbino, Assisi, and Siena, as well as to some lesser lights such as Bibbiena and Anghiari. It also includes some of the most spectacular riding you will find anywhere in the world. If you want it all, the most famous cultural attractions as well as truly epic riding, this is the tour for you.

Day 1: Firenze—Bibbiena, 69 km/ 43 mi., R

Day 2: Bibbiena—Anghiari, 68 km/ 42 mi., R

Day 3: Anghiari—Urbino, 83 km/ 51 mi., R

Day 4: Urbino—Gubbio, 86 km/ 53 mi., PG-13

Day 5: Gubbio—Assisi, 63 km/ 39 mi., PG-13

Day 6: Assisi—Cortona, 98 km/ 61 mi., PG

Day 7: Cortona—Montalcino, 76 km/ 47 mi., PG-13

Day 8: Montalcino—Siena, 60 km/ 37 mi., PG

Day 9: Siena—Firenze, 97 km/ 60 mi., R

TOUR 7/ DAY 1

FIRENZE—BIBBIENA
69 km/ 43 mi. Degree of Difficulty: R

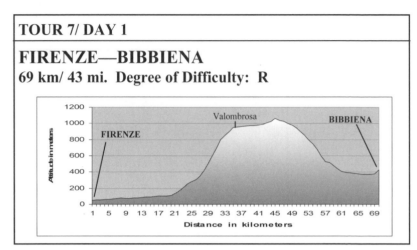

After a day or two padding the steaming pavement of **Firenze**, standing in line for everything from ice cream to unencumbered views, and breathing in exhaust fumes at every curb, you will be more than ready for this ride. It takes you far from the maddening crowds into the cool, quiet forest of the **Vallombrosa Nature Reserve**. Here a pine needle carpet caresses the edge of the road. The silent forest recedes into dark shadows. The only sound is a brook tumbling among rocks — and your own heavy breathing. You will have to work hard to reach this Nirvana, but it will be well worth the effort. And the second half of your day is all downhill.

Starting from the **Ponte Vecchio** bridge in downtown Firenze follow the south side of the river up stream along **Lungarno Torrigiani.** This is a one-way street against you, but there is a wide sidewalk along the river. Continue past the **Ponte alla Grazie** bridge to **Piazza F. Ferrucci** at the **Ponte San Niccolo.** Dash across this confusing intersection and get on **Via Orsini.** This is a big one-way boulevard going your way. Follow it to **Piazza Ravenna**. Here you bear right onto **Via Bracciolini,** which after the next intersection turns into **Viale Donato Giannotti.** This wide boulevard soon morphs again into **Viale Europa,** and you follow this tree-lined boulevard out of town watching for signs to **Bagno a Ripoli** and **Pontessieve.** Eventually the traffic and apartment blocks give way to rolling farm land and you are at last free of the city.

The road winds along the south bank of the river. There are olive groves and vineyards climbing the hills on the left, and the muddy river slumbering by on the right. About 10 km from Firenze you pass through the village of **Vallina**, which boasts a stop light and a few shops. Thus far the road has been flat, but beyond Vallina it begins to roll with small climbs and descents.

About 18 km from Firenze as the road comes down a gentle descent there is a left turn which crosses the river over to the town of Pontessieve. Go past this this turn and continue for another kilometer to the village of **Rosano**. Here there is another left turn and a bridge over to Pontessieve.

After crossing the river the road goes under the highway which follows the north bank of the river from Firenze. Follow the bulls-eye signs into the town center. The road weaves around through modern apartment blocks, back under the highway, over railroad tracks, and then climbs up to an intersection where you turn right at the sign for "Centro Storico" (the historical center). Just past this turn you will cross a bridge back over the river. Here you should get on the highway and head south in the direction of **Arezzo.**

The purpose of this exercise is to keep off the highway for as long as possible. You can avoid the confusing tour of gritty Pontessieve by getting on the highway earlier, but this gives you a kilometer or two of high-speed traffic. If you can find your way through town you are only on the highway for about 200 meters. You then get off at the exit with signs for route **N 70** to **Passo di Consuma** and **Poppi**.

From the bottom of the exit ramp the road immediately begins to climb. A series of steep switchbacks winds up the hillside, but you will soon come to a right turn for the town of **Pelago**. Turning here the road descends down to this pretty medieval town perched on a low hill. This is a good place to take a break and recharge. From here the long climb up to **Vallombrosa** begins.

From Pelago the road descends into the valley below town and then begins to climb. It starts out mildly, but within a kilometer you will be out of the saddle and puffing. The next 9 km go relentlessly up. You will pass through a series of cute villages clinging to the hillside. **Paterno** is first, then **Tosi**, and above them all is **Pian di Melosa**. The views over the vineyards below get progressively more spectacular as you climb. Above Pian di Melosa pasture land gradually gives way to woods and then deep, dark forest. Here it is quiet and cool. A babbling brook keeps you company before the road switchbacks deeper into the forest. These are the woods that spawned fairytales of wolves and witches. The congestion of Firenze will seem very far away.

Four kilometers above Pian di Melosa you will reach the imposing edifice of the **Abbazia di Vallombrosa**. Its high walls and tower protect its monastic solitude in a park-like setting. There are also a few shops where you might find refreshment.

As you approach the gates of Vallombrosa there is a left turn with a sign for **Consuma**. After visiting the monastery follow this road deeper into the forest. It meanders for eight peaceful kilometers through the dark woods gently climbing most of the way.

About 43 kilometers from Firenze you return to N 70, the main road to Poppi and **Bibbiena**. As you emerge from the forest you should turn right on the main road and continue uphill for another 2 km. Here you will enter the village of Consuma, a pretty one street town with several shops and restaurants as well as a few hotels. One kilometer above the town you will finally reach Passo di Consuma at 1060 meters (3,476 ft.) above sea level. Firenze is at 50 meters (164 ft.). Your reward for all that climbing is the next 23 km, which is all downhill.

You sail off the summit and plummet down and down. There are one or two short climbs on the way down just to keep the blood pumping but the operative word is down. All the way down there are marvelous views over forest and pastures filled with wildflowers. About 6 km down you blow through the hamlet of **Scardacchia.** At about 15 km you pass through **Borgo alla Collina.** Finally the grade begins to moderate as the road rolls you out into a broad valley. The castle of Poppi is visible directly ahead perched on a high hill. The road skirts around the modern village nestled at its feet. If you have reached your limit, Poppi makes a good alternative overnight stop. Its old section on top of the hill exudes medieval charm. There are several hotels and commercial campgrounds in the area.

Another 5 km across the flat valley floor brings you to the foot of the short climb up to **Bibbiena**. A steep series of switchbacks leads you up through the modern outskirts to a square just below the city walls. There is a park and several cafes here. Just across from the park there is a bike shop. Cobblestone streets snake through gates up into the old part of town. There are four hotels in Bibbiena, but in July and August it is wise book ahead.

Degree of Difficulty: Between Firenze and Passo di Consuma you gain 1010 meters (3,313 ft.) in elevation. This is over 45 km, although most of the gain is in the 15 km between Pontessieve and Vallombrosa. With loaded panniers, this will be heavy going particularly in the summer heat.

On the plus side there is very little traffic above Pelago and the Vallombrosa forest is shady and cool. You may notice on the map that the main road, N 70, goes directly from Pontessieve over Passo di Consuma, but be advised: it is just as steep, has no shade, and has plenty of traffic. Rating: R.

Highlights: The highlight of this route is the quiet ride through the Vallombrosa forest. The following 23 km descent down through meadows of wildflowers isn't bad either. The medieval towns along the way, Pelago, Poppi, and Bibbiena are a bonus.

km	Place Name	Cafes	Shops, Mkts	Lodging	Camping	Bank	Bike Shop	Quaintness Rating
10	Vallina	●	●					
18	Rosano	●	●	●		●		
20	Pontessieve	●	●			●		
26	Pelago	●	●	●		●		***
28	Paterno	●	●					**
30	Tosi	●	●					**
31	Pian di Melosa	●	●					**
35	Vallombrosa	●	●	●				***
44	Consuma	●	●	●				*
45	Passo di Consuma	●		●				*
51	Scardacchia	●	●					
60	Borgo alla Collina	●	●					**
64	Poppi	●	●	●	●	●		*****
69	Bibbiena	●	●			●	●	*****

Tour 7/ Day 1 Firenze—Bibbiena

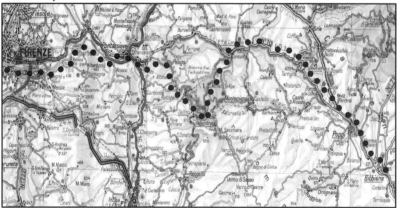

Touring Club Italiano, Auth. 04 November 2002

Photo by Doug Knisley

TOUR 7/ DAY 2

BIBBIENA—ANGHIARI
68 km/ 42 mi. Degree of Difficulty: R

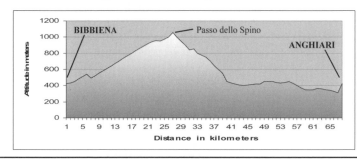

This route starts with a long climb (27 km/ 17 mi.) from **Bibbiena** to **Passo dello Spino**. A breathtaking descent follows which takes you down to the shores of **Lago di Montedoglio**. The ride ends with an easy spin to the spectacular hilltown of **Anghiari**.

From Bibbiena you follow signs for **Chiusa della Verna** and **Pieve Santo Stefano** on **N 208**. You don't get much time to warm up before hitting the big climb of the day. It pretty much starts at the gates of town. But it does begin gently. You meander up into wooded hills and pasture with occasional views down over Bibbiena. Just when you've gotten into a rhythm there is a steep descent down to a bridge over a creek with an equally steep climb up the other side. The road continues to wind up hill. There should be little traffic, and the views into the valley below are spectacular.

About 14 km from Bibbiena you pass through the village of **Dama** which consists of a restaurant/ bar. A few kilometers later you begin to catch glimpses of the Franciscan monastery of **La Verna** built high on a rocky outcrop. This is where St. Francis received "the miracle of the stigmata," wounds like those of Jesus on the cross. On weekends car-loads of Italians arrive to visit this holy site and to hike in the nearby national forest.

The climb levels out as you approach the monastery buildings and then drops down to the town of Chiusa della Verna. This pretty village of stone buildings is set among tall dark evergreens. There are several restaurants and cafes here in case it is time for a break. However, you are not yet at the top. There is another 3 km of climbing before you reach the Passo dello Spino at 1055 meters (3,460 ft.).

From the top of the pass the road drops like a stone for 13 km down to Pieve San Stefano. Wide sweeping switchbacks with wonderful views over rolling forested hills take you down and down. A few kilometers from the summit the village of **Compito** flashes by. Two kilometers later the road levels out briefly as you pass through **Montalone.** All too soon the descent ends at the busy main street of Pieve Santo Stefano.

When you reach the intersection with the main road through Pieve Santo Stefano, turn right following signs for **Sansepulcro.** The road parallels the Autostrada. After about 3 km look for a right turn with signs for **Lago di Montedoglio, Fermole,** and **Sigliano.** You will pass under the Autostrada and then over a bridge where the road turns left at the hamlet of Fermole. After about a kilometer the road meets the lake shore and follows it around the west shore. There are a few short climbs and descents as the road clings to the steep slope down to the water. After about 7.5 km you reach a bridge across to the south shore of the lake.

Once across the bridge the road runs along the base the foothills of the wide Tiber River valley. After about 4 km you will see the walls and towers of Anghiari high up on the ridge to the left. There is a short climb up a series of switchbacks to town.

Anghiari is one of the most interesting hilltowns you will find anywhere in Tuscany. There are no huge parking lots for tour buses here, no trinket shops, and few postcard stands. There are tiny twisting stone alleyways and window boxes full of flowers, traditional family-run trattorias with menus only in Italian. There are four hotels in town as well as a few private rooms for rent. You will not have to book ahead except perhaps in August. If you get stuck for accommodations you can ride the 7 km across the flat valley to the larger town of Sansepulcro.

Degree of Difficulty: Of the 68 km of this route, nearly half of them are uphill. But it's actually not as bad as it sounds. The grade is not steep and the 5-star scenery is enough to keep you entertained the whole way up. Rating: R.

Highlights: With fantastic mountain scenery, smooth roads, and little or no traffic, this is a 5-star ride. Ending your day in undiscovered Anghiari is icing on the cake.

km	Place Name	Cafes	Shops, Mkts	Lodging	Camping	Bank	Bike Shop	Quaintness Rating
14	Dama	●						
23	Chiusa della Verna	●	●	●	●	●		***
30	Compito	●						
32	Montalone	●						*
41	Pieve Santo Stefano	●	●	●		●		*
51	Tizzano	●						*
59	Motina	●	●	●				
68	Anghiari	●	●	●		●	●	*****

Tour 7/ Day 2 Bibbiena—Anghiari

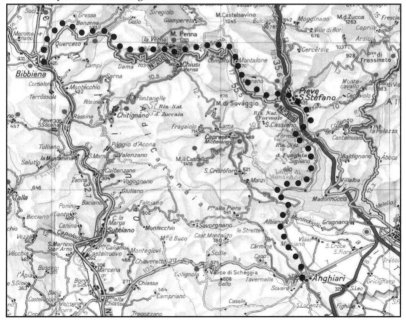

Touring Club Italiano, Auth. 04 November 2002

TOUR 7/ DAY 3

ANGHIARI—URBINO
78 km/ 49 mi. Degree of Difficulty: R

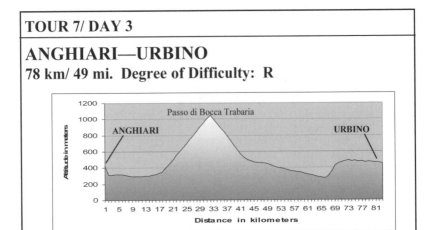

Like the previous stage this route also includes one long climb—a 15 km (9 mi.) spin up to **Passo di Bocca Trabaria.** At no more than a 7% grade it is really not difficult, and the views over the Tiber River valley are stupendous. Once you reach the top of the pass the next 34 km are all downhill as far as **Urbania.** To reach enchanted **Urbino** there is a 5 km grind up above Urbania, but it is well worth the effort.

Starting from **Anghiari** you drop down to the valley floor in the direction of **Sansepulcro.** About 1 km below town look for a right turn with a sign for **San Leo** and **Arezzo.** A few kilometers on a flat road through farm land bring you to San Leo and an intersection with the main road between Sansepulcro to Arezzo. Dashing straight across this busy road you continue in the direction of **Pistrino.** At this unassuming village out in the middle of the valley follow signs right through town in the direction of **San Giustino.** You are now cutting across the valley towards the mountains to the east that you will soon be climbing.

San Giustino is a pleasant town with a good bike shop in case you need a repair. Weave your way through town following the signs for **Urbino.** The road begins to climb almost immediately. It winds up out of the valley at a gentle grade. You are never out of the saddle, and there are spectacular views to keep you entertained the whole way up.

About 7 km above San Giustino you get a brief break from the climbing when you hit a plateau of green pasture. It lasts for about 1 km before the grade gradually increases. Ahead you can see the final switchbacks up to the top of the pass. At 15.5 km above San Giustino (32 km from Anghiari) you crest out on the Passo di Bocca Trabaria at 1049 meters (3,440 ft.). Hold on to your handlebars, the next 34 km are all downhill.

The road noses over the top of the pass and then falls away to the left. Down and down you fly through tight switchbacks with an unbelievable vista ahead into the valley below. About 6 km down from the summit you will pass the pretty mountain town of **Lamoli**. The grade lessens here as you roll down the river valley. About 14 km from the summit (46 km from Anghiari) you will pass the medieval village **Borgo Pace** perched on the hillside across the river. Farther down the valley you will come to **Mercatello sul Metauro** and **Sant'Angelo in Vado** where you can pull off the road and pedal down the cobbled streets past ancient stone houses. After 34 km of pleasant down grade you will reach the outskirts of Urbania. This quaint town with tree-lined boulevards has an impressive fortress on the banks of the river. If you want to call it day, Urbania is a possible option. It only has two hotels, but it is a pretty town to explore. It is another 17 km to Urbino.

To continue on to Urbino watch for a left turn as you approach Urbania. There is a huge villa off to the left, a hunting lodge for the Dukes of Urbino. Just beyond this villa as you enter town you will see a left turn with signs for Urbino. Turning here a set of tight switchbacks takes you above Urbania. The steep grind goes on for 5 km to the top of a ridge. From here there are awesome views over range after range of steep hills in every direction.

You roll along the top of the ridge for about 8 km. As you come round a bend the city of Urbino suddenly appears before you. It is a magical sight of blond brick towers and domes. The road contours along the hillside and delivers you to a broad square below the gates of the city. During the summer months this square is likely to be crowded with cars and tour buses. Urbino is one of the most famous Renaissance cities in Italy, and it richly deserves its popularity. This means that during July and August the touring cyclist with 83 km in his legs will want to have advance hotel reservations.

Degree of Difficulty: The climb up Passo di Bocca Trabaria is not steep, but it is long. The climb up above Urbania is not as long, but it is steep. Coming at the end of the day you can count on it to be challenging. Although the other 63 km of the ride are flat or down hill these two climbs qualify as adult entertainment. Rating: R.

Highlights: The climb and the descent of Passo di Bocca Trabria is nothing short of spectacular. This is bicycle touring at its best: a satisfying slog followed by a long sleigh ride down hill past crumbling stone villages with sleepy cafés offering a cold drink and a snack. Coming over the last hill to the sight of the fairytale city of Urbino should cap a near perfect day in the saddle.

km	Place Name	Cafes	Shops, Mkts	Lodging	Camping	Bank	Bike Shop	Quaintness Rating
3	San Leo	•	•					
7	Pistrino	•	•					
11	San Giustino	•	•	•		•	•	**
35	Lamoli	•						***
45	Mercatello	•	•	•				***
52	Sant'Angelo	•	•	•		•		***
62	Urbania	•	•	•		•	•	****
78	Urbino	•	•	•	•	•	•	*****

Tour 7/ Day 3 Anghiari—Urbino

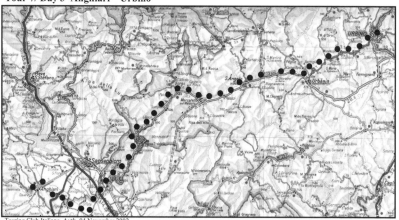

Touring Club Italiano, Auth. 04 November 2002

TOUR 7/ DAY 4

URBINO—GUBBIO
86 km/ 53 mi. Degree of Difficulty: PG-13

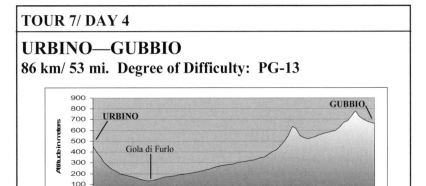

This route takes you from the Renaissance palaces of **Urbino** into the rustic outback of the Marches. It winds through the awesome **Furlo** gorge, past medieval **Cagli**, up and down a few stiff climbs, and finally brings you at the walls of **Gubbio**, a medieval fortress built over Roman ruins. For this route you will need climbing legs and extra film.

From the "Piazza di Tour Bus" below the gates of Urbino you should follow the signs for **Roma**. This takes you down a steep busy road towards the Autostrada. This is not especially pleasant riding but at least it is downhill. After about 4 km the grade lessens as you reach the valley floor. The road rolls past the villages of **Fermignano** and **Canavaccio.** Just beyond Canavaccio the road merges onto the Autostrada. You have to bear left to avoid the on-ramp. At this point the traffic mostly disappears.

About 15 km from Urbino you will enter the village of **Calmazzo.** As you come into town you will see a mass of green Autostrada direction signs next to a bus shelter. There is also a curious giant cement building in the shape of an inverted cone just beyond the bus stop. You must make a sharp right turn at the bus shelter. Only after making the turn will you see the sign for **Furlo.** The road zig-zags through a residential section of town, crosses an overpass above the highway, and comes down the other side into the village of **Pagino.** Following the road through the sleepy neighborhoods of Pagino you soon come to an intersection with a huge white sign for Furlo to the right.

You are now on the **Via Flaminia,** an ancient Roman road built by order of the Roman Consul Gaius Flaminius in 220 B.C. The road is barely wide enough for two cars to pass, but you won't see many anyway. A kilometer or two from the turn you will see the mouth of the **Gola di Furlo,** the Furlo gorge. Sheer granite walls close in on you as you pedal up the gentle grade. Through the bottom of the gorge flows an unnaturally green turbid river. Soon you come to a stop light at the mouth of a tunnel. This tunnel was cut by the Romans in 76 B.C. as part of a highway improvement project, and being only two ox carts wide, modern automobiles can only pass through one direction at a time. The tunnel is only about 50 meters long.

You finally emerge from the narrow gorge at the town of Furlo, a pleasant spot with a grassy park next to the river. Keep pedalling up the valley following signs for **Acqualagna**. Two kilometers from Furlo you will pass through **Pelingo**, a town remarkable mostly for its huge brick factory. Three kilometers later you will enter the medium-sized town of Acqualagna, which offers little attraction besides a good bike shop. At the center of Acqualagna you will come to an intersection with signs for **Citta di Castello** to the right and **Cagli** to the left. Bearing left here you will shortly come to another intersection with signs for Cagli to the left and **Smirra** to the right. You want to go right here in order to avoid getting on the **N 3** highway. The road to Smirra continues on to Cagli along the original Via Flaminia. It is shady and quiet and blissfully traffic free, but the pavement hasn't seen much attention since the end of the Roman era.

Cagli is a pretty medieval town and also has a good bike shop. It is on the right just as you climb the gentle grade up to the old section of town. Pedal through the main square of Cagli and explore some of its back alleys. Its most memorable feature is the huge fortified bastion at the far end of town. It is all that remains of a huge fortress that once guarded the valley. You will pass it on the way out of town following signs for **Roma** and **Cantiano.** Be careful not to follow the signs onto the N 3 highway. You want to follow the street named Via Flaminia out of town. This is the ancient Roman road and it parallels the highway through the narrow valley to Cantiano. Although it is unclear on the map, the old road does not go through any tunnels.

Ten kilometers from Cagli a broad valley opens to the left and you can see the tile roofs of Cantiano. Follow the bulls-eye signs into the town center. A wonderful little ruined castle glowers down at the town from a hilltop. At the center of town there is a pleasant square with a fountain and park benches. Continue past the square following signs for **Chieserna**.

Just past the square the road begins to climb. Steep mountain crags surround the valley. As you climb the moderately steep grade hay fields and vineyards give way to forest. About 4 km from Cantiano you will pass through the village of **Fossato.** Just above Fossato you will come to Chieserna. Things begin to take on an alpine look here, and there is a left turn for a ski area as you pass through town. You continue straight. The grade begins to get more serious the higher you climb.

About 2 km above Chieserna the climb finally reaches a saddle in a dense forest between rocky peaks. Crossing this pass you almost immediately dive down the other side. Smooth switchbacks take you down through lush woods into a narrow valley. Four kilometers of marvelous descent bring you to **Valdorbia,** a restaurant/ bar at an intersection with the road between **Scheggia** to **Sassoferrato.** You turn right here and head towards Scheggia.

You are now in a narrow wooded valley with steep rock walls. There will be very little traffic and the road is smooth. A barely perceptible uphill grade takes you up the river valley. Three kilometers from Valdorbia you will pass through the pretty hamlet of **Ponte Calcara**, which has a road-side café. Two kilometers farther on you reach Scheggia.

At Scheggia you will intersect again with the busy N 3 highway. You should turn right on N 3 and pedal about 500 meters up a gentle grade past town. At the sign for **Gubbio** turn left off the main road.

From here the road strikes off across a beautiful landscape of green pastures. Ahead you will see a solid barrier of mountains that you must cross. It looks daunting, but the grade up to the top is not difficult. Seven kilometers of easy climbing winds you up to the continental divide of the Italian peninsula. There is a shrine to the Virgin Mary at the top marking the spot. From here it is 5 km of beautiful sweeping switchbacks down a narrow gorge to the fortified gates of Gubbio.

Gubbio is perched on hillside overlooking a broad valley ringed by mountains. Its medieval walls climb high up the ridge to a ruined fortress. Below the fort medieval houses huddle along narrow streets. Magnificent palazzos face ornate churches across the squares. At the foot of the town just outside the walls there is a Roman amphitheater and other ruins. Take your time to explore this exquisite town. There are more than a dozen hotels, and you should have no trouble finding a place to stay even during the summer months.

Degree of Difficulty: There are two climbs on this route that will get your attention. Both are about 6 km long but have only short sections which are really steep. The rest of the ride is easy flats or descents. Rating: PG-13.

Highlights: The Furlo gorge will be the highlight of this ride. Its dramatic sheer rock walls and narrow, nearly deserted road will percolate up in your memory for months to come. The descent through the trees down to Valdorbia will also probably make your top-ten list. My personal favorite is the quiet, serene stretch from Valdorbia to Scheggia. Finally the descent down to the medieval walls of Gubbio will end a great day of riding.

km	Place Name	Cafes	Shops, Mkts	Lodging	Camping	Bank	Bike Shop	Quaintness Rating
7	Fermignano	●	●	●		●		**
10	Canavaccio	●	●	●				
15	Calmazzo	●	●					
21	Furlo	●	●	●				***
23	Pelingo	●	●					
26	Acqualagna	●	●	●		●	●	
29	Smirra	●	●					
34	Cagli	●	●	●		●	●	****
44	Cantiano	●	●	●		●		**
50	Chieserna	●	●	●				*
56	Valdorbia	●						
59	Ponte Calcara	●						*
61	Scheggia	●	●					
73	Gubbio	●	●	●		●	●	*****

Tour 7/ Day 4 Urbino—Gubbio

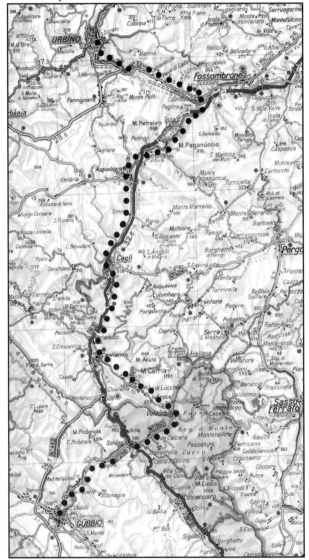

Touring Club Italiano, Auth. 04 November 2002

TOUR 7/ DAY 5

GUBBIO—ASSISI
63 km/ 39 mi. Degree of Difficulty: PG-13

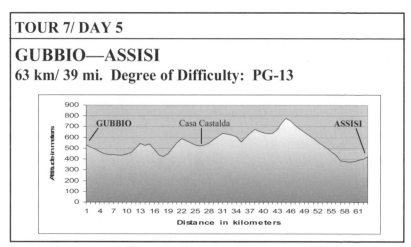

This route leads you into the green heart of Umbria. The trick for getting from **Gubbio** to **Assisi** is to avoid the heavy truck traffic that dominates the three main roads out of the valley. The route described here leads you into the mountains where few cars or trucks venture mostly because of the steep curvy hills. As a result you will have these torturous roads mostly to yourself. They lead up and down the Umbrian hills and finally to a long descent which brings you to the back door of Assisi. Along the way you will pass through marvelous scenery sprinkled with tiny villages.

The route begins at the walls of Gubbio. You follow **Via di Porta Romana** south following signs for **San Marco, Padule**, and **Gualdo Tadino.** The road weaves through the residential streets of modern Gubbio. You will soon pass through the suburbs of San Marco and Padule. Just beyond Padule look for a right turn with signs for **Perugia** and **Casa Castalda.** This takes you to an intersection with the main road between Gubbio and Gualdo Tadino. Cross over the highway and continue straight across the flat valley. After 2 km you will pass a left turn with a sign for Gubbio; continue straight. As the road reaches the far side of the valley it turns south paralleling the range of hills bordering the valley. You will cross a bridge over the Saonda River and then begin to climb into the wooded hills.

The road climbs steadily past olive trees and hay fields. After about 5 km you top out on the ridge and are rewarded with magnificent views back across the valley towards Gubbio. A screaming descent follows taking you down a series of tight switchbacks into the valley of the Chiasco

River. Crossing over the river you climb a short distance to the village of **Colpalombo,** a sleepy narrow spot in the road. From here the road climbs steeply for another kilometer. This is pretty much the pattern for the day: short steep climbs followed by short steep descents as you wind through the rolling forested hills of the Umbrian outback.

A few kilometers from Colpalombo you will pass through the equally sleepy village of **Carbonesca**. All along this route you will see great stone farmhouses perched on the slopes of overgrown hills. Many of these have been turned into Agriturismos, and you will see signs for them at every intersection.

Beyond Carbonesca the road climbs briefly and then at about 26 km from Gubbio you will roll down to the village of Casa Castalda. This pretty town sits on a low hill with most of its medieval walls intact. The few narrow streets and shops behind its gates are interesting to explore.

At the far end of town in the direction of Gualdo Tadino there is a right turn with signs for **Colle Mincio** and **Osteria di Morano.** Turning here the road from Casa Castalda climbs deeper into the lush green hills. After 2 or 3 km contouring along a hillside you will pass a right turn for Valfabbrica. Just beyond this turn the road turns to dirt, but it is in good shape and is perfectly rideable. The dirt section takes you past Colle Mincio, a collection of tall stone buildings. From here the road descends down into a narrow valley between rolling wooded hills. A short climb brings you up to Osteria di Morano where you meet the pavement again and turn right following the sign for Assisi.

From Osteria di Morano you descend for about 1 km before once again climbing. This time you are out of the saddle for about 2 km until you reach the top of a high ridge. There are spectacular views over rolling waves of green hills in every direction. Gradually the road goes into a steep descent down into a narrow valley that runs out ahead of you. Steep switchbacks weave back and forth down the hillside. You begin to catch glimpses of the Rocca Maggiore castle above Assisi. The road eventually hits the bottom of the valley and follows the river bed for a few kilometers before gradually climbing the south side of the valley towards the walls of Assisi. You will arrive at the **Porta Perlici** gate at the upper end of the town. This has the advantage of allowing you to ride down the steep cobblestoned streets rather than up.

Assisi is wonderful and well-preserved. It is perhaps the most famous of the Italy's hilltowns. It sits high above the broad Vale di Spoleto plain, and the views down over its pink tile roofs are awesome. The quaint streets and buildings and of course the Basilica of St. Francis have been drawing tourists and pilgrims for centuries. By dint of this popularity don't expect to have this place to yourself; in fact don't expect to be able to ride your bike down those narrow cobblestone streets. You will be cheek-by-jowl with your fellow travelers like nowhere else except perhaps the Ponte Vecchio in Firenze. Needless to say, it is necessary to book your accommodations well in advance if you wish to stay up in the old section of town. In a pinch you might be able to find a room down in the valley at the town of **Santa Maria delli Angeli.**

Degree of Difficulty: This ride is relatively short and there are no monster climbs, but don't take it lightly. All the up and down riding can wear you out, especially on a hot mid-summer's day. Rating: PG-13.

Highlights: This route takes you from one medieval gem to another. Gubbio and Assisi are at the head of the hilltown hit parade. In between you get a taste of the lush green remoteness that gives Umbria its sobriquet as the "Green Heart of Italy."

km	Place Name	Cafes	Shops, Mkts	Lodging	Camping	Bank	Bike Shop	Quaintness Rating
3	San Marco	•	•					
5	Padule	•	•					
18	Colpalombo	•						*
22	Carbonesca	•						*
26	Casa Castalda	•	•					***
38	Osteria di Morano	•	•					**
63	Assisi	•	•	•		•	•	*****

Tour 7/ Day 5 Gubbio—Assisi

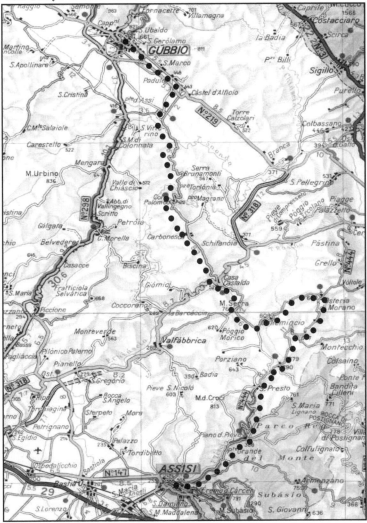

TOUR 7/ DAY 6

ASSISI—CORTONA
98 km/ 61 mi. Degree of Difficulty: PG

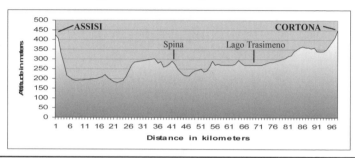

This is a beautiful ride through rolling hills. There are no big climbs until you reach the final pitch up to **Cortona**. The route takes you on quiet roads through fields of wheat and sunflowers. You will pedal along the shores of **Lago Trasimeno** past its beaches and campgrounds. Despite the length this is an easy ride.

From **Assisi** you point the handlebars down the steep hill to **Santa Maria degli Angeli.** It lies 5 km straight down a series of broad switchbacks. At the bottom of hill you enter the confusing streets of Santa Maria. Finding you way through this town will be the hardest part of your day. Essentially try to head straight across the valley away from Assisi and follow the signs for **Costano** and **Bettona** where you can find them. The congestion of Santa Maria falls away once you cross over the Autostrada and soon you are out on the flat plain pedaling on a quiet country road with hardly a car in sight.

About 4 km from Santa Maria you will pass a right turn for Co-stano; continue straight for Bettona which you can see perched high on a hill on the opposite side of the valley. About 8 km from Santa Maria you will hit an intersection at the modern village of **Passaggio.** Here you turn right following the signs for **Torgiano.** A few hundred meters from this turn there is a left turn which climbs up to Bettona. This is a wonderful hill town with its walls and fortified gates intact. There is a pleasant cobble-stone piazza at its center. It you have the legs and the inclination it is worth the short steep climb to check it out and enjoy the view. Otherwise you can pass by this turn and continue towards Torgiano.

As you approach Torgiano follow the bulls-eye signs leading you to the center of town. Torgiano is a large busy town with some remnants of its walls and towers. It sits on a low hill overlooking the broad Tevere River valley. The city center signs bring you to an intersection where you can turn left to head into town or bear right following the signs for **Perugia.** Turning right you will descend down into the flat valley towards the Autostrada. About 1.5 km from this turn you will come to an intersection with signs for Perugia and **San Martino in Campo** to the left. You should turn left here following the signs for San Martino.

You will be able to see and hear the busy Autostrada just ahead. You will cross the highway on an overpass and soon enter the modern town of San Martino in Campo. Following the main road through San Martino in Campo you will come to a large traffic circle where you bear left following the sign for **San Martino in Colle.** This smaller road leads you up out of the flat valley through vineyards to the ridge opposite Torgiano. The views from the top extend to Perugia in one direction and all the way down the valley to **Todi** in the other.

At the top of the gentle climb you will meet an intersection with **N 371**. You should turn left here following the sign for **Marsciano**. Pedaling along the top of the ridge you will pass through San Martino in Colle and continue straight on N 371. You continue on through the next village of **Santa Enea** and after about 5 km you will see a right turn for the towns of **Olmeto** and **Spina**. If you reach the town of **San Valentino** you have missed the turn and must backtrack.

From N 371 the road descends down past the village of Olmeto into a shallow valley and then climbs gently up the other side towards Spina. As you look at the map you may think this is a circuitous route to reach Cortona, but the reason lies at Spina. No semi-precious stone, this is a ten carat diamond of a tiny walled hamlet forgotten by the march of time and tour buses. It must have started out as a small castle with four round towers at each corner and two gates through to its courtyard. Over the centuries the walls and towers were co-opted into housing and its courtyard crammed with more stone tenements of uncertain structural integrity. It is now a warren of tiny alleys between leaning walls and window boxes. Best of all it is completely unsullied by postcard stands and gift shops. It offers a wonderful contrast to Assisi.

From Spina you roll out of "town" following the signs for **Castiglione della Valle.** The road meanders through rolling hills of olive groves and sunflowers. After about 2 km you will pass a right turn for Perugia; continue straight. Following a short climb the road sails down a hill into a broad flat basin. The road here is lined by fig trees, and if you catch the right season the aroma of ripe melons wafts across the road from the surrounding fields.

Castiglione della Valle is indeed a castle or rather was. Like Spina its walls and towers have now been converted into housing. The jumble of houses and towers crowd together on a rock above the valley floor. The road skirts around its base and comes to a fork on the far side. You bear right here following the signs for **Mugnano** and **Magione.**

From Castiglione della Valle the road gradually climbs. After about 4 km you will cross over **N 220,** a busy main road into Perugia. The signs for Mugnano lead you through a pleasant countryside of olive trees and pasture land. Soon you crest a hill and a broad bowl-shaped valley spreads out before you. At its center is the small town of Mugnano. As you descend down towards the town the road splits allowing you to circle around the outside of town or cut directly through it. Mugnano has a quaint medieval section, and it's worth while to take the short cut through town. You pop out the other side and continue across the flat valley following the signs for Magione and Lago Trasimeno.

About 4 km from Mugnano you will pass a large super market which seems a bit far from any customers. Just beyond the market the road climbs up the rim of the volcanic crater which forms Lago Trasimeno. At the top there is a magnificent view across the lake.

From the top of the ridge you descend steeply down to an intersection with the main road that circles the lake. Turning right here you go about 2 km on the fairly busy road before there is a left turn with signs for **San Feliciano.** This road takes you down closer to the water. Terraced olive groves climb the hillside to your right up to the quaint village of **San Savino.** You continue along the lake shore. You will pass several pizzaria/bar-type establishments. About 3 km from San Savino you will enter the pleasant lake-front town of San Feliciano.

San Feliciano is a busy summer resort. There are many shops and markets. It has a boardwalk along the water and launch service out to **Isola Polvese** which sits just offshore. Just outside town there are two commercial campgrounds down on the water.

About 1 km north of San Feliciano you will pass the interesting ruins of **Castello di Zocco.** You can see the remains of walls and towers but there is no sign or marker to identify what it is or was. Just beyond this mysterious site you will reach **Monte del Lago,** a cute village built high on a rock promontory jutting out over the lake. There is a short steep climb up to it, and it is worth a stop to explore its few streets and admire the view.

From Monte del Lago the road descends back down to the lake shore. You will pass a beach-bar and campground at **Toricella**. Just beyond Toricella the road cuts under a highway overpass. You will see a sign for **Passignano,** the next town along the lake, but this leads you onto the divided highway. You can avoid the highway by going straight ahead in the direction of **Castel Rigone**. After about a kilometer there is a right turn which veers away for Castel Rigone, but if you continue straight the road will take you into Passignano.

Passignano is a sporty place with campgrounds and hotels and a ruined castle overlooking a yacht harbor. There is a boardwalk along the water with cafes and outdoor tables. Follow the signs for **Tuoro** through town.

About 5 km outside of Passignano you will reach a 4-way intersection with signs for Tuoro and **Umbertide** to the right and **Borghetto** to the left. You want to go straight following the sign for **Arezzo**. About 1 km past this intersection the road begins to climb away from the lake. You wind gently up through terraced olive groves with spectacular views across the water towards **Castiglione del Lago**. Three kilometers of easy climbing bring you a to an intersection where you bear right following the sign for **Cortona**. About 2 km from here you will reach another intersection at the edge of the town of **Riccio**. Here there are signs for Arezzo, Firenze, and Orvieto, but surprisingly none for Cortona. You turn right here in the direction of Arezzo.

Riccio has a few shops but is otherwise uninspiring. At the far end of town you will get your first view of Cortona high up on its hill. Just beyond Riccio there is a right turn with a sign for **Ossaia**. Turning here gets you off this busy main road.

A gentle climb takes you through quiet Ossaia. You then roll down into a broad flat plain which runs to the base of the Cortona climb. About 3 km on this flat straight road brings you to an intersection with a sign for Cortona to the left. The long climb up to town starts here.

The climb up to Cortona starts out gently going by walled estates and olive groves. After about a kilometer you merge with the main road up to town. The climb is never steep and the scenery is such that even the traffic won't bother you. On the way up you will pass **Santa Maria di Calelunaio**, a great hulking brick basilica that now seems abandoned. A few more switchbacks and you will reach the gates of the city. Unfortunately the real climbing starts here, or maybe it's time to start hiking. The cobblestone streets are steep and slick all the way up to the main square.

Cortona has great restaurants and shops to explore as well as an impressive castle at the very top of the hill. In addition to its many hotels it has a rare youth hostel in a converted monastery. But as with any of the popular hilltowns of Tuscany and Umbria, if you want to stay in the old section or even nearby, it is best to book ahead during the summer months.

Degree of Difficulty: Although fairly long, this is not a hard ride. There are a few short climbs but the only real grind is the final 4 km climb up to Cortona. Rating: PG.

Highlights: Apart from the beautiful countryside, the time-capsule village of Spina will be among the memorable sights of the day. The ride along the shores of Lago Trasimeno is also very pleasant. Cortona is a classic Italian hilltown largely free of the tourist trinket shops that plague Assisi.

km	Place Name	Cafes	Shops, Mkts	Lodging	Camping	Bank	Bike Shop	Quaintness Rating
5	Santa Maria delli Angeli	•	•	•		•	•	*
23	San Martino in Campo	•	•					
41	Spina	•	•					*****
46	Castiglione della Valle	•	•					***
52	Mugnano	•	•	•		•		***
60	San Feliciano	•	•	•	•	•		*
75	Passignano	•	•	•	•	•	•	**
98	Cortona	•	•	•		•	•	*****

Tour 7/ Day 6 Assisi—Cortona

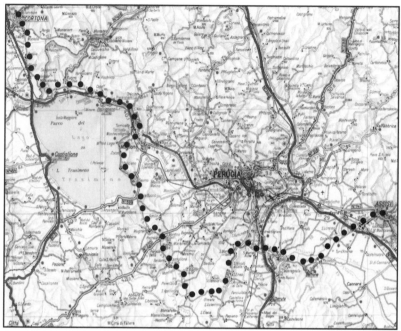

Touring Club Italiano, Auth. 04 November 2002

TOUR 7/ DAY 7

CORTONA—MONTALCINO
76 km/ 47 mi. Degree of Difficulty: PG-13

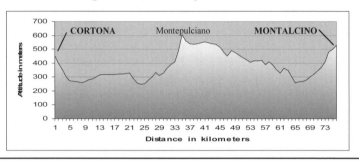

This route takes you down across the broad, flat agricultural valley below **Cortona** and up to the aerie heights of **Montepulciano**. From there 30 km of more or less uninterrupted descent take you down to the foot of the final 9 km climb up to **Montalcino**. Along the way you pass through stunning Tuscan countryside and the quaint towns of **Pienza** and **San Quirico**. This route has two stiff climbs, but the rest of the ride is over easy rolling terrain.

From the gates of Cortona you sweep down broad switchbacks to the busy town of **Camucia**. Go straight through town following the signs for **Siena, Sinalunga,** and Montepulciano. Just beyond town you cross a set of railroad tracks and a murky canal and come to a fork where you bear left for Montepulciano. The road stretches out straight ahead of you.

About 6 km from Camucia you will cross over the **N 75** highway. The road continues through broad expanses of farm land and sleepy villages. At every major intersection there are easy-to-follow signs for Montepulciano. About 21 km from Cortona you will pass through the pleasant town of **Valiano**. You can see Montepulciano ahead spread across the top of a high ridge. At 25 km from Cortona you cross over the **A-1** Autostrada and enter the busy suburb of **Stazione di Montepulciano**. The climb up to the old city begins here.

It starts out gently. You follow the signs in the direction of **Gracciano**. About a half kilometer beyond Gracciano you will hit an intersection with the main road, and the grade gets steeper. The last kilometer up to the city gates is a leg-buster.

Montepulciano commands a magnificent site high above the surrounding plains. The slopes below it are combed with grape vineyards. Its medieval palazzos and crenulated walls are well preserved, and there are several cafes where you can sit at outdoor tables and the watch the less fortunate travelers who had to drive up that hill.

After seeing the sights you should follow signs for Pienza out of town. You are soon zooming down a long gentle hill below the city. There are marvelous views back up at its walls and towers as you cruise along. This is Tuscan scenery at its best: rolling hills, vineyards, and wheat fields. The hilltops are crowned with a jumble of ancient stone houses with the inevitable church tower poking above. The pleasant coast down to Pienza is interrupted only by a short, steep climb up to its shady main square. Pienza is an interesting town, a reputed masterpiece of Renaissance urban planning. It's worth investigating the main street inside its gates.

From Pienza you continue down into the Orcia River valley. To your left you will have magnificent views of hulking **Monte Amiata** and next to it the solitary tower on the muffin-shaped hill of **Radicofani.**

It is 9 km from Pienza to San Quirico d'Orcia. Although this is a major road up to Montepulciano, the traffic is barely noticeable. As you roll up to the gates of San Quirico you will see signs to Siena to the right. You should follow these across an overpass above the busy **N 2** highway. Just after the overpass look for a left turn with signs for **Torrenieri.** This puts you on the original Roman **Via Cassia** which parallels the modern highway. It will take you to Torrenieri in blissful traffic-free solitude.

As you come into the center of Torrenieri you will come to a 4-way intersection with signs for Montalcino to the left. Turning here the road leads you out of town and onto the Via Cassia highway. The cars will be speeding by but there is a wide shoulder and you are only on it for about 2 kilometers.

You will soon reach a right turn off the Via Cassia for Montalcino. The final climb of the day begins here. It starts out gently and takes you up through golden wheat fields. About the time the wheat gives way to olive trees the grade begins to increase. About 4 km from the Via Cassia you are really working. But by 6.5 km from the main road the grade becomes more forgiving and you are lured on by magnificent views of the castle and walls of Montalcino. The entire climb is about 9 km but only the middle part is hard.

Montalcino is a smaller, quainter version of Montepulciano. There are about 8 hotels in or near town as well as a number of private rooms for rent. Nevertheless in July and August it is best to book ahead.

Degree of Difficulty: This is an easy ride except for the two climbs up to Montepulciano and Montalcino. Rating: PG-13.

Highlights: Montepulciano is the first highlight of the day, followed by Pienza and the wonderful descent down to San Quirico. The scenery along this route is as beautiful as any in Tuscany. Montalcino is the prize at the end of the day with its quaint streets and shops and impressive citadel over-looking the valley.

km	Place Name	Cafes	Shops, Mkts	Lodging	Camping	Bank	Bike Shop	Quaintness Rating
5	Camucia	•	•	•		•		
21	Valiano	•	•					*
25	Stazione di Montepulciano	•	•	•			•	
35	Montepulciano	•	•	•		•		*****
48	Pienza	•	•	•		•		*****
57	San Quirico	•	•	•		•		***
65	Torrenieri	•	•	•				*
76	Montalcino	•	•	•		•	•	*****

Tour 7/ Day 7 Cortona—Montalcino

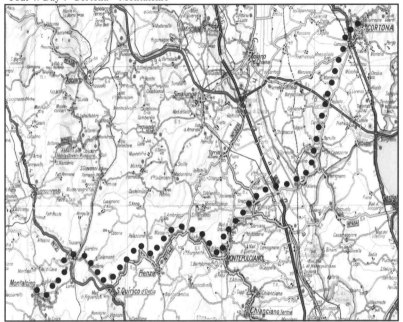

Touring Club Italiano, Auth. 04 November 2002

Photo by Geri Walsh

TOUR 7/ DAY 8

MONTALCINO—SIENA
60 km/ 37 mi. Degree of Difficulty: PG

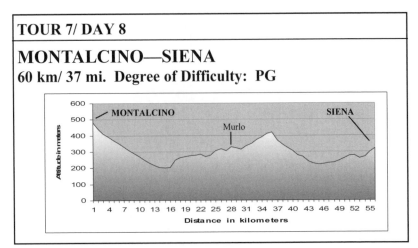

This route takes you through the beautiful Sienese hill-country. Quiet roads wind through vineyards and olive groves past medieval towns at **Buonconvento** and **Murlo**. The towers of **Siena** are visible over the hills for almost half the ride.

From **Montalcino** you begin the day by riding back towards **Tor-renieri.** About 2 km below the city walls there is a left turn with a sign for Buonconvento. Turning here you descend steeply through vineyards and olive groves for about 3 km. As the grade lessens you roll through wheat fields to an intersection with the busy **N 2** highway. You turn left here and pedal along the flat valley towards Buonconvento. After about 2 km you can bear left off the highway and head into Buonconvento. This takes you through its modern outskirts, but you soon reach the medieval section on the north side of town. Take some time to explore inside its brick battlements; its narrow streets and overhanging houses exude a sense of the careworn use spanning the centuries.

The main road through town jogs around the west side of the medieval walls. As you pedal along look for a left turn with a signs for **Bibbiano.** This road strikes off across the flat valley through fields bordered by cypress trees. You can see abbeys and villas set off the road in stands of trees. High up to the left you can see Montalcino clinging to its hilltop. About 1.5 km from Buonconvento you hit a short, steep climb that takes you up out of the valley. At the top there is an intersection with Bibbiano to the left and Murlo to the right. Turning right you cruise along the top of the ridge with spectacular views across rolling hills and into the valley.

The road is smooth, there is almost no traffic: this is great riding. You follow the signs for Murlo through every intersection. After about 10 km you descend down a gentle grade and can see the town, a tiny circular walled village, perched up on a hill. The short climb up to its gate is worth the effort. Inside its gate there is a cafe, a few shops, and a museum of Etruscan artifacts.

Back on the main road you will soon reach the modern outskirts of **Vescovado di Murlo.** The main road climbs up around the central part of town. Just beyond town there is an intersection where you bear left following the sign for **Casciano di Murlo.**

From here the road begins to descend and you shoot past the hamlet of **Lupompesi** down into a forested valley. High up on the next ridge you can see the dramatic ruins of the **Torre di Cervoli** fortress, once the front line in the wars between Siena and Firenze. At the bottom of the descent you will cross a bridge over a murky stream and begin to climb. The road winds up through low forest for about 2 km. You will pass a dirt path which leads up to the Torre di Cervoli castle in case you want to explore it.

On the road to Murlo

The climb tops out at **Palazzina,** an Agriturismo. Beyong Palazzina a steep drop of about 100 meters takes you down to an intersection where you turn right for **Ville di Corsano.** From here you descend down through a shady woods. It gets steeper and begins to twist and turn into switchbacks. As you break out of the trees the view ahead extends across a beautiful scenery of olive groves and wheat fields. Beyond the far hilltop you can see the towers and spires of Siena. After about 2.5 km there is a brief flat as you pass a left turn for the town of **Grotti,** then the road drops away again for another kilometer down to the village of Ville di Corsano.

From Ville di Corsano the road crosses a broad flat valley and climbs a far hillside lined with olive trees. Ancient stone farm houses sit at the end of dusty tree-lined lanes. At the top of the hill you enter the village of **Costafabbri.** The roads passes through a quiet residential neighborhood and meets **N 73,** one of the main arteries into Siena.

Busy N 73 takes you the rest of the way into Siena. There is no shoulder, and the cars are going fast. A few short ups and downs bring you to a confusing traffic circle. Follow the bulls-eye sign for the city center and the **Porta San Marco** gate. After climbing a broad boulevard up to the city walls you will enter the pedestrian zone in the old section of the city.

Siena is Tuscany's second city, behind only Firenze as a tourist attraction. If you want to stay inside the old section of the city during the summer months you will have to book well ahead.

Degree of Difficulty: There are just enough climbs on this route to bump it from G to PG. It is really not a difficult ride, and the scenery is so spectacular you will hardly notice the climbs. Rating: PG.

Highlights: The undisputed highlight of this ride will be the spectacular Tuscan landscape. Quiet, traffic-free roads, magnificent scenery, the occasional sleepy village offering an espresso or a glass of sparkling mineral water — this is 5 star riding.

km	Place Name	Cafes	Shops, Mkts	Lodging	Camping	Bank	Bike Shop	Quaintness Rating
15	Buonconvento	●	●	●		●		***
29	Murlo	●	●					****
31	Vescovado di Murlo	●	●	●		●		
32	Lupompesi	●						**
45	Grotti	●	●					*
47	Ville di Corsano	●	●					*
54	Costafabbri	●	●					
60	Siena	●	●	●	●	●	●	*****

Tour 7/ Day 8 Montalcino—Siena

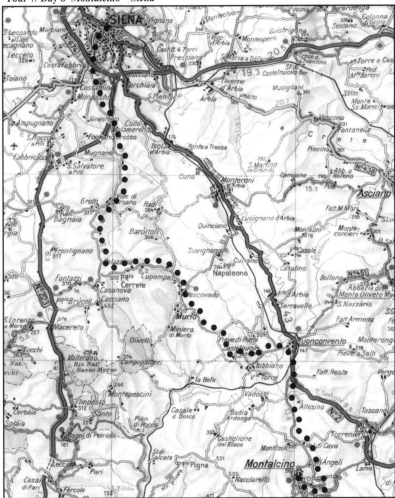

Touring Club Italiano, Auth. 04 November 2002

TOUR 7/ DAY 9

SIENA—FIRENZE
97 km/ 60 mi. Degree of Difficulty: R

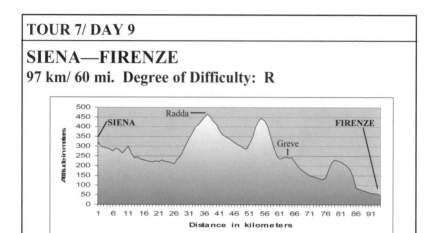

This ride takes you through the heart of the Chianti wine region. And while you might expect to be riding through vineyards all day, you actually spend most of your time in shady forested valleys. This is a beautiful ride that takes you through the famous towns of **Radda in Chianti** and **Greve in Chianti** and delivers you relatively painlessly to downtown **Firenze**.

From the **Piazza del Campo** in central **Siena** follow **Via Banchi di Sopra**, the narrow main street west towards **Porta Camollia.** The name of this street soon changes to **Via dei Montanini**. After several blocks you will come to a fork where **Via Giuseppe Garibaldi** veers off to the right and goes down a steep hill. Follow via Garibaldi until you reach the **Barriera San Lorenzo**, a gap in the city walls. Once through the walls turn right on **Viale Don Giovanni Minzoni**. It sweeps down around a bend to another right turn with signs for **N 408** and **Montevarchi.** Turning here you will pedal through a couple of busy traffic circles. Just keep following the signs for Montevarchi out of town.

A short climb takes you out of the suburbs of Siena. You go up and down a few hills and then descend down to a bridge at the town of **Ponte Bozzone.** Here you are at last free of the traffic congestion of Siena. You will climb gently up through a quiet forest and at the top of the hill pass the hamlet of **San Giovanni.** There are great views from here back at the towers of Siena. From San Giovanni the road drops down a steep descent to the village of **Pianella.** You continue following signs for N 408 and Montivarchi.

Beyond Pianella the road starts down a shady wooded valley. It is quiet and serene; there should be little traffic as you coast easily down hill.

About 20 km from Siena on N 408 you will come to a left turn for Radda in Chianti. Turning here you immediately begin to climb out of the forested valley. It starts out gently but gradually gets steeper. Soon you are switchbacking up through slopes of vineyards and olive groves. There is a huge villa crowning the hill on your right.

After 6 km of climbing you reach an intersection at the top of a ridge. There are signs for Montevarchi to the right and Radda to the left. Turning left you descend down to a saddle where there is right turn for Greve in Chianti and Firenze. Radda is directly ahead up a short, steep climb. Radda is a wonderful walled town, as pretty as any in Tuscany. It is worth the climb to explore its streets and shops.

To continue on to Firenze you return to the intersection at the saddle below Radda and follow the signs for Greve and Firenze. The road loops around under a brick overpass and then goes down a steep descent to the floor of a river valley below. You pedal easily down this valley through pasture land and stands of trees. There are occasional glimpses of vineyards on the hillsides above and great views back towards Radda. About 13 km of wonderful riding brings you to **Lucarelli**, which consists of a café/ restaurant in a shady hollow. It also marks the beginning of the stiff climb up to **Panzano in Chianti.**

Just above Lucarelli you will reach an intersection with **N 222,** the **Via Chiantigiana,** and the traffic picks up a bit. You turn right and continue up the hill towards Panzano and Firenze. Two kilometers of climbing wind you up to the central square in Panzano. There are great views the whole way up over the forested valley below.

Panzano has several shops and cafes and wonderful views but does not have the medieval quaintness of Radda. The main road passes through town and immediately dive-bombs down a hill on the other side. Almost 4 km of steep descent takes you down to a pleasant shady valley. The road continues flat or gently down to the town of Greve in Chianti. When you reach a traffic light you can continue straight or turn left to explore the pretty town. It has a large square and several outdoor cafes. At about the half-way point, it makes a good lunch stop.

About 2 km past Greve you will reach a fork where you can go right for **Strada in Chianti** or left to the town of **Ferrone.** If you go left you trade a long steep climb for a shorter steep climb by way of Ferrone. Both routes take you to Strada in Chianti. Going left is somewhat easier if a bit less scenic.

Assuming the weight of your panniers pulls you left towards Ferrone, the road continues down the Greve River valley for another 9 km. This is easy riding through pleasant countryside until you enter Ferrone, whose most notable feature is its several brick factories. As you roll through town keep an eye out for a right turn with a sign for Strada in Chianti. This is where the shorter steep climb you traded for begins. It goes up for 3 km. At the top you will meet an intersection with N 222 just on the outskirts of Strada. Here you turn left to continue on to Firenze.

The Via Chiantigiana, N 222, rolls on towards Firenze along the top of a ridge. There are great views left and right over neat rows of grape vines. After about 5 km you hit a descent down to the modern town of **Grassina**. A long tree-lined boulevard leads you out of town towards the congestion of Firenze. Follow the signs for N 222 past the Autostrada overpass to a large traffic circle. Bear left across the traffic circle onto **Via Benedetto Fortini.** This will take you down to the river where you turn left to pedal down stream to the **Ponte Vecchio**.

Firenze is the premier tourist destination in Tuscany. If you want to stay in the hotel of your choice in the area of your choice, you must book months in advance.

Degree of Difficulty: This route is long and relatively hard. It features three significant climbs. Between those climbs it is easy riding down river valleys, but the three walls will likely take their toll. Rating: R.

Highlights: This ride is about quiet riding and shady valleys—until you reach Firenze. The route takes you past charming medieval Radda sitting on its high hill and sophisticated Greve with its outdoor cafes. It delivers you with relative ease to the banks of the Arno River in downtown Firenze. Except for the last few kilometers through the city it provides a great last day for your tour.

km	Place Name	Cafes	Shops, Mkts	Lodging	Camping	Bank	Bike Shop	Quaintness Rating
9	Ponte Bozzone	●	●					
11	San Giovanni	●						
13	Pianella	●	●					
37	Radda in Chianti	●	●	●		●	●	*****
50	Lucarelli	●						*
56	Panzano in Chianti	●	●	●		●		**
62	Greve in Chianti	●	●	●		●	●	***
70	Ponte di Gaviano	●						
75	Ferrone	●	●					
79	Strada in Chianti	●	●	●		●		*
81	Poggio alla Scala	●						
84	Poggio Ugolino	●	●					*
89	Grassina	●	●	●		●		
97	Firenze	●	●	●	●	●	●	*****

Tour 7/ Day 9 Siena—Firenze

TOUR 8

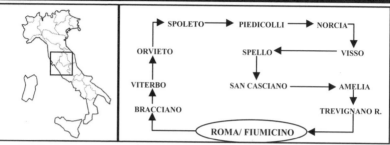

ROMA/ FIUMICINO—NORCIA—ROMA/ FIUMICINO
12 Days, 845 km/ 524 mi.

This tour traverses the rolling hills of Tuscany and the high mountain passes of Umbria. It is designed to thread together some of the very best rides I could discover in Italy. It is challenging; there are some epic climbs and equally epic descents. And while it skirts many of the well known hilltowns, it will lead you to equally charming more off the beaten path destinations.

Day 1: Roma/ Fiumicino—Bracciano, 63 km/ 39 mi., PG

Day 2: Bracciano—Viterbo, 76 km/ 47 mi., PG-13

Day 3: Viterbo—Orvieto, 55 km/ 34 mi., PG

Day 4: Orvieto—Spoleto, 87 km/ 54 mi., PG-13

Day 5: Spoleto—Piedicolle, 69 km/ 43 mi., PG-13

Day 6: Piedicolle—Norcia, 67 km/ 41 mi., PG

Day 7: Norcia—Visso, 51 km/ 32 mi., R

Day 8: Visso—Spello, 69 km/ 43 mi., PG

Day 9: Spello—San Casciano dei Bagni, 98 km/ 61 mi., PG-13

Day 10: San Casciano—Amelia, 80 km/ 50 mi., PG

Day 11: Amelia—Trevignano Romano, 70 km/ 44 km, PG

Day 12: Trevignano R.—Roma/ Fiumicino, 60 km/ 37 mi., G

TOUR 8/ DAY 1

ROMA/ FIUMICINO—BRACCIANO
63 km/ 39 mi. Degree of Difficulty: PG

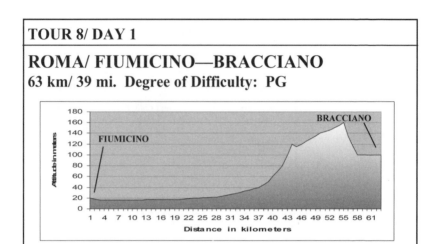

This tour begins and ends at the **Leonardo da Vinci International Airport** in the town of **Fiumicino** just west of **Rome.** If you are flying into Rome, this is where you will land. To ride your bike away from the airport, the only reasonable route is north past the seaside resort of **Fregene**. This town also provides the best choice for accommodations near the airport. There is a Hilton Hotel in the airport itself, but if you want something less expensive within riding distance of the airport, Fregene is your best option. For a detailed description and map of how to get out of the airport, see the **Airports** chapter.

It is about 16 km of flat riding from the airport terminal building to Fregene. The road jogs north around the end of the runways and strikes off through flat agricultural fields. About 9 km from the airport you will come to a blinking yellow traffic light with the right turn for **Roma**. Continue straight past this intersection for about 4 km to a second blinking yellow light. Here there will be a left turn and a sign for Fregene. If you do not intend to stop in Fregene, continue straight following the signs for **Maccarese**.

The road continues north and gradually curves around to the east. At about 22 km from the airport the flat, tree-lined road brings you to the bustling modern town of Maccarese. Go past the shops and markets and up over a railroad overpass. Coming down the other side of the overpass turn left following the signs for **Via Auralia.** The road parallels the railroad tracks for about 2 km until you come to a fork. Straight ahead there are signs for **Torrimpietra.** You should bear right following the sign for Via Auralia.

From this turn the road narrows down and goes through a wooded section and over a curious wooden bridge that creaks under your wheels. It would be great riding except for the traffic which can be heavy, particularly on summer weekends as Romans flock to the beaches. About 1 km from the turn you will come to the Autostrada, the Via Auralia highway. Signs to the left point to **Civitavecchia** and to the right for **Roma.** You want to go straight following signs for **Santa Maria di Galaria** and **Anguillara.** Once past the Autostrada the traffic diminishes and soon you are in quiet, rolling farmland.

About 7 km from the Autostrada you will reach a 4-way intersection. Go straight across on **Via di Santa Maria di Galaria.** This quiet road follows the Arrone River valley for about 4 km and then gradually begins to climb into the hills. The climb continues for 3.5 km and gets steeper as you go. You finally top out on a ridge with wheat fields and vineyards dropping away on all sides. Santa Maria di Galaria, a collection of forlorn stucco buildings, is there to greet you. The road continues along the ridge line for about 2 km and then descends down to a 4-way intersection. Here you turn left following the signs for **Bracciano** and **Ostia Nuova.**

Lago di Bracciano

You are now on the busy **Via Claudia Braccianese.** After about 200 meters you will pass a right turn for Ostia Nuova and Anguillara; continue straight. The road rolls past fields of wheat, corn, and sunflowers bordered by trees. After about 4 km you will see a right turn for **Vigna di Valle** and **Lago di Bracciano.** Turning here you get off the main road, and after a short climb get your first glimpse of the lake below. The road descends down through shady woods past a right turn for Anguillara. Once you reach the lake shore the road turns north and travels clockwise around the lake. As you pedal along the shore you can see the fairytale fortress of Bracciano ahead overlooking the lake.

You will pass several hotels and commercial campgrounds as you approach Bracciano. There are several more hotels in the town itself. Bracciano is built up above the lake, and to reach it you will have to climb a short but quite steep hill. You may prefer to stay in a hotel down on the lake at **Bagni di Bracciano**, a resort right on the water. You can then climb up to explore Bracciano without your panniers. You should have no trouble finding a room here, except perhaps in August when it would be wise to book ahead.

Degree of Difficulty: At 63 km (39 mi.) from the airport this can be a long first day on the bike. There is one long climb up to Santa Maria di Galaria, but the effects of jet lag, the stress of dodging cars on the way out of the airport, and getting used to your fully-loaded bike will conspire to make this a challenging day. Rating: PG.

Highlights: The long blissfully quiet stretch up the Arrone River valley will be just the antidote you need after escaping the airport traffic. The view over Lago di Bracciano as you crest the ridge and the quiet ride along the lake shore is lovely. The cobblestone streets below the Disneyland castle of Bracciano will be fun to explore. And finally the sunset over the lake from an outdoor café will provide the perfect end to your first day in the saddle.

km	Place Name	Cafes	Shops, Mkts	Lodging	Camping	Bank	Bike Shop	Quaintness Rating
9	Focene	●	●					
16	Fregene	●	●	●				*
22	Maccarese	●	●	●		●		
45	Ostia Nuova	●	●					
63	Bracciano	●	●	●	●	●	●	****

Tour 8/ Day 1 Roma/ Fiumicino—Bracciano

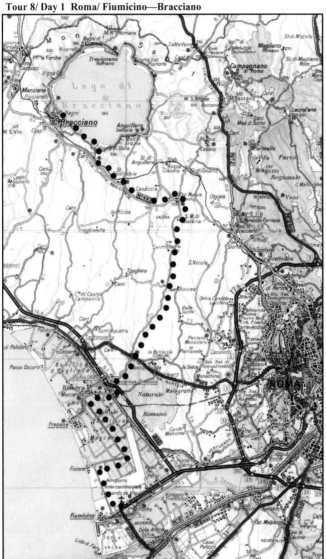

Touring Club Italiano, Auth. 04 November 2002

TOUR 8/ DAY 2

BRACCIANO—VITERBO
76 km/ 47 mi. Degree of Difficulty: PG-13

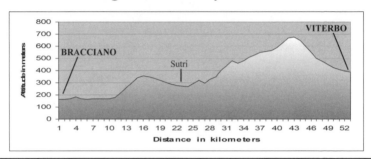

This route to **Viterbo** circles around the base of the Cimini Mountains and trades the panoramic views of Lago di Vico (see Tour 4) for visits to several medieval hilltowns. It is 21 km longer than the Lago di Vico route but has less climbing. It takes you through dense forests and rolling wheat fields, classic Italian countryside that is littered with ruins dating back to Etruscan times.

The route begins on the lake shore below **Bracciano**. You strike off clockwise around the lake in the direction of **Trevignano Romano.** This is a beautiful stretch of road with magnificent views over the water. There are a couple of short climbs and descents as the road weaves its way through the olive groves climbing the slopes above the lake.

About 10 km from Bracciano you will see a left turn with a sign for **Sutri.** Turning here the road immediately begins to climb steeply. As you wind your way up the mountainside there are spectacular views over Lago di Bracciano and the lake-front town of Trevignano. After about 3.5 km of sustained climbing the grade gradually lessens as you reach the summit. If you happen to do this ride on a clear day, the view back into the lake will be unforgettable. Two kilometers of more or less flat riding over the top of the ridge bring you to the descent down the other side. At 25 km from Bracciano you will hit an intersection with **N 2**, the **Via Cassia**.

You turn left on the Via Cassia and follow the signs to Sutri, which is about 2 km down the road. As you approach Sutri there are spectacular Etruscan tombs along the left side of the road. A few hundred meters beyond the tombs you will see the town built up on the cliff-side on the opposite side of the narrow valley. Sutri is a gem of a medieval village complete with ramparts, towers, fortified gates and tiny cobblestone streets.

Leaving Sutri follow the signs in the direction of **Fabrica di Roma**. A short distance down the road you will pass through the hamlet of **Fonte Vivola.** At each intersection you come to, simply follow the signs for Fabrica di Roma. You are now on a quiet country road with hardly any traffic. The trees give way occasionally the views up the slopes of Monti Cimini above you to the left. Wheat fields, vineyards, and olive groves roll away to your right. About 14 km from Sutri (37 km from Bracciano) you will reach an intersection with a left turn for Fabrica di Roma. You can see its tile roofs and the tower of its castle a short distance up hill. This quaint medieval hilltown is well worth the short climb up to its gates to explore its narrow streets. To continue on, you return to this intersection and follow the signs for **Vignanello.**

The 8 km to Vignanello contour along the slopes of the mountainside. There are several short, steep climbs as the road negotiates it way through the eroded hillsides. Vignanello sits on a long rocky outcrop above neat rows of olives trees and grape vines. As you come into town, follow the bulls-eye signs to the historic town center. When you reach the main street, turn right onto **Corso Jiacomo Matteotti** and follow the signs out of town in the direction of **Soriano nel Cimino.**

Leaving town the road plunges down into a narrow river valley and climbs just as steeply up the other side. This up and down pattern continues for the next 9 km until you hit a really steep climb up to Soriano. This classic hilltown is dominated by its fortress, the Castello Orsini. Narrow lanes weave past stone houses up the steep slope to the castle walls.

On leaving Soriano follow signs for **Viterbo.** This will take you down into a narrow ravine below the old city and of course up the other side. The road then rolls through a dense chestnut forest for about 8 km until you reach an intersection with **N 204.** Here you turn left in the direction of Viterbo.

About 4 km down the road you will reach the pleasant town of **Bagnaia**. It is famous for the ornate gardens of the summer palace of the bishops of Viterbo. A tall round tower defends the main gate into the old section of town and its labyrinth of alleys and streets. From Bagnaia it is a gentle 5 km descent into Viterbo.

The historic section of Viterbo is enclosed by impressive walls. A ring-road circles the walls, and massive gates allow access into the old section. The road from Bagnaia brings you to the northeast corner of the walls. If you go straight when you reach the busy intersection with the ring-road, you will soon reach the Porta Fiorentina gate which allows you to duck inside the walls and escape the traffic. Viterbo is a university town, and there are plenty of hotels. You should have no difficulty finding a place to stay even during the summer months.

Degree of Difficulty: This ride has two long climbs. The first one comes after a 10 km warm-up along the shores of Lago di Bracciano. The climb up out of the lake's volcanic basin is 3.5 km and steep. The second climb is the slog up to Soriano nel Cimino. It is not really steep until just below the town. There are also lots of other little ups and downs along the route to keep you loose. Rating: PG-13.

Highlights: The highlights of your day will be visiting the quaint medieval towns of Sutri, Fabrica di Roma, Vignanello, Soriano, and Bagnaia. Each of their castles and walls and cobblestone squares will seem more picturesque than the last. The quiet riding through this lovely countryside is bicycle touring at its best.

km	Place Name	Cafes	Shops, Mkts	Lodging	Camping	Bank	Bike Shop	Quaintness Rating
23	Sutri	•	•	•		•		*****
42	Fabrica di Roma	•	•	•		•		***
50	Vignanello	•	•	•		•		***
58	Soriano	•	•	•		•		****
71	Bagnaia	•	•	•		•		***
73	La Quercia	•	•					
76	Viterbo	•	•	•		•	•	***

Tour 8/ Day 2 Bracciano—Viterbo

Touring Club Italiano, Auth. 04 November 2002

TOUR 8/ DAY 3

VITERBO—ORVIETO
55 km/ 34 mi. Degree of Difficulty: PG

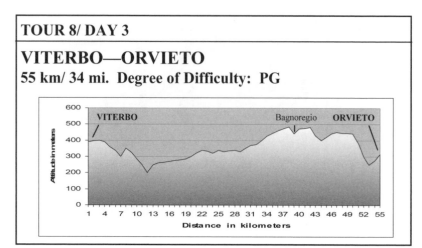

This route takes you through beautiful countryside past medieval hilltowns to **Orvieto,** which is perhaps the quintessential Italian hilltown. Orvieto sits atop sheer sandstone cliffs. Its rambling stone houses crowd to the very edge. Church spires and towers rise above the red tile roofs. At its center is a cathedral which rivals any outside of Rome. If you can some-how time your ride to arrive at Orvieto at sunset when its walls are lit up in golden light, you will be rewarded with one of the most marvelous sights in all of Italy.

Starting from the **Porta Fiorentina** gate in the old section of **Viterbo,** turn right and retrace your steps in the direction of **Bagnaia.** The road climbs gently up a tree-lined boulevard for 2 km to the town of **La Quercia**. As you enter the main square of town look for a left turn with a sign for **Vitorchiano.**

The road to Vitorchiano plunges down a steep descent through overgrown pastures and fields. This is immediately followed by an equally steep climb up to an overpass above a highway at the modern town of **Paparano**. From Paparano the road descends again for about 2 km to the gates of the medieval village of Vitorchiano.

You will find no tour buses parked at Vitorchiano — at least not yet. There are no trinket shops, no post card stands, not even a Tourist In-formation Office. This is the kind of treasure that you only discover by accident. Behind the burly fortified gate you will find delightful twisting alleys with laundry strung overhead. Tiny markets and shops are squeezed into narrow doorways. There is a feeling that life toils on here as it always has, oblivious to the outside world.

Vitorchiano is built out on a tongue of crumbling rock above a brushy ravine. On leaving town the road descends steeply into this ravine for about 2 km. On the way down you get great views back up at the jumble of stone house perched on the cliff. At the bottom of the descent the road crosses a bridge over a soupy stream and then climbs steeply up the other side. You will pass a right turn with a sign for **Sippicciano**; continue straight. The road rolls along through open fields and occasional stands of trees. About 18 km from Viterbo you will pass through the quiet town of **Magugnano.** Follow signs for **Montefiascone** and **Bagnoregio** through town. The road continues more or less flat for about 5 km until you reach an intersection with the main road from Viterbo. Turn right here following the signs for Bagnoregio.

Orvieto

From this turn you will be pedaling along the side of a ridge. Across the valley to your left you will be able to see the spires of Montefiascone. The road then begins to roll through farm land and patches of forest. At about 38 km from Viterbo you will begin to see a remarkable stone village built on a high point of rock off to your right. This is the village of **Civita di Bagnoregio.** It rivals Vitorchiano for charm but is not quite undiscovered.   It is the site of the original medieval town of Bagnoregio, which was abandoned over time due to its crumbling rock foundations. What remains is a wonderful time capsule of a medieval town. It is connected to the modern town by a pedestrian causeway across a steep ravine and is worth a detour off the road to explore.

From Bagnoregio the road descends steeply from town and then climbs up to a traffic circle. Here you bear right in the direction of **Orvieto**. The road descends for about 2 km and then rolls along the top of a ridge-line. At about 50 km from Viterbo you will pass through the pleasant village of **Canale.** At this point the view down over Orvieto opens up before you. If you happen to reach this point in the late afternoon with the golden rays of the sun lighting up the cliffs and walls of Orvieto you could have a near-religious experience. The road sails down a long series of switchbacks, and the view seems only to improve as you approach the city. Unfortunately you will be wrenched out of your reverie when you hit the bottom of the descent and have to face the steep 3 km climb up to the city gates. Hopefully the dramatic sight of the cliff-side pock-marked with ancient Etruscan tombs will be enough to distract you from the effort.

At the top of the climb you pass through the massive city gates Orvieto into a labyrinth of cobblestone streets. You will not be alone here; in fact it may be too crowded to ride your bike down the main street. There is no shortage of accommodations for the legions of visitors who tramp through here each day, but most of the hotels are down below near the train station at **Ovieto Scalo**. If you want to stay in the old section of the city, which is much more interesting, it is best to book ahead in the during the summer months.

Degree of Difficulty: The hardest climb of the day will be the last one up to the gates of Orvieto. There are several other shorter, steeper climbs to tackle, but none that are likely to provoke more than mild profanity. Rating: PG.

Highlights: Vitorchiano, Civita di Bagnoregio, and Orvieto are three of the most spectacular hilltowns you can find anywhere in Italy. The riding to get to these towns is quiet and mostly traffic-free. This is 5-star touring.

km	Place Name	Cafes	Shops, Mkts	Lodging	Camping	Bank	Bike Shop	Quaintness Rating
2	La Quercia	•	•					
8	Paparano	•						
10	Vitorchiano	•	•	•				*****
18	Magugnano	•	•					
38	Bagnoregio	•	•	•		•		*****
55	Orvieto	•	•	•		•	•	*****

Tour 8/ Day 3 Viterbo—Orvieto

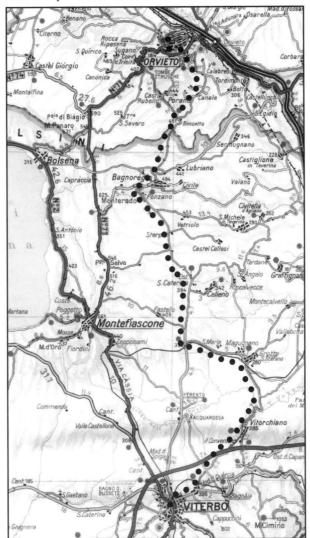

Touring Club Italiano, Auth. 04 November 2002

TOUR 8/ DAY 4

ORVIETO—SPOLETO
87 km/ 54 mi. Degree of Difficulty: PG-13

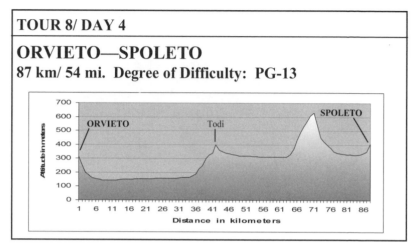

This is a fairly long route with some significant climbing. It takes you from **Orvieto** to the classic hill-top town of **Todi** and then on to **Spoleto**.

From the old section of Orvieto follow the signs down the steep descent to **Orvieto Scalo.** This is a busy modern suburb built around the train station. Weave your way through town and get on the main road heading south in the direction of **Roma.** Just outside of town this becomes a wide secondary highway that parallels the train line and the Autostrada. It is not particularly scenic, and there is a fair amount of traffic traveling at speed, but it is rideable. About 12 km from the old city (7 km from Orvieto Scalo) the road jogs left across the valley going over the Autostrada and the unnaturally green Tevere River. On the far side of the river there is an intersection where you continue straight following the sign for Todi.

A short distance upstream the road meets **Lago di Corbara** and runs along the shore. It is reasonably scenic; there are a few quaint stone farm houses set in pastures across the lake. You can expect a fair amount of traffic on this road, and it goes by fast. On the plus side the road is almost flat as it travels up the valley towards Todi. You stay on this road for about 16 km (31 km from Orvieto) until you reach a right turn with a sign for Todi. The main road crosses the river and continues up the opposite side of the valley. You continue straight and begin to climb. After about 2 km you will hit a series of steep switchbacks which bob and weave up through vineyards and olive groves towards the city walls. There are great views back down the valley.

It is a steep grunt up to Todi, but it is worth the effort. This wonderful walled town has preserved all its medieval charm without acquiring too many modern accoutrements. Steep cobblestone streets wind up to a square at the top of the town. There are many shops and cafes here, and as it is about the half-way point of the ride, it makes a good lunch stop.

From Todi follow the signs for **Acquasparta**. From the central square at the top of the town a screaming descent down slick cobblestone streets rolls you out the city gate. At the intersection outside the walls bear left following the signs for Acquasparta. The road contours along the side of the ridge with great views back towards Todi then descends down into the valley. The road to Acquasparta follows the river and is flat and mostly traffic–free.

The town of Acquasparta is up on your right off the main road. Just as you pass by it, look for a left turn with a sign for **Spoleto**. The road crosses under the Autostrada highway and then begins to climb up the ridge opposite Acquasparta. It grinds relentlessly up for about 8 km, but the views over the patch-work countryside below are spectacular. As you near the top of the climb it becomes more heavily forested. Soon you are speeding down the other side. If anything the views over the tiny villages on this side of the pass are even more spectacular.

About 3 km down from the summit you will flash through the tiny hamlet of **Firenzuola**, a collection of stone huts surrounded by olive groves. At about 6 km from the top you will roll through **Crocemaroggia** which has a few shops. Just beyond Crocemaroggia the downhill grade peters out and you have to pedal again.

As you approach Spoleto the rural farmland gives way to warehouses and factories, and then modern apartment buildings. Just about the time you are deciding that there is nothing special about Spoleto you will catch a glimpse of the old city with its forbidding fortress high above. If you follow the bulls-eye signs and the brown "Centro Storico" (historical center) signs you will soon come to the old city walls. Narrow cobblestone streets will lead you up to the charming old section of town.

There are plenty of hotels in Spoleto, but you should try for one as high up in the old section as possible. Even during the summer months you should have no trouble finding a room unless you arrive during a festival.

Degree of Difficulty: At 87 km this is a long day. There are two tough climbs, up to Todi and up above Acquasparta. However, these uphill sections represent only about 10% of your day. The rest of the ride is flat or downhill. Rating: PG-13.

Highlights: The highlights of this ride will be tough climbs, spectacular descents, easy cruising, and unforgettable views. For cultural content there are the lovely hilltowns of Todi and Spoleto, which would be all the more impressive had you not just come from Orvieto.

km	Place Name	Cafes	Shops, Mkts	Lodging	Camping	Bank	Bike Shop	Quaintness Rating
41	Todi	●	●	●		●		*****
62	Acquasparta	●	●	●		●		*
77	Crocemaroggia	●	●					
81	Baiano	●	●					
87	Spoleto	●	●	●	●	●	●	*****

Tour 8/ Day 4 Orvieto—Spoleto

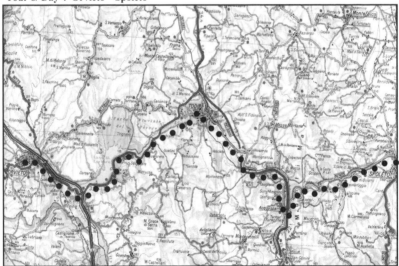

Touring Club Italiano, Auth. 04 November 2002

TOUR 8/ DAY 5

SPOLETO—PIEDICOLLE
69 km/ 43 mi. Degree of Difficulty: PG-13

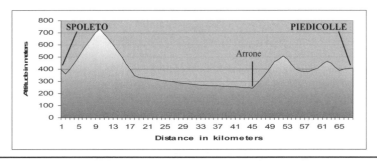

This is a magnificent ride. It starts with a long climb first thing in the morning when it is cool. This is followed by a wonderful cruise down the Nera River valley to the town of **Arrone**. From here another long climb takes you up into the rugged mountains of Umbria. Then you drop down into a broad agricultural valley which leads to the town of **Rieti**. At the head of this valley you will find the tiny village of **Piedicolle**. The only business in Piedicolle is the **Albergo—Restorante Peppe Parco alle Noci.** It is a country inn set in a lovely park-like setting, and is worth the journey all by itself.

Your day begins with a short steep descent down through the streets of **Spoleto** to the valley below. Initially you should follow signs to **Norcia** and **Cascia.** This will lead you north of town to an on-ramp for **N 3**, the busy **Via Flaminia** highway. Go past the on-ramp and continue up hill following signs for **N 395** to Norcia. This beautiful quiet road climbs up through pasture and stands of trees affording breathtaking views down into the valley. After about 10 km of climbing you reach the crest of the **Forca di Cerro.** From here you sail down 9 km of twisting switchbacks into the Nera River valley. As you coast down you will see a tiny stone village perched on the opposite side of the valley. This is the village of **Vallo di Nera**, a wonderful tiny hilltown largely forgotten by the march of modern times. The short climb up to its walls is well worth the effort.

When you reach the main road in the valley, **N 209**, turn right following the signs for **Terni.** The access road for Vallo di Nera is on the left about 1 km down the road. You will continue down the Nera valley on route N 209 for the next 26 km. This gentle downhill takes you past tiny stone villages heaped up on rocky promontories above the valley floor. Occasionally you will see ruined watch towers built up on the steep slopes above the river. If you happen to do this ride on a weekend, you will be joined by hundreds of local riders — some in garish team jerseys in tight packs of 60 or more riders, others in tee-shirts out for a spin on their three-speeds. They will come in all sizes, ages, and degrees of fitness, and they are almost entirely male. There seem to be very few Italian women out on the weekend rides.

The wonderful 26 km spin continues all the way to the town of Arrone. The modern section of town is along the road and has hotels, shops, and supermarkets. The medieval section is across the river high on a rocky outcrop. Watch for a left turn with signs for Arrone, **Piediluco**, and **Rieti.**

Above Castiglione

As soon as you cross the river over to Arrone you begin to climb. The road skirts around the old section of Arrone and continues up a narrow side-valley that cuts into the mountains. The road winds back and forth up the steep slope. About 2 km above Arrone you will pass through tiny **Castiglione**, which has a few stone houses and a bar/ restaurant. Terraced olive trees march up the hillside above Castiglione. You will know you are nearing the top when the olive trees give way to forest and finally pasture. It is about 6 km of sustained climbing to the top, but you are rewarded with a 5 km descent down the other side through stands of trees with intermittent views of the lake-side town of Piediluco and its hilltop fortress.

At the bottom of the descent you will hit an intersection where you turn left following signs for Rieti. The road skirts around Piediluco and begins to climb away from the lake. After two or three kilometers of gentle climbing a stunning view opens up before you as you crest the ridge. Patch-work fields dot a broad valley ringed with mountains. At the far end you can see the spires of city of Rieti. From here broad switchbacks swoop to the valley floor.

At the bottom of the descent you will meet an intersection with a left turn for **Rivodutri** and **Leonessa**. Turning here the road proceeds up to the very head of the valley. About 3 km from the intersection you will come to a right turn with a sign for Piedicolle and the Albergo—Restorante Peppe Parco alle Noci.

The road goes over a clear stream and to the right you will see the shady lawns of the inn. You really can't miss it as there is nothing else there. The Peppe Parco alle Noci is a country inn with clean simple rooms and an excellent restaurant. It has been run by the Servi family for 35 years, and it is their warmth and hospitality which makes this hotel a destination. You can contact the hotel through its website at www.paginegialle.it/parconoci, or by telephone at 390746 685755. The mailing address is listed in the Appendices.

There is a certain risk in relying on this one hotel. You could arrive and find out there is wedding and the place is booked. So it would be prudent to book ahead. If you decide to risk it and find the hotel is full, you can ride down the valley to Rieti about 15 km away where there are many hotels.

Degree of Difficulty: There are two big climbs on this route. The one above Spoleto is about 10 km, and the one above Arrone is about 6 km; both will have you working hard. The rest of the ride is an easy spin, especially the 26 km down the Nera River valley. Overall this is a great ride, but the two climbs bump up the degree of difficulty. Rating: PG-13.

Highlights: The climb up above Spoleto with the views over the city and into the valley beyond is unforgettable. The Nera River valley with its many tiny hilltop towns is equally delightful. The climb up through the olive groves above Arrone and the views into the Rieti valley are also spectacular. Finally you get to spend the night at a wonderful undiscovered country inn with friendly proprietors and a great restaurant.

km	Place Name	Cafes	Shops, Mkts	Lodging	Camping	Bank	Bike Shop	Quaintness Rating
21	Vallo di Nera	●	●					*****
24	Castel San Felice	●						****
25	Sant'Anatolia di Narco	●	●					***
27	Scheggino	●	●				●	*****
34	Macenano	●	●					***
39	Ferentillo	●	●					
45	Arrone	●	●	●		●		***
48	Castiglione	●						**
69	Piedicolle	●		●				***

Tour 8/ Day 5 Spoleto—Piedicolle

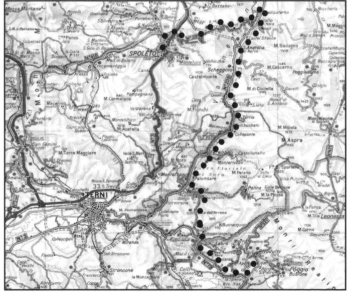

Touring Club Italiano, Auth. 04 November 2002

TOUR 8/ DAY 6

PIEDICOLLE—NORCIA
67 km/ 42 mi. Degree of Difficulty: PG

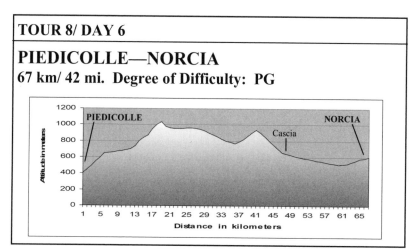

This route takes you through the remote hinterlands of Umbria. In contrast to the rolling wheat fields of Tuscany, here you will see a dramatic landscape of deep valleys and high forested mountains. This rugged country is sparsely populated, and you will have the road to yourself.

From sleepy **Piedicolle** you continue up the valley to the town of **Rivodutri.** The valley walls close in as you climb higher. Rivodutri sits above a steep slope with a long view down the valley towards **Rieti.** On the final approach to the town you will pass a ruined tower guarding the last tight switchback below the walls.

From Revodutri follow the sign for **Leonessa.** The road continues higher up the mountainside. About 6 km from Piedicolle you will reach an intersection at the town of **Valliola.** Here you turn right onto **N 521**, the main road to Leonessa.

From Valliola the road contours along a steep, forested ridge. The trees keep the road shady and cool. As you approach the village of **Fucetto,** about 14 km from Piedicolle, the grade increases. From here the road climbs up the side of a mountain valley, and at 18.5 km you enter a tunnel. Fortunately the tunnel is only about 50 meters long and marks the summit of the climb. On the far side a vast bowl-shaped valley opens up below you. The road drops away in a broad curve. At the bottom of the descent there is a remarkable bridge high above the valley floor that gently rolls you out onto the plain. The view all the way down is spectacular.

About 3 km beyond the bridge there is a right turn for Leonessa. This is a ski resort town, and you will see the chairlifts snaking up the mountainside. Leonessa boasts a ruined castle and a pleasant medieval section, but unless you need a snack or water, it is not worth a detour. Opposite the right turn for Leonessa there is a left turn for **Cascia,** your next destination.

The road to Cascia heads due north away from Leonessa. It's long and straight and slightly downhill. You spin along for the next 10 km into a river valley. You will pass the medieval town of **Monteleone** built high up on a ridge and the modern village of **Ruscio** down in the valley next to the road. Just beyond Ruscio the valley narrows down to a dramatic rock-walled gorge. The road then crosses the river and begins to climb its way out. It snakes up for about 4 km and then falls away in a steep 7 km descent down to the bustling town of Cascia. Here you will find many cafes and a shady roadside park. Cascia is a great place to take an break.

From Cascia you continue down the main road below town. At length you will come to an intersection with a profusion of signs. You need only look for the one to **Norcia** which points straight ahead. This takes you down a gentle 12 km descent along a narrow river valley. It ends at the village of **Serravalle,** where you pick up N 396, the main road to Norcia.

The last 7 km to Norcia on N 396 go gently uphill. There will be a little excitement when you encounter a 200 meter-long unlit tunnel. If a car catches you in there it will sound like a freight train. A few kilometers beyond the tunnel you will reach the gates of Norcia.

Norcia is a beautiful town with its medieval walls intact. Inside narrow streets snake past shops and open air cafes. The main square is dominated by a statue of Saint Benedict commemorating his birth place. The culinary specialty in this region is wild boar, and stuffed boars' heads seem to be a favorite decoration in the shops. There are several hotels to choose from both inside and outside the walls. Norcia is far enough off the beaten path that you should not need reservations even during the summer months.

Degree of Difficulty: Most of the climbing on this route occurs early in the ride when it should be cool. There is a steep section up to Rivodutri and again up to the tunnel above Leonessa, but for the most part this is a relatively easy ride. Rating: PG.

Highlights: The view towards Rieti from above Rivodutri is spectacular. The descent on the way down to Leonessa is also unforgettable. The rugged countryside, the quiet roads, and the long uninterrupted descents make this a great ride.

km	Place Name	Cafes	Shops, Mkts	Lodging	Camping	Bank	Bike Shop	Quaintness Rating
4	Rivodutri	●	●					**
6	Valliola	●						*
17	Fucetto	●						*
25	Leonessa	●	●	●		●		**
35	Ruscio	●	●	●				
48	Cascia	●	●	●		●		***
67	Norcia	●	●	●		●		****

Tour 8/ Day 6 Piedicolle—Norcia

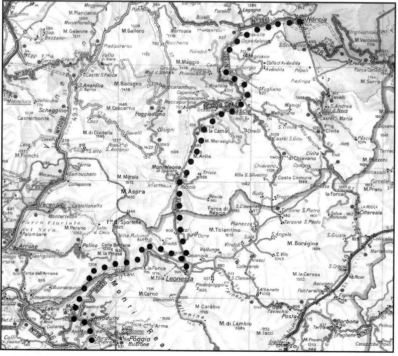

Touring Club Italiano, Auth. 04 November 2002

TOUR 8/ DAY 7

NORCIA—VISSO
51 km/ 32 mi. Degree of Difficulty: R

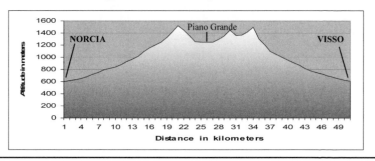

Today's ride takes you through some of the most spectacular scenery in all of Italy. This route leads you up out of the **Norcia** valley to an alpine basin called the **Piano Grande.** Here you will find the tiny village of **Castelluccio** perched on a knoll overlooking a verdant expanse of wildflowers. It is a long grind to get up there, but worth every pedal stroke. And once at the top you get to enjoy a 20 km descent down to the walled town of **Visso.**

From the gates of Norcia head south from the old section of town following signs for **Ascoli Piceno.** This road is fairly busy and goes through a modern commercial district, but after about 3 km you turn left off the main road at the signs for Ascoli Piceno and Castelluccio. The road immediately begins to climb, but there is almost no traffic.

At 7.5 km from Norcia you will reach a traffic circle where you bear left in the direction of Castelluccio. As you climb higher the view over the Norcia valley gradually opens up. The road switchbacks up the mountainside, but the grade remains gentle. The views are spectacular all the way up.

At 19 km from Norcia you will reach an intersection where again you turn left for Castelluccio. The road soon climbs above timber line and on the grassy slopes of the mountain you may see horses grazing or a sheep-herder and his dogs tending their flock. As you approach the top of the climb the grade begins to steepen. Just below the summit you will pass a restaurant/ bar called the **Refugio Perugia**. It is another 500 meters to the top — 20.5 km from the gates of Norcia.

The view down into the Piano Grande basin is absolutely breathtaking. A screaming 3 km descent takes you down to the broad flat meadow, which even in August is filled with a profusion of wildflowers in every color; it is truly incredible. A ruler straight road takes you across the basin towards Castelluccio. On the way across you will pass a right turn for Ascoli Piceno. About 2 km beyond this turn you begin the fairly steep 1 km climb up to the town.

Castelluccio sits on a hill overlooking the broad expanse of the Piano Grande. It has a slightly down-at-the-heels atmosphere, but there are a couple of cafes, shops and the Hotel Sibilla. At the height of the summer you will find this town bustling with outdoor enthusiasts—hikers, hang gliders, horseback riders, mountain bikers, fellow bike tourers, and more. After the long climb up from Norcia, this makes an ideal stop for lunch.

From Castelluccio follow the signs out of town for Visso. A steep descent takes you down to another broad meadow of wild flowers. About 3 km across you begin to climb up to the **Passo di Gualdo**. A steep 1 km climb gets you to the top of the pass where there are marvelous views back towards

Piano Grande

Castelluccio. There is a spring at the top where you can splash your face or re-fill water bottles. From here it is 20 km downhill to Visso.

From the top of the pass the road plummets down into a narrow wooded valley. About 3 km down from the summit (37 km from Norcia) you will pass a hotel/ restaurant. About 7 km down you will flash by the tiny stone village of Gualdo. It has a pretty church and a sign for a pizzeria. Down below you can see the tile roofs of other villages clinging to the sides of the steep valley. The grade down this side of the Piano Grande is extremely steep and you would not want to ride it in the other direction.

At 44 km from Norcia you will come to the town of **Castelsantangelo**. It features a ruined tower overlooking the town and a few shops and cafes. There is also a sign for a rare campground nearby.

From Castelsantangelo the road descends more gently down the valley. About 6 km below the town you will pass a huge fish farm along side the road. The tanks seem to almost overflow with fish. Another kilometer and you will reach the walls of Visso. There are the crumbling remains of a castle on a rock overlooking the town. A fork below the castle directs you through a short tunnel to the right or along the walls to the left. You should bear left and skirt along the walls. After a short distance you will reach an intersection with signs for **Roma** to the left and **Macerata** to the right. Turning right will take you into the quaint square at the center of Visso. Unfortunately the town suffered heavy damage during the earth quake of 1997, and you may see buildings still shored up with baulks of timber. Otherwise this is a delightful medieval town undiscovered by modern tourism. There are two hotels in Visso and a third one about 1 km away in the hamlet of **San Antonio** in the direction of Macerata. You are far off the beaten path here, and there should be little competition for rooms.

Degree of Difficulty: With nearly 20 km of continuous climbing from Norcia to Piano Grande this is a challenging ride. The grade, however, is mild most of the way. You may find the steep descent down to Castesantangelo more fatiguing, as you will be bent over your brakes all the way down. Rating: R.

Highlights: This ride is about the views — all the way up and all the way down. The green velvet bowl of wild flowers in the Piano Grande is absolutely spectacular. If you could do only one ride in Italy, this might be it.

km	Place Name	Cafes	Shops, Mkts	Lodging	Camping	Bank	Bike Shop	Quaintness Rating
20	Refugio Perugia	●						**
30	Castelluccio	●	●	●	●			****
41	Gualdo	●						***
44	Castelsantangelo	●	●		●			**
51	Visso	●	●	●	●	●		****

Tour 8/ Day 7 Norcia—Visso

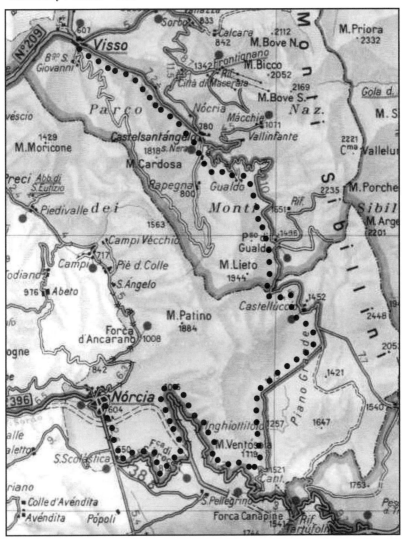

Touring Club Italiano, Auth. 04 November 2002

TOUR 8/ DAY 8

VISSO—SPELLO
69 km/ 43 mi. Degree of Difficulty: PG

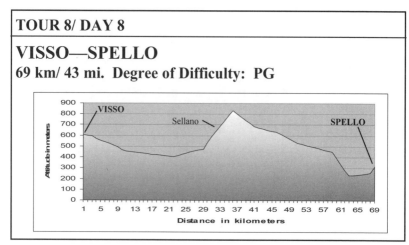

This route rolls down the Nera River valley from **Visso** to **Borgo Cerreto**, a distance of 22 km downhill! At Borgo Cerreto the climbing begins, but the real work of the day does not come until you approach the town of **Sellano**.   After about 7 km of steep grade you coast down hill again to the town of **Foligno,** a distance of 27 km. From there it is 6 km of flat riding to the spectacular medieval town of **Spello.**

Starting out from Visso you follow the signs for **Roma** and **Terni**. If you find yourself going uphill, you have made a wrong turn. The road descends gently down the narrow forested valley. Like the ride from **Spoleto** to **Piedicolle** (Tour 8/ Day 5) this is effortless riding, and if you care to pedal you will make good time.

At 19 km from Visso you will approach the town of **Treponzo,** and here the valley narrows down to a dramatic gorge. Beyond Treponzo, past a turn for **Norcia,** you will come to the village of Borgo Cerreto, which has a gas station and a few shops. The picturesque old part of Borgo Cerreto is built on a rock above the road. You turn right here at the sign for Sellano.

The road to Sellano strikes off up a side valley. It follows the Vigi River into the rugged countryside. The grade going up the valley bottom is very mild and is just enough to get you warmed up for the steep section coming up. About 7 km from Borgo Cerreto the valley narrows down and the road begins to switchback up one side. You can see Sellano ahead, but this is not the end of the climbing; it goes on for another 4 km above Sellano. The town itself is on a dramatic site with views over the surrounding mountains. It was founded by the Romans 2000 years ago and has a won-

derful historic feel. Unfortunately it was at the very epicenter of the disas-
trous earthquake of October, 1997, which damaged much of the region.
Sellano got the worst of it and many of its buildings are still under repair.
At almost half-way up the climb Sellano provides a convenient place for a
break and is interesting to explore as well.

Above Sellano the road continues to climb past the adjacent village of **Villamagina** and up to a high forested ridge. Once at the top you
are rewarded with a spectacular view back towards Sellano and down into
the next valley. The road falls away, and down you go. At each intersection you come to, follow signs for **Casenove.** The road sails down into a
pleasant forested valley punctuated by occasional farm houses and pastures.

Forty-six kilometers into your day you will reach the town of **Rasiglia.** This town is remarkable mostly for its ruined castle and curtain wall
that crowns a low hill above the houses and shops along the river. About 2
km below Rasiglia you will come to the town of **Serrone.** This is a village
with streets so narrow a stop light has been set up to allow cars to pass
through one way at a time. Like all the towns in this region Serrone suffered heavy damage in the '97 earthquake. Many buildings appear to have
been braced with timbers and abandoned to the slow pace of reconstruction.
Casenove, a few kilometers farther down the valley is in similar condition.
Here you meet **N 77**, a fairly busy road which takes you down to Foligno.

Foligno is a bustling, modern town. The trick is to navigate your
way through town without getting shunted off in the wrong direction. As
you come into town on N 77, first follow the bulls-eye signs to the city
center. Once you have crossed a set of railroad tracks, then look for signs
to **Assisi.**

As you emerge on the far side of town watch for a right turn with
a sign for **San Lorenzo Vecchio.** This takes you back over the railroad
tracks. About 50 meters past the tracks there is another right turn that takes
you under a highway overpass. On the other side of the overpass you will

find a sign for Spello. This puts you on the road that parallels the east side of the highway and that will take you directly to the gates of Spello. If you miss this turn you will get diverted out into the broad flat valley and have to find your way back across the highway.

Spello is a wonderful medieval hilltown which rivals better-known **Assisi** in charm but without the legions of tourists. Inside its walls you will find a warren of narrow cobblestone alleys and streets, Roman ruins, quaint shady piazzas, and clear fountains. There are several hotels to choose from, but this close to Assisi it is best to book ahead.

Degree of Difficulty: This ride has only one obstacle: the 7 km climb up past Sellano. Otherwise it is mostly downhill. Rating: PG.

Highlights: The long gentle descents on this route are marvelous. The villages of Treponzo, Sellano, and its close neighbor Villamagina add to its enjoyment. Lower down the valley Rasiglia and Serrone are also wonderful relics of the long history of Umbria. Finally there is Spello which rivals any hilltown in the region for quaintness and charm.

km	Place Name	Cafes	Shops, Mkts	Lodging	Camping	Bank	Bike Shop	Quaintness Rating
14	Casali Belforte	●		●				
19	Treponzo	●	●					***
22	Borgo Cerreto	●	●					**
32	Sellano	●	●	●				****
33	Villamagina	●	●					**
46	Rasiglia	●	●					**
48	Serrone	●	●					*
49	Casenove	●	●					
63	Foligno	●	●	●		●	●	
69	Spello	●	●	●	●	●		*****

Tour 8/ Day 8 Visso—Spello

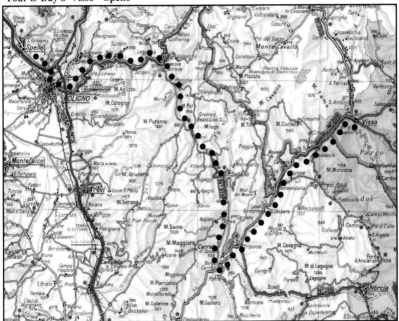

Touring Club Italiano, Auth. 04 November 2002

TOUR 8/ DAY 9

SPELLO—SAN CASCIANO DEI BAGNI
98 km/ 61 mi. Degree of Difficulty: PG-13

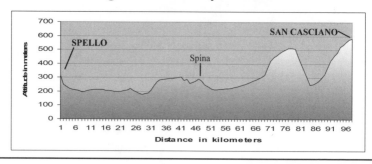

This is a relatively long route with most of the hard riding coming at the end. During the early part of the ride you have great views across the valley towards **Assisi** and **Perugia**. Later you pass the remarkable tiny walled villages of **Spina** and **Castiglione della Valle**. Finally after some heavy lifting you reach the medieval jewel of **San Casciano dei Bagni**, where you can soak away any aches and pains in the 2000 year-old thermal springs.

Leaving **Spello** from its south gate ride north along the base of its walls in the direction of Assisi. A few hundred meters up the road you will see a left turn with signs for the town of **Cannara.** Turning here you strike off across a flat expanse of agricultural land. After about 8 km you will reach this busy farming town on the banks of the canalized Topino River. At Cannara you turn left and cross the river following signs for **Bettona** and **Torgiano.** This takes you across to the far side of the valley. Here the road turns north and runs along the base of the mountains.

The medieval hilltown of Bettona sits high up on the mountain-side facing Assisi across the valley. It is a short steep climb up to town but worth the effort. Its medieval walls are intact and it has an untouristy air. Past the turn for Bettona the road continues flat for about 5 km before gradually climbing up to Torgiano.

As you approach Torgiano initially follow the bulls-eye signs to the city center. When you reach a busy intersection with the old section of town to your left, bear right following the signs for Perugia. This will bring you down into the broad valley on the other side of Torgiano. After about

1.5 km you will reach another intersection with signs for Perugia and **San Martino in Campo** to the left. Turning here the road leads you to the Autostrada which roars off towards Perugia; you cross over the overpass to San Martino in Campo.

San Martino in Campo is a modern suburb of Perugia. Riding past the supermarkets and shopping centers you will soon come to traffic circle where you bear left following the sign to **San Martino in Colle.** Two kilometers of flat riding across the valley brings you to a short steep climb up through neat rows of grape vines. At the top of the ridge you hit an intersection with **N 371** and signs for **Marsciano** to the left. Turning here you roll through the unremarkable town of San Martino in Colle and continue along the top of the ridge in the direction of Marsciano.

As you pedal along the ridge you will pass through several small towns. About 7 km from San Martino in Colle look for a right turn with a sign for **Olmeto.** If you reach the town of **San Valentino** you have gone too far and missed the turn.

The road to Olmeto goes down into a shallow valley, then up the ridge on the far side. Beyond this ridge it again drops down into another valley followed by climb. Ahead you can see a collection of buildings at the top of a round hill. This is the wonderful walled village of **Spina.** It was once a castle with towers at each corner of its walls, but gradually over the centuries it has been converted into housing. Today you find an almost comical example of urban planning gone awry. Inside the formidable gates is a rabbit warren of alleys just wide enough for a donkey cart that weave between and beneath lurching and leaning stone and beam houses. It is one of the most interesting and original medieval villages you will find anywhere.

From Spina follow the signs for **Castiglione della Valle.** The road rolls through beautiful hills of vineyards, olive groves, and fields of sunflowers and wheat. You know you are well off the beaten tourist path because the only cars that pass are battered Fiats, not roaring Mercedes. About 5 km from Spina you will begin a easy tree-lined descent into a flat valley. Ahead you can see the curious town of Castiglione in Valle built hap-hazardly up on a rock. The main road circles around the base of town and reaches a fork on the far side. Here you bear left here towards **Monte Petrolio** and **Tavernelle.**

The road follows a shallow river valley past Monte Petrolio to an intersection with **N 220.** You turn left here and pedal through the modern town of Tavernelle. N 220 continues up the valley past a giant bottling plant with two huge red and white smoke stacks. At the town of **Piegaro** the valley narrows down and you reach a steep series of switchbacks which climb up the head of the valley. At the top the road settles back to a gentle grade. About 9 km above Piegaro, 78 km from Spello, N 220 meets **N 71.** Here you turn right following the sign to **Citta della Pieve**, which you can see just up the road. As you pedal towards Citta di Pieve watch for a left turn with a sign for **Ponticelli.**

Ponticelli lies at the bottom of a beautiful descent down through ancient gnarled olive trees. The town itself is a gritty railroad depot, but you pass quickly through it and cross the valley. After crossing the railroad tracks follow the signs for **Piazze** and **San Casciano die Bagni.**

A steep climb greets you on the far side of the valley, but above the hamlet of Piazze the grade lessens. When you finally crest the hill, a gentle descent takes you down to the walls of San Casciano dei Bagni.

San Casciano is a delightful place with the relaxed, unhurried atmosphere of a thermal spa. There are plenty of hotels in town, but the more charming ones are in the old section. In this forgotten corner of Tuscany there should be no need for reservations.

San Casciano dei Bagni

Degree of Difficutly: This is a long ride with many rolling hills to climb. The only major climb is the last one up to San Casciano. Rating: PG-13.

Highlights: This is wonderful, quiet route through lovely rural countryside largely free of traffic. You will pass the interesting medieval towns of Bettona, Spina, and Castiglione in Valle. Finally you end up in largely undiscovered San Casciano dei Bagni.

km	Place Name	Cafes	Shops, Mkts	Lodging	Camping	Bank	Bike Shop	Quaintness Rating
8	Cannara	●	●			●	●	
29	San Martino in Campo	●	●			●		
34	San Martino in Colle	●	●	●		●		
47	Spina	●	●					*****
52	Castiglione della Valle	●	●					***
62	Tavernelle	●	●	●		●		
84	Ponticelli	●	●					
98	San Casciano dei Bagni	●	●	●		●		*****

Tour 8/ Day 9 Spello—San Casciano dei Bagni

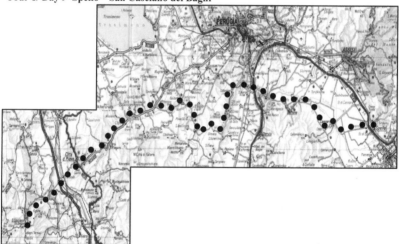

Touring Club Italiano, Auth. 04 November 2002

TOUR 8/ DAY 10

SAN CASCIANO DEI BAGNI—AMELIA
80 km/ 50 mi. Degree of Difficulty: PG

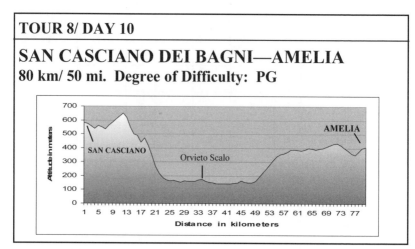

This route crosses your outbound track at **Orvieto** and continues on to the ancient hilltown of Amelia. This is mostly easy riding on quiet roads except in the immediate vicinity of Orvieto.

From **San Casciano dei Bagni** you head south out of town in the direction of the spa facilities. The road gently descends for several kilometers and then climbs up to an intersection with signs for **Acquapendente** to the right and **Allerona** and **Orvieto** to the left. From this intersection you can see the quaint village of **Trevignano** just down the hill in the direction of Acquapendente. It is built on a razor-thin spur of rock with a tiny castle at one end.

Turning left towards Orvieto you climb for about 1 km into a cool forest. The grade gradually eases as you climb. At 10 km from San Casciano you will reach an intersection where you turn right following the signs for Allerona and Orvieto. After a short climb the road crests the ridge and begins to descend down through a wonderful pine forest with pic-nic tables set off in the deep carpet of pine needles. You will pass two roadside springs where you can fill water bottles. The descent continues down and down through the trees for several more kilometers. After a brief flat you will break out of the trees and descend down to the town of Allerona. This quaint town sits high on a steep slope with commanding views over the valley below. A brief climb takes you up to its fortified gate. The road then skirts around below the historic section and plunges down through terraced olive trees into the valley.

After 10 km of almost uninterrupted descent you will reach the valley floor at the gritty town of **Allerona Scalo.** As you enter town you will pass under an elevated railway line that looks like a modern Roman aqueduct. On the way down the main street of town keep a sharp look out for a right turn with a blue Orvieto sign. This turn is easy to miss, and if you reach an overpass for a spur line of railroad tracks, you have gone too far.

From Allerona Scalo the road travels through the flat valley past miles of vineyards. You can soon see Orvieto built high atop its sheer cliffs. As you approach the town you will enter a commercial area, and the traffic increases. Eventually you will come to a busy intersection where you bear left to skirt around the base of the old city to **Orvieto Scalo.**

From busy Orvieto Scalo you follow the signs for the A-1 Autostrada to **Roma.** This puts you on a road with a wide shoulder heading south down the valley. About 7 km from Orvieto Scalo the road makes an abrupt left-hand jog across the turbid Tevere River in the direction of **Todi.** Just across the bridge there is a right turn with a signs for **Baschi, Alviano** and **Amelia.**

Turning here you get off the main road and continue down the valley on a quiet country lane which parallels the noisy Autostrada. About 2 km from this turn (45 km from San Casciano) you pass through the bustling village of Baschi. It has a wonderful medieval section built up on a rock. In a clash of historical contexts it over-looks the modern super-highway just below.

From Baschi the road continues down the valley for another 3 km whereupon you reach a left turn with signs for Amelia and **Narni.** This turn takes you up a side valley before doubling back and climbing the slopes of a high ridge above the Tevere River valley. This climb goes on more or less continuously for the next 7 km but never at a very steep grade.

At 59 km from San Casciano you will pass through the village of **Guardea.** It is a prosperous place with many shops and a ruined castle on the hillside above. A few kilometers later the wonderfully medieval town of Alviano comes into view. It has a sturdy castle with round towers facing the road and a jumble of stone houses crowding behind it. The road continues rolling along the side of the ridge with great views across the valley.

At about 70 km from San Casciano you begin a long descent and as you come around a bend the hilltop town a Amelia suddenly appears across a deep ravine. The road descends down to a dam at the head of the ravine immediately beneath the walls of the city. A final gentle climb brings you to a square before the ancient city gates.

Amelia has one of the most dramatic settings of any hilltown you will see. The town is built up a steep hill. Around its base there is a massive wall. The foundation stones of this wall are said to pre-date the Romans and even the Etruscans. Inside the walls it is easy to get lost in the maze of narrow streets that zig-zag their way up the steep hill. In a few places you will see plexi-glass plates over exposed paving stones about a foot below the street level. These are sections of Roman road built 2,000 years ago. At the very top of the town there is an octagonal tower constructed with stones looted from earlier Roman buildings. Amelia is a fascinating place, and best of all, you will have it mostly to yourself.

There are several hotels to choose from both inside and outside the walls. The Tourist Information Office is just outside the main gate and can give you a list of accommodations, maps, etc. Amelia is a bit off the beaten path, so you should have no trouble finding a place to stay even in the high season.

Degree of Difficulty: This is not a difficult ride. There are one or two long climbs, but they re not steep. And by this point in your tour, you'll be so fit you will hardly notice them. Rating: PG.

Highlights: Without question the highlight of your day will be the 10 km descent down through the forest to Allerona Scalo. The quiet meandering road from Baschi to Amelia is a 5-star ride. Finally there is Amelia.

km	Place Name	Cafes	Shops, Mkts	Lodging	Camping	Bank	Bike Shop	Quaintness Rating
18	Allerona	•	•					***
24	Allerona Scalo	•	•					
35	Orvieto Scalo	•	•	•		•		
45	Baschi	•	•					***
59	Guardea	•	•					*
70	Lugnano	•	•					**
80	Amelia	•	•	•		•		*****

Tour 8/ Day 10 San Casciano dei Bagni—Amelia

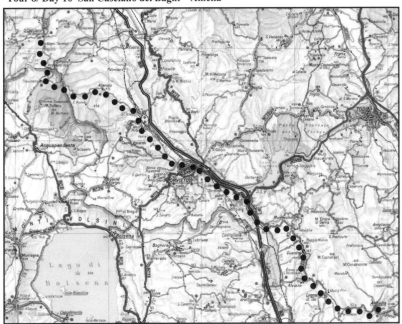

Touring Club Italiano, Auth. 04 November 2002

TOUR 8/ DAY 11

AMELIA—TREVIGNANO ROMANO
70 km/ 44 mi. Degree of Difficulty: PG

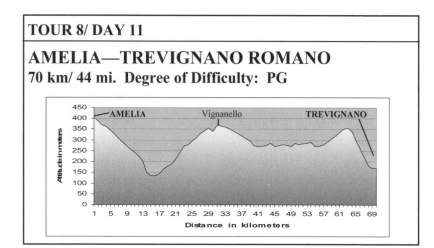

This ride takes you back down into the Tevere River valley and up the rugged slopes of the Monti Cimini. You will pass through several small towns set amid terraced slopes of olive trees. This is wild off-the-beaten-path countryside with lovely scenery and little traffic. After a final climb up the flanks of Monti Sabatini you drop down to the lake-front town of **Trevignano Romano,** where a shady café and a cold drink await you.

From the ancient walls of **Amelia** follow the signs for **Orte.** They take you on a long 15 km descent down into the broad Tevere River valley. The views are spectacular all the way down; this is a great way to start the day. At the base of the descent you will pass under the Autostrada highway and cross the river to the town of Orte. Built up on a rock above the river, Orte has a marvelous medieval section. As a major cross-roads it is also a busy place, and you should expect to encounter heavy traffic. Navigate your way through town following the signs for **N 204** to **Viterbo.**

About 1 km outside of Orte you will come to a left turn with a sign for **Vasanello.** This gets you off the busy main road. A few kilometers down this road you will roll into the central piazza of Vasanello. It has a great castle and a few shops. From Vasanello follow the main road out of town in the direction of **Soriano** and **Vignanello.**

About 5 km from Vasanello you will hit an intersection where you turn right following the sign for Soriano. A few hundred meters down the road you must turn left in the direction of Vignanello. You are now back on your outbound track and things should look familiar.

After a short descent you begin the climb up to Vignanello. This is about the half-way point of the ride and makes a good place to break for lunch. Back on the bike roll down the main street of town and look for the left turn onto **Via Roma.** Follow the signs for **Fabrica di Roma** down the steep descent below town.

Eight kilometers of rolling hills will bring you within sight of Fabrica di Roma. Follow the signs for **Sutri** through the intersection below the town.

Fourteen kilometers from Fabrica di Roma you will pass below the gates of Sutri. If you didn't explore this quaint town on your way north don't miss the opportunity to do so now. Its medieval walls, narrow streets, and Etruscan tombs are worth seeing.

A "villa" on the slopes of Monti Cimini.

From Sutri you head south on the **Via Cassia** for about 1 km to the right turn at the sign for Trevignano Romano. This takes you back over Monti Sabatini and into the basin of Lago di Bracciano. The climb is a little gentler going up this side and the view over the lake as you crest the top is nothing short of spectacular. The steep descent down to the lake will have you sitting on your brakes. At the bottom turn left to reach Trevignano. It is only a kilometer down the road.

Trevignano is a popular resort destination for Italians. It has a pleasant lake-front promenade and several inviting cafes where you can enjoy "la vita dolche." During the traditional vacation month of August you may have trouble finding a place to stay here. If you strike out in town, there are several more hotels and a few commercial campgrounds along the lake in the direction of **Anquillara.**

Degree of Difficulty: Compared to some of the other rides described in this tour, this is an easy day. There are some long hills and a lot of short ones, but none of them are particularly difficult. Rating: PG.

Highlights: The 15 km descent from Amelia down winding switchbacks into the valley of the Tevere River is nothing short of awesome. Beautiful views, effortless riding, it is a great way to start your day. The quiet roads and rolling hills of vineyards and olive trees between Vasanello and Sutri is also excellent riding. Finally the steep descent into the basin of Lago di Bracciano is icing on the cake.

km	Place Name	Cafes	Shops, Mkts	Lodging	Camping	Bank	Bike Shop	Quaintness Rating
15	Orte	●	●	●		●	●	**
23	Vasanello	●	●	●		●		***
31	Vignanella	●	●	●		●		***
39	Fabrica di Roma	●	●	●		●		***
54	Sutri	●	●	●		●		*****
70	Trevignano R.	●	●	●		●		***

Tour 8/ Day 11 Amelia—Trevignano Romano

Touring Club Italiano, Auth. 04 November 2002

TOUR 8/ DAY 12

TREVIGNANO—ROMA FIUMICINO
60 km/ 37 mi. Degree of Difficulty: G

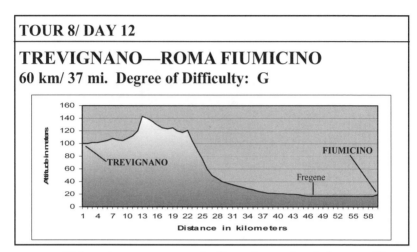

This route returns you to the Rome international airport at **Fium-icino**. While it is possible to ride all the way to the airport in time to catch an afternoon flight, it would make for a very hectic day. A better option would be to spend your last night in **Fregene** and ride the last 17 km (10 mi.) to the airport the following morning. The entire route to the airport at Fiumicino is described here; you can decide whether to stop at Fregene based on your own travel arrangements.

From **Trevignano Romano** follow the signs out of town towards **Anguillara**. This takes you clockwise around the lake. It is mostly flat, shady riding with little traffic. About 5 km from Trevignano you will pass a left turn with a sign for **Roma;** you continue straight. About 12 km from Trevignano you will reach another left turn with signs for Anguillara Saba-zia and Roma. After a short, steep climb you will reach the main street leading into Anguillara. You should turn left following the sign for Roma.

This is a busy road as it rolls through the suburbs of town. Eight kilometers from Anguillara you will reach an intersection with **N 493**, the **Via Claudia Braccianese** at **Ostia Nuova**. You should turn left here fol-lowing the sign for Roma. About 100 meters down the road there is a sec-ond intersection where you turn right at the sign for Fregene. This retraces you outbound route from the airport.

Once off the Via Claudia Braccianese the traffic disappears, and you are back to pleasant rural roads through rolling fields. The road fol-lows the ridge-top for a few kilometers. At **Santa Maria di Galaria** the road abruptly drops away into a descent down the Arrone River valley.

The next 10 km are an easy downhill spin. Follow the signs for

Fiumicino and Fregene past the Autostrada interchange. At 42 km from Trevignano you will reach a "T" intersection with signs for **Torrimpietra** to the right and Fregene to the left. Turning left you parallel a set of railroad tracks for about 1 km to the bridge over the tracks at **Maccarese.** At the top of the overpass you should turn right and roll down into the main part of town. The road passes right through Maccarese and continues on to Fregene.

At 47 km from Trevignano you will reach a blinking yellow traffic light. This marks a right turn which will lead you into Fregene, a pretty sea-side resort. There are several hotels here in case you decide to spend the night. See the **Airports** chapter for more information.

To continue on the **Leonardo Da Vinci International Airport** you continue past the blinking yellow light. The road is straight and flat almost all the way. Fifty-three kilometers from Trevignano (6 km from Fregene) you will hit a 90 degree turn to the right which parallels the end of the airport runways. After a kilometer or so there is another 90 degree turn to the left and a sign for the town of **Focene.** Turning left here you pedal along next to the runways for 7 km to a 4-way intersection with a sign for the town of Fiumicino to the right, and "Aeroporto" to the left. Turning left at this intersection a straight, busy road takes you towards the airport. Look for a green sign for Roma and a yellow sign for Ostia; it will be your second left turn. This turn leads you up onto the broad boulevard which rolls in to the airport terminal buildings. For a more detailed description of the approach to the airport see the Airports chapter. From Trevignano Romano it is 60 km flat to the airport terminal.

Degree of Difficulty: There is only one climb on this ride, not counting the railroad overpass. The climb up to Anguillara from the lake is steep but only a few hundred meters long. The rest of the ride is flat or downhill. Rating: G

Highlights: Unfortunately your best riding is now behind you. The ride along Lago di Bracciano is pretty. The long descent down the Arrone valley is quiet and traffic-free. But nothing on this ride will compare to the past 11 days of riding.

km	Place Name	Cafes	Shops, Mkts	Lodging	Camping	Bank	Bike Shop	Quaintness Rating
13	Anguillara	●	●	●	●	●	●	**
21	Ostia Nuova	●	●					
35	Maccarese	●	●	●		●		
43	Fregene	●	●	●		●		*
50	Focene	●	●					
60	Fiumicino	●	●	●		●		

Tour 8/ Day 12 Trevignano Romano—Roma/ Fiumicino

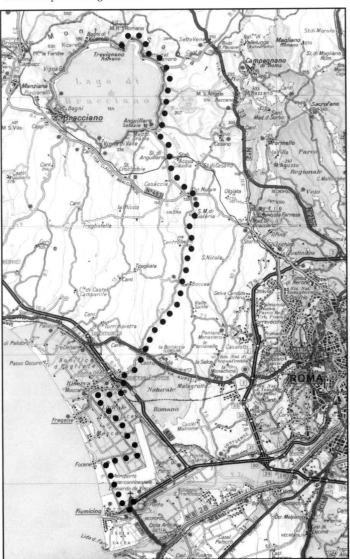

Touring Club Italiano, Auth. 04 November 2002

Spedaletto

APPENDIX A

FURTHER READING

Guide Books

The Rough Guide, Tuscany & Umbria. I found this guide to have the best coverage of out-of-the-way places. It is readable and easy to use, offers hotel and restaurant suggestions. It is a little heavy on art history and British "attitude," but is very useful. Paperback. $18.95.

Cadogan Guides: Tuscany & Umbria. Another good guide to off-the-beaten-path destinations. Offers both hotel and restaurant suggestions. Also a little heavy on art history. Paperback. $19.95.

The Blue Guide: Tuscany, and **The Blue Guide: Umbria.** Thorough guides to both regions. Detailed coverage of the principal tourist destinations. Not quite as good off the beaten path. Succinct and informative; offers hotel and restaurant recommendations. But you have to buy two books if you want coverage of both regions. Paperback. $24.95 each.

The Michelin Green Guide to Tuscany. Good coverage of the principal tourist sites. Fully half the guide is devoted to Firenze. Readable, easy to use, and a handy size. Does not cover Umbria or the Marches region, nor does it offer hotel and restaurant suggestions. Paperback. $20.00

The Michelin Green Guide to Italy. Good coverage of the principal tourist sites throughout Italy, including Tuscany, Umbria, and the Marches. Nothing off the beaten path, but a good general overview. No hotel and restaurant recommendations. Paperback. $20.00

The Michelin Red Guide to Italy. The last word on hotels and restaurants. If it's in here, it will be great. No text, just ratings. Not limited to the principal tourist centers, this guide covers it all — from quaint country inns buried in the hills to 5-star luxury resorts. It is perhaps most valuable for its restaurant recommendations. There is nothing worse after a long day in the saddle than to put up with poor service and bad food. It does take some time to master the ratings system, but you will not be disappointed. Hardback. $26.00.

Rick Steve's Italy. Good coverage of the principal tourist destinations in Italy, including Tuscany, Umbria, and the Marches. Very readable. $18.95.

Other

Anybody's Bike Book, a Comprehensive Manual of Bike Repairs, by Tom Cuthbertson. If you don't know how to do it, this book will teach you. Easy to follow instructions and great illustrations on how to fix almost any bike problem. It might be overkill to bring it along on your tour, but if it gets you out of a jam, it would be worth the extra weight. Paperback. $14.95.

The Complete Idiot's Guide to Learning Italian. A genuinely useful book for learning a bit of the language. I know it sounds like homework, but it helps to be able to ask a few questions and understand the answers. This book is also full of interesting insights into Italian culture. Paperback. $18.95.

APPENDIX B

INTERNET SITES

General Tourism Sites

Italy

www.italiantourism.com. The official site of the Italian Government Tourist Board for North America. A wealth of information for anyone Italy-bound. In English.

www.enit.it. The Italian State Tourism Board. Great information on all regions of Italy. Has English version; simply click on the British flag.

Tuscany

www.turismo.toscana.it. The official site for the tourism board for Tuscany. Great info on hotels, agriturismos, campsites, etc. English version.

www.terraditoscana.com. A great resource for learning about Tuscany. Has helpful descriptions of principal tourist destinations and a great photo gallery. Also has links to local tourist boards of various towns. English version.

www.volterratur.it. The official website of the municipality of Volterra. Good information on this historic city and the surrounding region. English version.

www.bardotti.com. A commercial site devoted to the Chianti region of Tuscany. Excellent information on lesser-known destinations. Good photos too. In English.

www.valdichiana.it. The Val di Chiana is the region along the eastern edge of Tuscany on the border with Umbria. Its principal tourist destination is Montepulciano. This site provides some historical information, and lists hotels and restaurants. English version.

http://new.elbalink.it. This is the official tourism site for the island of Elba. It is a great site for researching beaches, hotels, etc. English version.

Umbria

www.umbriaonline.com. This is a commercial site, but it offers thumbnail descriptions of all towns and many small villages in Umbria together with hotel and restaurant information. English version.

www.aboutumbria.com. Another commercial site. Not quite as useful as umbriaonline.com, but worth checking out. English version.

www.regione.umbria.it. This is the official government site, but it is in Italian only.

Marches

www.turismo.marches.it. This is an extremely well-done government site. It has a wealth of information about this region with links to other resources. English version.

www.marcheworldwide.org. An English language site set up by the Marches Regional tourism board. It links you to many of the same sites as turismo.marches.it. A great resource for more detailed information about this region.

Lazio

www.regione.lazio.it. The Lazio region includes Rome and the area from the Fiumicino airport north to Lago di Bolsena. The first few days of any tour originating at Fuimicino travels through this area. This official website contains a lot of information, unfortunately in Italian only.

www.viterboonline.com. Viterbo is the principal city in northern Lazio. This excellent English language site provides a wealth of information about the region.

Airports

www.adr.it. The official website for the Rome/ Fiumicino international airport.

www.pisa-airport.com. The official site for the Pisa international airport.

www.safnet.it. The official site for the Firenze international airport.

Hostels

www.hostels.com. "Every hostel, everywhere." Over 6,000 listed worldwide. In English.

Camping

www.icaro.it. "Easy Camping, a guide to Italian campsites." Lists campgrounds throughout Italy. English version.

www.camping.it. In Italian and German only, but you can use the map to locate campgrounds and find contact information.

Bicycle Touring

www-math.science.unitn.it/bike. The Trento Bike Pages, the greatest compendium of bicycle touring knowledge and experience on the Web. This site contains hundreds, maybe thousands, of bike tour travelogues from virtually every country you can think of. An incredible resource. Note the hyphen after the www.

www.florencebikepages.com. The Florence Bike Pages, an English language online bicycle touring guide to Florence written by a native. Offers several itineraries complete with maps, altitude profiles, etc. My only observation is that the author apparently doesn't mind riding in heavy traffic.

www.sheldonbrown.com/articles. This guy is the guru, and you don't have to climb the mountain to consult him; he has put it all on the Web. Everything you ever wanted to know about bikes, biking, bike touring, bike repair, etc. An incredible resource for cyclists.

www.velovista.net. "Your link to an on-line community of adventure cyclists." Good advice on the soup-to-nuts of bicycle touring. Many useful links.

www.adventurecycling.org. The Adventure Cycling Association: "No one knows more about bicycle touring than our organization and its 41,100 members." A good website with a lot of useful information.

Miscellaneous

www.slowtrav.com. Slow Travelers is a great website that advocates traveling slowly by renting "villas" in Europe from which you take side trips. Has a lot of excellent information on living and traveling in Italy and elsewhere.

www.onebag.com. "The Art and Science of Traveling Light." A must read for bike tourists.

APPENDIX C

TOURING GEAR SOURCES

The following is a list of mail order houses for cycling equipment. Prices tend to be cheaper than in your local shop, but not always. It always pays to compare prices.

bike nashbar   Huge inventory of gear.
P.O. Box 1455
Crab Orchard, WV 25827-1455
1-800-627-4227
www.nashbar.com

The Colorado Cyclist   Helpful staff. Good prices.
3970 E. Bijou Street
Colorado Springs, CO 80909-6806
1-800-688-8600
www.coloradocyclist.com

Cyclosource
Adventure Cycling Association   The sales arm of the Adventure Cycling Association.
P.O. Box 8308   ture Cycling Association.
Missoula, MT 59807-8308   Touring gear for touring
1-800-721-8719   cyclists.
www.adventurecycling.org

Excel Sports   Hign end gear. Slick website.
2045 32nd Street
Boulder, CO 80301
1-800-627-6664
www.excelsports.com

Old Man Mountain Products   Manufacturer of bike racks.
23 S. Fairview Ave.
Santa Barbara, CA 93117
1-888-439-6445
www.oldmanmountain.com

Schwab Cycles   Good stuff, good prices, good
1565 Pierce Street   service. Call for their catalog.
Lakewood, CO 80214
1-800-343-0243e-mail: schwabike@aol.com

APPENDIX D

BICYCLE RENTAL SHOPS

Many bicycle retail and repair shops in Italy will rent out bicycles. The hard part is locating them in advance and ensuring that you get the kind of bike you want, that it fits, etc., etc. Here is a list of shops that I understand rent out bikes. This is hardly an exhaustive list, only the ones I happen to know about. I have no information about to the quality of their bikes or their service.

Firenze

Florence by Bike   According to their website they
Via San Zanobi 120   rent MTB, road, hybrid, and
50129 Firenze, Italy   "city bikes." They also arrange
Tel. (39) 055 488992   guided and self-guided tours of
www.florencebybike.com   the area.

Siena

D.F. Bike
Via Massettana Romana 54
53100 Siena, Italy
Tel. (39) 0577 271905
e-mail: dfbike@biemmepro.it

They advertise having 40 MTB bikes and 4-5 road bikes available for rent.

Pienza

Cicloposse
Via 1 Maggio 27
53026 Pienza, Italy
tel./ fax (39) 0578 749983
www.cicloposse.com

According to their website they rent road and hybrid bikes. They also offer guided and self-guided tours of the area.

Poggibonsi (Near San Gimignano)

Ciclosport Porciatti
Via Trento 82
53036 Poggibonsi, Italy
Tel. (39) 0577 938507
Fax (39) 0577 996732
www.ciclosportporciatti.it

Offers 10 MTB and 5 road bikes for rent, but can provide more as needed.

Urbania

Happy Bike
Via Leopardi 28
61040 Urbania, Italy
tel. (39) 0722 319010
www.happybike.it

They offer racing, touring, and MTB bikes for rent.

APPENDIX E

SOURCES FOR TCI MAPS

Touring Club Italiano
www.touringclub.it
English version. You can order any map they print.

Tamasee.com
Travel and Outdoor Books and Maps
401 W. Main street
Walhalla, SC 29691
Tel. 888 770 5463
www.tamasee.com

Omni Resources
1004 So. Mebane Street
P.O. box 2096
Burlington, NC 27216
tel. (336) 227-8300
fax (336) 227-3748
www.omnimap.com

Maps, Guides, and More
www.mapsguidesandmore.com.

The Travel Guide Warehouse
www.travelguidewarehouse.com

LanguageQuest Traveler
Tel. (800) 622-3574
www.languagequest.com

APPENDIX F

ROME/ FIUMICINO AIRPORT HOTELS

At Leonardo da Vinci International Airport

The Hilton Rome Airport
Via Arturo Ferrarin
00050 Fiumicino, Italy
Tel. (39) 06 65258
Fax (39) 06 652.56. 525
www.hilton.com
Convenient and expensive.

At Fregene

The seaside town of Fregene is 16 km (10 mi) from the airport. It has three hotels. Each is rated three stars, and offers clean, relatively inexpensive rooms plus a restaurant. During the summer months you should make advance reservations. You can book reservations over the Internet by doing a search for the hotel's name. This will bring up dozens of on-line hotel booking services.

The Golden Beach Hotel
Via Gioiosa Marea 63
00050 Fregene, Italy
Tel. (39) 06 665.60.250
Fax (39) 06 665.61.095
English speaking, helpful staff. Two blocks from the beach.

Hotel Corallo
Via Gioiosa Marea 140
00050 Fregene, Italy
Tel. (39) 06 665.60.121
On the beach and a little more expensive.

Villa Fiorita
Via Castellammare 86
00050 Fregene, Italy
Tel. (39) 06 665.64.590
Fax (39) 06 665.60.301
On the main street of town. Features "American bar, Ristorante, Pizzaria."

APPENDIX G

VOCABULARY FOR THE BIKE SHOP

English	**Italian**
Bicycle/ bike	Bicicletta/ bici ("beeshee")
Frame	Telaio
Fork	Forcella
Saddle	Sella
Seat post	Reggisella
Seat post bolt	Dado di reggisella
Handlebars	Manubrio
Brakes	Freni
Brake lever	Comandi freno
Brake cable	Cavo freno
Gear shift	Comandi
Gear cable	Cavo pignono
Cable housing	Guaina
Wheel	Ruota
Rim	Cerchione
Spoke	Raggio
Hub	Mozzo
Axel	Asse
Tire	Pneumatico

Inner tube	Camera d'aria
Patch	Toppa
Tire pump	Pompa
Tire valve	Valvola
Derailleur	Cambio
Freewheel	Ruota libera
Chain	Catena
Chain link	Maglie
Grease/ Oil	Lubrificante
Pedal	Pedale
Crank	Manovella
Cleat	Gioco
Nut	Dado
Bolt	Bullone
Washer	Rondella
Screw	Vite
Ball bearings	Cuscinetti
Lock	Lucchetto
Bike rack (for bags)	Rastrelliera per biciclette
Car rack (for bikes)	Portabiciclette
Garage (to store the bike)	Garage

INDEX

Bold indicates maps

ACKNOWLEDGEMENTS

This guide could not have been written without the encouragement and support of family and friends. Amy, Emily and Rocky Cleveland were patient and enthusiastic during the research of routes throughout Italy. They did not mind being dragged up long climbs to test the accuracy of my difficulty ratings system. Geri Walsh, Doug Knisley, Karin Budding, and George Squibb graciously agreed to review an early draft of the manuscript and offered many valuable suggestions for content and format. Geri Walsh and Doug Knisley were also the first to "field check" the guide on their own first bike tour of Tuscany. Their observations confirmed my hopes and fears for the book: The rides are great, but the hills may be underrated. They also contributed several excellent photographs.

Dick Mansfield at Vitesse Press was generous with his time and advice and was more helpful than he knows. I would also like to thank the Iniziative Speciali division of Touring Club International for allowing me to reproduce portions of their excellent maps of Italy in this edition.

David Cleveland
Boulder, Colorado